RED ☆ ☆ ☆
RISING

THE WASHINGTON CAPITALS STORY

TED STARKEY

ECW PRESS

Published by ECW Press
2120 Queen Street East, Suite 200, Toronto, Ontario, Canada M4E 1E2
416-694-3348 / info@ecwpress.com

Library and Archives Canada Cataloguing in Publication

Starkey, Ted
Red rising : the Washington Capitals story / Ted Starkey.

ISBN 978-1-77041-105-0
ALSO ISSUED AS: 978-1-77090-307-4 (PDF); 978-1-77090-308-1 (EPUB)

1. Washington Capitals (Hockey team). 2. National Hockey League. 1. Title.

GV848.W37S83 2012   796.962'6409753   C2012-902749-9

Editor for the press: Michael Holmes
Cover and type: Troy Cunningham
Cover images: "Tampa Bay Lightning v Washington Capitals - Game Two" © 2011
G Fiume | Getty Images; "Hockey Background" © Brad Calkins | Dreamstime.com
Printing: Thomson Shore   5   4   3   2   1

Printed and bound in the United States

STRUCK BY LIGHTNING, CAPITALS BOTTOM OUT

Washington Capitals defenseman John Carlson skated behind his own net, collected the puck and looked up-ice at the canvas in front of him. 2011–12 had been rough through 62 games — the Capitals were in a playoff berth dogfight in the tightly packed Eastern Conference. They'd been hit with several key injuries and had even experienced a mid-season coaching change. The fact that their postseason hopes were still in question was unusual for a team that had enjoyed tremendous regular-season success in recent years, winning the Presidents' Trophy in 2009–10 and having been the East's top seed two years running.

Even though players were glancing at the out-of-town score-board, they knew only one score really mattered: the one on the high-definition screen that hung over center ice. Right now it showed the Capitals trailing the New York Islanders by two with less than four minutes remaining in regulation. Despite their struggles, the Caps still owned one of the league's best home records, but they'd been frus-trated by Islanders goaltender Evgeni Nabokov. The sellout crowd of 18,506 was looking for a reason to cheer when Carlson decided to skate out from behind the cage toward his right and delivered a long pass to

Jason Chimera at center. The winger tipped the pass into the corner of the Isles' zone, out-raced a pair of defensemen and chipped the puck back to Mathieu Perreault. The center took the feed and sent it across the goal line to Troy Brouwer, who was parked just at the far side of the blue paint and tipped the puck past Nabokov with 3:29 to play.

The crowd roared its approval, with the fans — and the players — sensing that perhaps a Washington comeback was possible. While the Capitals buzzed as the clock wound down under a minute, the crowd tried to do its part, rising during a timeout taken with 31.8 seconds left in regulation by Capitals legend-turned-coach Dale Hunter. Tonight's game was Washington's 136th consecutive sellout — three years had passed since a Capitals home game had had any empty seats, and that crowd also had gained a reputation around the league as one of the loudest in the NHL. Washington fans created an impressive visual display: a majority of them wore the team's signature red sweater.

The ensuing draw was in the Islanders' end. Washington center Jeff Halpern — who grew up a Capitals fan, just a few miles away from the city limits in Potomac, Maryland — was able to send the puck back to winger Brooks Laich. The veteran forward ran a quick give and go with defenseman Dennis Wideman. After Laich took the return pass, he wound up and fired through traffic in front of the net. The shot grazed off Troy Brouwer's stick and in past Nabokov, sending the crowd into a frenzy with just 25.5 seconds left in regulation. The six players on the ice mobbed Laich, and the team's superstar captain, Alexander Ovechkin, pumped his fist.

With the two-goal deficit erased, all that was left was a player to complete the storybook ending.

Early in overtime the Islanders broke into the Capitals' zone, but defenseman Mike Green poke-checked the puck free to Ovechkin. The top pick of the 2004 NHL draft picked up the disk and gained steam along the boards; Islanders defenseman Travis Hamonic skated backward, looking to defend. Once Ovechkin reached the faceoff circle in the New York zone, he fired a wrist shot. The puck whistled by Hamonic's skate and through Nabokov's pads. The goalie could only tilt his head back and look toward the building's rafters; Ovechkin skated to the corner and the entire Capitals roster mobbed their captain. The fans pounded on the glass in celebration behind them.

The overtime win eventually led to celebratory dance music in the Capitals' locker room, and a large media contingent entered and surrounded the Russian at his corner locker. In the other corner, Brouwer, still wearing all his gear, also answered questions in front of a mob of cameras and recorders. He talked about the two goals he'd scored, but made a point of explaining that the fans fueled the comeback. "We could feel the positive energy in the building, and it's so much more fun to play at home," he said.

Dale Hunter spoke to the media in a crowded room underneath the stands — and the local journalists would use his words to backbone their improbable comeback stories. It's a tale local hockey fans have read time and time again — ever since the seemingly down-and-out franchise underwent the transformation that made it one of the league's most visible and successful.

Back when the 2003–04 regular season was drawing to a close, labor woes began to spread the dark shadow of pending doom over the NHL's member cities. Washington, however, was a gloomy place even before the Capitals' painful 82-game campaign of disintegration mercifully made its way into late March.

The very real threat of an extended work stoppage put the entire 2004–05 season in jeopardy. The game's economic landscape looked destined for a major overhaul, with the league's owners determined to install a hard cap to control player salaries. Sensing what was on the horizon, the Capitals' management took a gamble with both the team's fan base and its roster by electing to try to completely overhaul the team as the season wore on.

The Capitals shed most of their expensive veteran salaries, trading the team's popular stars for prospects and draft picks in an effort to get a jump on a new economic system — one that was still to be determined by a collective bargaining agreement (CBA) that was months away from being hammered out in the bitter and protracted negotiations between the NHL and the National Hockey League Players' Association (NHLPA).

The result of a season's worth of dumping players and their pricey contracts — not to mention the fact that some of the remaining players weren't thrilled to be part of the kind of rebuilding project not seen in America's capital since the NHL franchise first arrived in 1974 — led to the Capitals and their fans suffering through the worst season in decades, and the team nearing its lowest point in the team's 30-year history.

On March 30, 2004, with less than a week to go in the regular season, the purple-hued scoreboard at then–MCI Center hanging above center ice featured the names of familiar rivals: Capitals and Penguins, a showdown that would normally attract a sellout crowd. The former Patrick Division foes had fought through seven bitter playoff series the previous dozen years and produced some of the most memorable moments in the two teams' histories — legacies that had become entwined since the Penguins beat the Caps en route to their first Stanley Cup title in the spring of 1991.

On this night, however, the team names and uniforms were pretty much the only common threads between the players on the ice and the two teams' successful pasts as they skated at the seven-year-old arena in Washington's Chinatown neighborhood, battling to stay out of the league's basement. The sounds of blades cutting into the ice and the players' chatter was clearly audible thanks to the rather small number of souls in attendance.

While the Capitals were no strangers to the playoffs in their previous 21 seasons — missing the cut just three times between the 1982–83 and 2002–03 seasons — the only postseason hope for Washington that spring would be landing the chance of picking first overall in the NHL draft.

Washington and Pittsburgh were in the unusual position of battling for that top pick and the chance to select a young Russian named Alexander Ovechkin, perhaps the best player to come through the draft since the Penguins took Mario Lemieux in 1984.

While the official attendance that night was listed as 13,417, the number of empty purple seats certainly outnumbered actual fans in the stands. Wide open spaces throughout the arena created a surreal setting. Like the Capitals, the Penguins were also seriously rebuilding. They were a shadow of their former selves, but with a young nucleus, Pittsburgh had rebounded from a terrible start — at one point being a league-worst 11–42–5–4 — to making a run at climbing out of the league's basement.

The Capitals' netminder, Matt Yeats, had trouble hooking on with an East Coast Hockey League team when the year started. With the roster upheaval, however, the Alberta native had signed with the Caps on March 19 and was making his third straight NHL start when the Penguins arrived. Yeats was looking for his first-ever NHL win.

Journeyman forward Trent Whitfield, who had scored only six times all season, was able to notch a pair of goals for Washington — the first time he had ever scored more than a single point in an NHL contest. Jeff Halpern, a Maryland native, had scored one of the more memorable playoff goals for Washington in Game 4 of the 2001 Eastern Conference Quarterfinals against the Penguins to square the series, and he also had a goal in the 4–2 win, essentially assuring that the Capitals would not finish with the worst record in the league. Afterward, Halpern told reporters the victory did more to take the sting out of losing than create a sense of accomplishment by avoiding the cellar. "The guys in the locker room obviously want to win," Halpern told the Associated Press. "For the last two or three weeks, any chance you get to have a win, it gives you two days when you don't have to think about losing. At this point, sometimes that's enough."

"I would love to play in a meaningful game or be in the playoffs where those plays, scoring a goal or making an assist, just amplifies that much more," he told the *Washington Times*.

The bright side was that a few young players who normally wouldn't get a shot in the show got a chance to play — even if they were playing in front of numbers more typical of an American Hockey League crowd than an NHL franchise.

"A bunch of young players got the opportunity to play, but at the same time, it was disappointing that we were going to be part of it but not a playoff team," Brian Willsie later recalled of that squad.

Matt Yeats celebrated his first — and what turned out to be his only — NHL win. "It's a great feeling," he told reporters. "I counted down the last seconds and gave myself a fist pump. I was cheering inside." After his five-game stint in Washington, "Yahtzee" never played in the league again.

Washington's win was its 23rd and, as it turned out, its last of the season. The Capitals finished with 59 points — just one ahead of the league's worst club, the Penguins. Tied with Chicago for the league's second-lowest point total, the Capitals held the "tiebreaker" and finished with the third-best chance at winning the NHL's draft lottery.

Clearly, the main reason for the sparse crowds at the end of 2003–04 was the fact the Capitals' fire sale had dealt away most of the team's recognizable stars. They plummeted to their worst record in a non-strike-shortened season since 1977–78, when the franchise was still dealing with growing pains of being a recent expansion team.

By the time the season had reached its last few games, the players wearing Capitals sweaters were a ragtag bunch comprised mostly of skaters called up from the team's American Hockey League affiliate in Portland, Maine, along with some waiver claims and players signed — like Matt Yeats — just to fill out the roster until season's end. It was the end of a rapid fall for the Capitals, who had qualified for the play-offs as a sixth seed in the Eastern Conference just 11 months earlier. The Capitals had finished 2002–03 with 39 wins and a respectable 92 points, falling just short of beating out the Tampa Bay Lightning for the Southeast Division title. What happened on the ice and in the stands in the 10 days of that first-round playoff series loss to the Lightning proved to be the catalyst behind the organization's plans for the future.

Matched up against the Bolts in the playoff series, Washington was able to jump out to a quick start, grabbing a 2–0 lead with a pair of wins in Tampa and looking like they would cruise past the young, inexperienced Tampa lineup.

But when the series moved north to the MCI Center for Games 3 and 4, Lightning coach John Tortorella made adjustments to his lineup and was able to grab momentum with two wins. The series shifted in Game 3 thanks to an ill-advised pair of penalties early in overtime that set up Vinny Lecavalier's goal just 2:29 into the extra frame. "If you look back on that series, [Lightning netminder] Nikolai Khabibulin was not very good," *Tampa Tribune* beat writer Erik Erlendsson recalled. "The goal that Brendan Witt scored to force overtime in that game was a terrible one for Khabibulin to let in, and you thought at the time Washington had all the momentum.

"Khabibulin wasn't very good, but [Jaromir Jagr takes a] penalty in overtime, and it was so obvious the [Ken Klee elbowing] penalty. You can't go down 5-on-3 with Vinny Lecavalier, Martin St. Louis, and at the time Dan Boyle and Vinny Prospal on the ice."

With the two-man advantage, Lecavalier poked a rebound past Washington goaltender Olaf Kolzig, snapping a Lightning 11-game MCI Center losing streak that stretched back four years.

More importantly, it gave the Lightning confidence, and the Caps weren't able to wrestle it back.

"That [Lecavalier goal] really changed the whole momentum of the series," Erlendsson said. "It's a cliché, but there's a big difference in being down 3–0 and down 2–1, and so that's obviously where that series changed, on that penalty."

Capitals coach Bruce Cassidy, the replacement for Ron Wilson — who had led the Capitals to their only Stanley Cup Finals in 1998 — wasn't able to respond to Tortorella's tweaks and counter the shift in the series. As a result, the Capitals were quickly run out of the playoffs with four straight losses.

"[Tortorella] took the momentum, and the Jeff Halpern–Steve Konowalchuk–Mike Grier line just could not contain Lecavalier, St. Louis and Prospal," Erlendsson recalled years later. "They're all calling them the MVP line, and they played like it. They just took over. Washington relied on Jaromir Jagr and Sergei Gonchar and Peter Bondra for offense, but it was actually Tampa's forwards that took over the series."

With the lack of a big-name playoff opponent — and playing back-to-back games over Passover and Easter afternoon — Washington's three home games in the series were several thousand fans short of sellouts. The empty seats certainly didn't make Capitals' owner Ted Leonsis very happy.

Leonsis, who purchased the club in 1999, had been aggressive in looking to boost the franchise's flagging ticket sales, not only by instituting more flexible ticket plans and making himself accessible to the fans, but also through adding some expensive pieces to the roster. With crowds noticeably below MCI Center's capacity — the deciding Game 6 was nearly 3,000 short of a sellout — Leonsis was visibly upset after the season came to an end. In his remarks to the press in the wake of the team's playoff loss, he hinted at big changes in the team's salary structure following the team's quick exit from the postseason.

"It's incredibly disappointing to have 14,000 people in the building for the final playoff game," he told reporters after the game. "I think the market has spoken and I have some real re-evaluating to do on the kind of investments we're going to make in the team because the city didn't respond. You cannot have a playoff game with 14,000 people with the kind of marketing and consumer focus that we've had."

"I do remember it was a little odd — although one of the games was played on Easter Sunday and right around Passover, that might have something to do with it," Erlendsson recalled. "I remember people like to say stuff about crowds in Tampa, but it's still a playoff game.

"You look around, and you see empty seats, and you wonder why the seats are empty. It's a playoff game. [MCI Center] wasn't empty by any means, and the fans who were there were loud and into it, but it is weird to look around and see that many empty seats — especially when they were up 2–0 in the series coming back home."

Years later, Halpern talked about how he felt the team was a playoff-caliber club, but with a labor dispute on the horizon, it was clear Capitals management elected to tear down the team instead of trying to tinker with the expensive lineup.

"I think we were really close, but there were things missing with that team that definitely showed up in the playoffs that we didn't address," he said. "It was either from a team standpoint or an organizational standpoint, I think there was a tremendous sense of frustration of 'what else do we need?'

"You see the group they have now, they know it's close and the players play the right way, and they're willing to add to those groups. As opposed to that year — they threw up their hands and started over.

"The beginning of dismantling of that team was that playoff series. It's unfortunate, we definitely lost a lot of good players because of it, but a lot of hockey people would argue sometimes you have to get worse before you get better."

In an office in Verizon Center overlooking now-bustling 7th Street, Leonsis reflected on his decision to alter the team's core after the 2003 playoff loss. "I think there was a general ennui that had set in around the city, around the team, around the fan base. We couldn't break through. The team certainly had 'star players' — Peter Bondra, Olie Kolzig, Sergei Gonchar, Jaromir Jagr, Robert Lang — and we couldn't connect. I got a sense the fan base didn't really like the team and we obviously weren't performing.

"Jagr's first year we didn't make the playoffs, [his second] we finished second to Tampa Bay, and you could sense it wasn't going to work. At the same time, there was the overhang that the league would look different because there was going to be a very difficult negotiation between the league and the union and so we better anticipate what the world would look like, and that was the big driver."

With a $51.1 million payroll, the franchise's management wanted to reduce that number significantly before the arrival of a hard salary cap. As a result, the 2003–04 Capitals were doomed to failure.

Over the summer, the Capitals openly told their fans they would not be making moves in the free agent market. They also not-so-quietly began looking to move the contract of their most expensive asset, Jagr. With the Czech star having signed a $77 million contract extension shortly after the team acquired him from the Penguins in a 2001 trade — and with five years still remaining on the deal — the idea of taking on the former Hart Trophy winner's contract was a difficult sell, despite his talent.

Poor playoff attendance, poor chemistry in the locker room and a poor start to the year led the team's management to elect to make radical changes early in the 2003–04 campaign. Management made its intentions clear to the players when they traded longtime Capital — and team captain — Steve Konowalchuk just six games into the season.

"The toughest year was [2003–04]," Jeff Halpern recalled years later. "Steve Konowalchuk leaving was the hardest because he was such an honest and hardworking player and the epitome of what you want a teammate to be, and once we lost him, it spiraled after that.

"To stick around and see that dismantling as a teammate of all those guys — it's sad to see those guys go. You try and make sense of it, but that was the toughest year that I had been here."

Brian Willsie, who was claimed from the Western Conference powerhouse Colorado Avalanche on the eve of the new season, came in expecting a chance to play for a playoff club, but instead wound up being part of a rebuilding project.

"The Caps didn't have a rough season in 2002–03, so we were expecting good things," he said years later. "Personally, it was an opportunity for me to play more and get in the lineup. It was a powerhouse [team] in Colorado and being a young guy trying to make my mark, but that [move] gave me the opportunity to solidify myself as an NHLer so I was excited to come. As the season went along, we saw that it was going to be the very early beginnings of a rebuild.

"We started trading players, traded Steve Konowalchuk just six games into the year . . . so that's the sense we got."

The end result was the club looking much different at the end of the season than the one that had convened at Piney Orchard Ice Arena in suburban Odenton, Maryland, in September 2003 for the team's

30th National Hockey League season — one that veteran defenseman Brendan Witt would later call "awful."

"We completely lost our momentum [in Game 3 of the Lightning series] and couldn't get it back," Capitals general manager George McPhee later explained to the *Washington Times*. "And I don't know that we've gotten it back this year. In training camp, there was the sense that we'd all failed. We have not rebounded from that at all.

"We really felt like we should have advanced farther last year, and the loss was really, really hard on this group. Then you go into the off-season, you can't lock people up [to] long-term [contracts] because of the uncertain [labor] situation, and it created a bad environment."

After blowing out the Islanders in the first game of the season, the Capitals would win just seven of their next 25.

After losing five straight following the season opener, the first move was trading away Konowalchuk — who was 31 and going to be an unrestricted free agent the following summer. The captain, who had been drafted by Washington in 1991, was sent west to Colorado on October 22. The Capitals picked up what they thought would be a less expensive alternative to the veteran in gritty forward Bates Battaglia, along with marginal prospect Jonas Johansson.

"That's what a guy plays for, the Cup," Konowalchuk told the *Times* after being traded to a contending Avalanche team that was just two years removed from the 2001 Stanley Cup title. "I've played my whole life for this opportunity. Still, it's tough [being traded]. You're in shock." The American-born Konowalchuk was a popular player in the dressing room and, despite not being one of the most talented Capitals, was a key part of the team's chemistry. Losing him, according to Halpern, was a huge blow.

"It was a shock because of how much respect I had for him as a player, as what a good player he was," Jeff Halpern said of the deal years later. "At that time, Bruce Cassidy was the coach, and Kono was only playing 10 or 11 minutes a game. He wasn't even killing penalties, or being able to do a lot of the things he did [well].

"I was sad to see him traded, but at that point, the writing was almost on the wall and he was able to go to Colorado and thrive. I was happy to see a friend do well there.

"But losing him was the start of a lot of head-scratching."

The trade didn't help spur the Capitals out of their early doldrums, as the team continued to spiral into the NHL's basement, amassing an 8–18–1–1 mark by December.

Not only was the on-ice performance ugly, things were also getting nasty in the team's dressing room, particularly as the 38-year-old Bruce Cassidy put himself in hot water with his own players.

Cassidy's job was already clearly in jeopardy when Brendan Witt told the *Washington Times* that the coach had implied his players were too worried about their sick children and pregnant wives instead of their jobs following a loss to the Devils in the Meadowlands on December 4. The words angered the players, and certainly cost Cassidy respect in the locker room. Less than a week after the story surfaced, Cassidy was gone.

"I don't think the players responded quite as good as we should have with [Cassidy], for whatever reason," veteran netminder Olaf Kolzig told the *Washington Post* right after the firing. "Some coaches seem to fit better for a team than others, and there's never a perfect coach out there — every coach has some fault — and every player has faults. Nobody is perfect, but for whatever reason he just didn't mesh with our team."

Assistant coach Glen Hanlon was promoted to replace Cassidy, and the former NHL goaltender was in charge of a roster that would rapidly deteriorate as the season progressed.

"Bruce was let go in December, and Glen Hanlon came in, who was a great coach," Brian Willsie recalled. "We were a close team, played for each other, and had a hard-working mentality . . . What we lacked in talent, we definitely made up for in hard work."

Jaromir Jagr, whom Leonsis had pushed hard to acquire from Pittsburgh in the summer of 2001 — reportedly over objections by McPhee and other Capitals hockey operations staff who didn't want to bring the Czech star to Washington — was the next player the team wanted to move. The New York Rangers had shown interest in picking up the veteran star since losing out to the Capitals in the trade talks with Pittsburgh in 2001. But without another apparent team willing to pick up the league's largest salary ($11 million per year), Rangers general manager Glen Sather was willing to wait patiently to see whether Washington would eventually agree to underwrite some of Jagr's salary.

After months of attempting to unload Jagr's massive contract, on January 23, 2004, the Capitals finally struck a deal to trade him to the Rangers for former Capital Anson Carter. The Capitals finally acquiesced: they'd pay a large chunk of Jagr's salary while he skated for one of their Eastern Conference rivals.

"This is a deal that we knew we had to make back in the summer," McPhee told reporters after the trade. "Jaromir's a tremendously gifted player, but we couldn't afford him. Jaromir could have scored 300 points a year, and we [still] couldn't afford him. When you have one player making a lot of money, it's hard to fill holes in other areas. Ultimately, we didn't have the resources to build a team to support him."

Persistent trade rumors had taken their toll on the team's former centerpiece; he was largely unimpressive in his final few months in a Washington sweater. "No matter how much you say to yourself, 'You're a professional. You've got to go to the game and play your best,' it's not easy because any game or any sport, if you want to play the best you can play, you have to be mentally ready," Jagr told the Associated Press just before the trade. "And it's not easy to do right now."

With the Capitals posting just a 14–27–5–2 record when the trade was made, the deal was a clear message that the team was going to continue to shed salaries and look to rebuild once the new CBA was hammered out over the next year.

"This was a contract that we had to move," McPhee told AP. "We couldn't go forward in our market in a new era with this type of deal."

"It didn't work the way everybody expected it was going to work," Jagr told reporters right after the deal, per the *New York Daily News*. "A lot of things maybe should have been done differently, but it didn't happen. It's too late to look back. I want to look forward. I apologize to all the people who are disappointed . . . I just did the best I could."

For Ted Leonsis, it was also the end of a massive contract he later called his biggest ever business mistake — in sport or otherwise.

Leonsis had amassed the bulk of his fortune when he sold his startup Redgate Communications to America Online in 1994 and cashed in on the rapidly growing internet company's rising stock value. With the high value of his stock and his net worth hovering near an estimated billion dollars in 1999, the AOL executive purchased the team from the club's founder Abe Pollin — along with a minority stake in the NBA's Washington Wizards and the MCI Center. More importantly, Leonsis had an eventual right of first refusal to buy the basketball team and arena if Pollin agreed to sell — or died.

When he purchased the Caps, Leonsis talked about a bold five-year plan to bring the Stanley Cup to Washington and make the team profitable. Instead, he had just three first-round losses and a sea of red ink to his credit in the four-plus years of his ownership.

With the bottoming out of 2003–04, it was a safe bet the Capitals weren't even going to be close to qualifying for the postseason. As the club rapidly shed salary commitments, Leonsis had to scrap his original five-year plan and take the sizeable risk of essentially starting from scratch. Clearly, the gamble to acquire and sign Jagr to a long-term $77 million contract extension had failed both on the ice and in the books.

"This [Jagr] trade is a good one in that it moves the largest player contract in the NHL to a team that can absorb it, and it provides us with options as we seek to improve our team," Leonsis told Washington's WTEM radio at the time.

Citing the "new economic" reality of the NHL, the team's owner acknowledged he had to look forward and shed as much payroll space as he could in preparation for a new salary cap era. "With our current payroll, our ability to improve was hindered as well as our flexibility to plan for the future as we move toward a possible new NHL business model," the owner said.

Leonsis had been one of the most accessible owners in professional sports, personally answering fans' e-mails, talking to ticket holders and always trying to stay connected to his customers. But with the Caps having their worst season in decades, he showed some of his personal frustrations. After a season ticket holder taunted him at the first home game against Philadelphia following the Jagr deal — holding a derogatory sign comparing the Caps' slide to the plummeting value of AOL stock and heckling him throughout another loss — frustration took over. The two met in the hallway afterward, and there was a physical altercation.

Leonsis reportedly ended up shoving the 20-year-old, leaving the Caps' owner "embarrassed" according to a team spokesman; Leonsis eventually called the fan to apologize for his actions.

While the altercation was minor — the fan elected not to press charges — the incident made national headlines; it certainly proved to be out of character for the largely gregarious owner. It also revealed both the discontent of the team's rapidly eroding fan base and the frustration of an owner with the state of his floundering, expensive and underachieving team.

Even with the club's biggest contract off the books, Washington wasn't done making major subtractions.

On February 18, the Capitals traded the franchise's all-time leading scorer and fan favorite, Peter Bondra, to the Ottawa Senators. The trade, which was an emotional move for both sides, landed a prospect named Brooks Laich and a draft pick.

Bondra had said in the weeks before the deal that despite the team choosing to rebuild he wanted to stay. When he was dealt, he found leaving the team that picked him in the 1990 draft difficult. "It's tough — this is home," a tearful Bondra told reporters. "It's hard to leave. I grew up here as a person and as a player. You hear the rumors . . . I kind of assumed at one point that it would happen. When I walked in the building this morning with my kids to skate before practice because they were off from school, and I saw George here, I told my kids, 'This is it. It's probably our last day here.'

"When George told me, I was so shocked and . . . my stomach had butterflies. It was almost . . . a breakdown. It was tough . . . I was here for 14 years, and all of a sudden it's gone."

"We're supposed to be big, tough guys, but there were a lot of tears this morning," McPhee told AP after the deal done. "We thought it was best for Peter. We worked harder to find the best place for him to play. Peter didn't want to leave. This wasn't something management and ownership wanted to do. We thought it was good for Peter and good for us."

"You absolutely can't replace a guy like Peter, the production he gave this team," Halpern told the *Washington Times'* David Elfin. "No one in this room is going to fill that void."

Less than two weeks later, another forward, Robert Lang, who was one of the rare bright spots in an otherwise dismal season (he had earned the only All-Star Game selection of his career that year), was shipped west to Detroit for a young prospect, forward Tomas Fleischmann.

Lang, who was tied for the NHL's lead in points at the time of the trade, certainly reflected the somber mood of the Capitals' locker room when he talked about his trade from the team mired near the bottom of the NHL standings to go to the defending Stanley Cup champion Red Wings. "This is no offense to anybody in Washington, but it's always great to go from a team that doesn't really have a bright future to go to a team with bright horizons," Lang told AP.

Another piece of the Capitals' core foundation, defenseman Sergei Gonchar, was traded to Boston less than a week later, with Washington picking up defensive prospect Shaone Morrisonn in return.

Gonchar showed no interest in being part of the rebuilding process, and had asked McPhee in February to be traded. "I grew up in Washington," Gonchar told the *Washington Times.* "I made a lot of friends on and off the ice and I will always keep my eye on the team, but I'm not sad. I've seen some friends go through this, and I know this is a step that I have to make. I need to move on for my career."

"Sergei Gonchar is an outstanding player, but given the uncertainty we are all facing next season and his impending unrestricted free agency thereafter, we thought it best to make the move to acquire young assets now," McPhee told reporters. "It's been difficult, but . . .

we're trying to do what we think is best for the hockey club in the near future."

The environment of constant trades, rumors and turnover certainly made for a strange vibe in the Capitals' locker room. "Especially back then, it wasn't a traditional hockey hotbed, but there were constantly rumors out of Canada and the newspapers are saying this guy's the next to move," Halpern recalled. "You kind of came to the rink every day expecting someone to move or be traded. It's a hard way to go about playing.

"One of the biggest things, I was a minus 16, I was one of the best on the team, and then when everyone got traded, I was at the bottom — just because everyone else had been traded."

With the team already seemingly headed for the bottom five and a spot in the NHL's draft lottery — and a potential franchise cornerstone like Ovechkin — outsiders couldn't help but note the rapid change in direction.

"You could tell they were going through transition," Erik Erlendsson said. "You could see a managerial change, a philosophical change. They had so much expectation for that team, maybe they didn't feel like they had the right leaders, the right personnel, the right balance, you don't want to say a team is playing for draft picks. Maybe they're testing the system, maybe they're looking around to see what they have, but when you see they bring players up like that, you can see there's a change in the thought process.

"Like the Penguins did back in 1984 [when they drafted Mario Lemieux], when a prize like Alexander Ovechkin is a potential reward, nobody's ever going to say they're trying to improve their draft status — but it does happen."

Around the NHL, teams were unsure what would transpire with the new CBA, as some of the league's spenders loaded up for one last shot with big payrolls, while others looked to cut their commitments to players past the season. Washington certainly was more than happy to try to deal some of their players to the Red Wings, Rangers and other clubs that would take their contracts.

As the trade deadline came and went, Michael Nylander, Mike Grier and even Anson Carter — the player Washington had picked up in the Jagr trade — were dealt away in exchange for prospects and draft picks that would be used to rebuild the team once the labor situation had settled.

Of the team's core veterans that departed, the only star that remained was Kolzig, who had led the team to the 1998 Stanley Cup Finals and won a Vezina Trophy as the league's top goaltender in 2000. Although his name had been mentioned in various trade rumors, the goaltender was pretty much all that was left after the dust settled.

"Since reaching the Stanley Cup Finals nearly six years ago, the nucleus of this team made the playoffs only three times, winning just five postseason games and failing to advance past the first round," Ted Leonsis wrote on the team's website after the trade deadline.

"Simply put, we had a high payroll with high expectations, and it didn't work out. So we are moving forward with an emphasis on getting younger, playing with passion and having a commitment to a team-first mentality. We have a wealth of young players either in Washington or in our system, and we have payroll flexibility that will allow us to make future moves to help the team."

Still, Leonsis had to defend against rumors the future of the franchise itself was in doubt.

"The Capitals are not moving and will not be contracted when the new CBA is in place," Leonsis wrote. "'We are located in a large market with a passionate fan base and great arena. [The ownership group] is committed to what is in the best interest of the long-term future of hockey and hockey in D.C. Our ownership group has invested significantly in losses during the last five years, probably more than any other NHL ownership group. What we are not committed to is a $50 million payroll for a team that is last in its division."

A good number of the players that had started the year in Washington were gone, so was most of the fans' enthusiasm.

"It wasn't the friendliest time," Comcast SportsNet's play-by-play announcer Joe Beninati recalled. "I remember the team had its marquee names ship out, and as those players changed, roster-wise, their fortunes in the standings kept tumbling, and the fans kept grumbling — and deservedly so.

"You think about it in comparison to the way the building vibrates now. It was quiet then, guys would come out for pregame warm-ups at 6:25 for those 7 o'clock starts, and Olie Kolzig would knock pucks away, and you could hear the pucks clatter on the ice and hear the guys whoo-hooing as they came onto the ice out of the dressing room, but there might be only 100 people or so in the arena. Totally different dynamic than what we enjoy nowadays."

Greg Wyshynski, now of Yahoo!'s popular Puck Daddy blog, noticed a very different demographic to the crowds as well. "It was an interesting time, you had the die-hards that followed the team from Landover coming here, but you simply didn't have the young, collegiate, 'Rock the Red' crowd coming. It was clique-ish, they had their die-hards, but by no means was it a widespread thing. It was a total niche sport."

"I was at a game right after Bondra had been traded, and there was hardly anyone in the stands," Ed Frankovic of WNST in Baltimore recalled. "There were maybe 5,000 actual people, because a lot of the team's stars were gone.

"It was uninspired hockey, and the team was positioning themselves to dump the rest of the season. There was no energy in the building. It was dark days for Capitals hockey."

The end result was a free fall, the Capitals going just 4–13–2–1 over the final 20 games of the campaign.

"You just look at the guys who were fortunate enough to wear an NHL jersey that year," Beninati recalled. "You never would have projected that. Things just got dismal, from February to March to April, and they only won three of the 14 games they played in March. By that time you knew the die had been cast, the organization was going to make a turn for the better and try to build through the draft, some astute trades and careful moves. Thankfully, that came to fruition."

In the short term, however, it certainly created a strange environment for both the Capitals and their opponents.

"It seems like ancient history, since the Thrashers were one of the best teams in the division and the Capitals were one of the worst in the league — but there was nobody at the games," said John Manasso, who covered the Atlanta Thrashers for the *Atlanta Journal-Constitution*. "It was laughable. I don't who was in charge at the time, if it was George McPhee's idea to rip that team apart or Ted Leonsis' idea. You can't see the long-range plans at the time and that's one of the problems being in the media — but I thought George McPhee should be fired.

"It was so bad. It was a disaster."

The silver lining to the slump was that the team put itself in position to try to grab the top pick in the draft lottery, which would take place a week after that March 30 home game against Pittsburgh.

Following the season finale in Pittsburgh on April 4 — which turned out to be the team's 46th loss of the campaign, its most since that 1977–78 season — Brendan Witt was asked if he was happy the turbulent season was finally over. "The year, the awful year, yeah . . . but as players we always enjoy playing, and now it's going to take a few days to sink in it's over," Witt told reporters.

While the season did mark the first time a Maryland native and a player who grew up a fan of the Capitals led his team in scoring, Halpern wasn't exactly happy. "It hasn't been a whole lot of fun," Halpern told AP after the game. "When you're losing games, it doesn't make any of the [individual stats] feel any good."

"We've battled through some situations that they will never experience again, the removal of players 10 minutes before games, a lot of things we've had to do as an organization," Hanlon told reporters. "[But] we've been in every game except the one against Buffalo at the deadline when we traded away Mike Grier. This group loves to play and plays hard."

For the Capitals franchise, the team was certainly at a crossroads.

"Washington isn't a Philadelphia, Montreal or Toronto where hockey's roots go very deep," Olie Kolzig told the *Washington Times* as the team cleaned out their lockers for the last time before what proved to be an off-season that would extend into September 2005. "It's still fragile territory. We've got the Redskins, the Orioles, the Redskins, and the Redskins. People have to see hockey. If we're not here for a year, they'll find something else to watch."

"All we can do is regroup, learn from this and try to make a positive out of it," Witt told the *Times*. "We don't want to go through this ever again."

"That season just spiraled the wrong way, but it was the trigger of what we enjoy now," Beninati said later. "They had to hit that rock bottom, and they did, and in glorious fashion. It was a long year. In the booth, you earn your keep; you do your best to keep the viewer interested when the product on the ice isn't what it can be.

"Looking at the names of the players they used, you realize how often they were dipping into the American Hockey League for their team, and just pulling up what they could to get by. It was a rough year to say the least."

The team had very little to build around after its worst season in decades.

"I think it was a huge risk," Ed Frankovic recalls. "Hockey in Washington was in dire straits. Go back to the 'Save the Caps' campaign in 1982 where the team was in danger of moving, they had some good young players coming up. They had a foundation of players, and the team's problems were more off-ice issues, with the amusement tax of Prince George's County, Maryland, and some of the financial problems the club had.

"This was Ted Leonsis saying he wanted to start over. They got rid of Peter Bondra, Jaromir Jagr and Steve Konowalchuk. These kind of guys had grown up in the organization or were guys people could relate to. Jeff Halpern and Olaf Kolzig were left as the face of the franchise . . . I remember going on the radio at WNST at the 2004 trade deadline, we thought it was going to be Olaf Kolzig's last day as a Capital. I guess Ted decided he had to keep somebody, and Olie was the face of the franchise."

While the Capitals franchise had certainly seen some dark days before — from recording an NHL-record low 21 points in its first season of 1974–75, to nearly leaving Washington in 1982 to several epic playoff losses, as a longtime observer of the franchise Frankovic thought nothing matched the low watermark of the spring of 2004. "This was probably the lowest point. There had been 30 years of the Capitals, and they really were starting over. They really had no one to build around.

"They still had Olaf Kolzig, who at that point was about to turn 34 and had 14 years of his career under his belt, so it's not like you're building around a 25-year-old goaltender. They really had no young quality players because their drafts had not been good. They were in bad shape on the ice, and if you aren't winning, people aren't going to be interested."

The *Washington Examiner*'s Brian McNally thought that although the shedding of salary was painful, it was necessary to turn a team that was an also-ran into a Stanley Cup contender. "I think . . . they knew the lockout was coming — I'm assuming they did — and had a good feel for what was going to happen . . . that maybe next season wasn't going to take place at all. As depressing as it was, they couldn't continue along that path.

"In the end, you realized they weren't a championship contender with that crew with Jagr. They had some promising young pieces, and it was a nice team, and Olie was at the height of his powers, but it wasn't going to happen.

"That Tampa series kind of smacked them in the face and said, 'They're younger than you, they're better than you, and they won a title [in 2004]. What are you going to do?' So, I think that they were taking a risk that the fan base wouldn't come back. But I think was a bigger risk to keep the status quo and not change. With any pro sports team, you have to roll the dice.

"If you're not building a championship team, you're just coasting, and you're never going to get to what they have now. Ted knew that, George knew that, and Ted gave George the latitude to take that risk and get rid of guys like Bondra.

"When you listened to sports talk radio, and they said, 'The Capitals traded Konowalchuk today,' you'd think the team wouldn't be good for five years — and they weren't — but in the end, it paid complete dividends."

Tim Lemke, who covered the business of sports for the *Washington Times*, also agreed that Leonsis gambled on making the team a true Stanley Cup contender instead of just a playoff contender, and that in the long run, it was his best move. "I think it was a bigger risk not to do it," Lemke said. "It was courageous, but ultimately smart to look at the team . . . and I don't know to what degree it was his decision . . . to be able to look at the team and ask, 'Can we win a Stanley Cup as we are currently assembled?'

"If the answer is no, what are you doing? If you can't win a championship with the players you have and the approach you're taking, what are you doing?

"They blew it up. They were lucky that they got a really special player, but they made some good decisions moving forward — and they had a plan. That's the key — *this is the plan; we're going to grow.*"

Asked if he thought that season was his most difficult as an owner, Leonsis conceded owning a National Hockey League team is — at least in the on-ice product — frustrating in trying to corral an elusive Stanley Cup title. "This is a very difficult business. Of all my businesses, this is the toughest. It has the most scrutiny, the most pixels [attention] washing over it, the most expectations and demands, and there's one winner and 29 losers every year. It's very binary . . . why when people win a championship, they cry like little children . . . because it's the hardest thing to accomplish in this business . . . to win a championship.

"I obviously thought [change] was less risky than staying the course. When you look around at pro sports, the teams that have been generationally really good to great and have won championships, for the most part, drafted their key players. They added around them, but the key generational players — Kobe Bryant, Larry Bird, Magic Johnson — all drafted. Vincent Lecavalier, they had just won the Stanley Cup [in 2004] — he was drafted. Sidney Crosby, Evgeni Malkin — drafted. We knew the draft would be very important, so we wanted to accumulate as many picks as we could.

"I had faith that if we were honest and transparent in what we were going to do and the team played hard, and played with passion, that the young kids would grow up and mature and the fans would fall in love with them."

Fortunately, the memories of a terrible, prolonged campaign were about to fade.

FROM RUSSIA
...WITH HOPE

Just two days after the regular season came to a merciful end, the Washington Capitals got their first bit of good news in months: they had won the NHL's draft lottery.

Despite having just the third-best odds of securing the top pick, Washington won the draw on April 6 and leapfrogged Pittsburgh and Chicago in the draft order, bumping the Penguins from the top spot and the Blackhawks down into third. This officially gave the franchise the chance to pick the dynamic young Russian touted as the number one prospect.

"Hopefully this is the first day of a new era," Capitals general manager George McPhee told reporters the day of the lottery. "We feel we were in some way rewarded for the difficult task we took this year. It's not easy restructuring your team, but it was something we had to do. We feel excited about the future . . . We certainly have some flexibility with the picks we have. You expect to get an impact player, someone who can really make a difference."

The prize was Alexander Ovechkin, a flashy and dynamic forward who had been dazzling scouts and reporters alike from a young age.

Ovechkin had jumped onto the world's hockey stage in Halifax, Nova Scotia, during the 2003 World Junior Championship, scoring a pair of hat tricks for the Russian team that won the gold medal. While NHL scouts had known the Russian prospect was a can't-miss player well before his name would be called in the draft, hockey fans across the Atlantic got their first real taste of the Russian's raw talent and skill during the tournament.

The Moscow-born son of a former Olympic basketball star and a professional soccer player, Ovechkin was a natural athlete who possessed a dynamic scoring touch — as well as a flair for the dramatic. When he was just 16, he was already skating with Moscow Dynamo of the Russian Superleague; he'd also already developed the gregarious personality that would help Washington attract fans once play eventually resumed.

Ovechkin missed being eligible for the 2003 NHL draft by just two days — he was born on September 17, 1985 — so despite his rising stardom, the 18-year-old spent a second season with Dynamo.

Once Washington secured the top pick, there were whispers that the Capitals would either trade the pick or use it to select fellow Russian forward prospect Evgeni Malkin, or even Medicine Hat defenseman Cam Barker. However, those whispers turned out to just be rumors, as Washington went ahead and made Ovechkin just the third first-overall pick in the franchise's history.

"You don't get a chance to pick in that spot very often," McPhee told reporters after making the selection official. "We were lucky to win the lottery and lucky to have a player of that ability sitting there. He was on our list as number one for a long time.

"He's an elite player with great character, and we hope he's going to be the type of player that plays hard and makes the difference in the big games, ultimately in the Stanley Cup Finals."

The team's first-ever top pick came back in the club's expansion year of 1974, but the player they picked, defenseman Greg Joly, was a bust. Two years later, the team selected another defenseman, Rick Green, in the 1976 NHL draft; Green was solid player who played well with the Caps. He later became part of Capitals history, as he was involved in the 1982 trade that brought Hall of Fame defenseman Rod Langway to Washington from Montreal, a trade that made the club a Stanley Cup contender for the next decade.

At 12 minutes past noon on June 26, 2004, in Raleigh's RBC Center, the fate of the Russian star and the Capitals franchise officially became intertwined. The 18-year-old was going to be the centerpiece of the floundering NHL team's rebuilding effort.

Despite the language barrier, Ovechkin did his best to speak English following his selection, and told reporters he "was ready to give my heart [to Washington]."

"I've been waiting for this day for maybe two years," he added. "It is very important to be number one. My mom and dad always said to try to be first. If you are second, you are second; if you're number one, you're number one."

For Leonsis' part, still cautious after the team's disastrous decision to build around Jaromir Jagr three years earlier, he explained to the *Washington Times* why the team elected to take a shot at picking Ovechkin. "We have so much work to do that we were entertaining trade [offers]," Leonsis told the paper. "Some teams made offers to us and while they were good, [we] felt we should build around this kid and the youth we have in the system."

Leonsis also mentioned he wanted to avoid the mistake he made of trying to build around Jagr — although not mentioning his former star by name.

"I've learned a lot, and I've learned that hockey is really a team game," he told the paper. "While there are parts that are special in their own way, I want to market the Washington Capitals. Our team needs to be a team, and this kid is a real team player."

"We could have done a trade for volume, but none of those players would have been as good as this guy," McPhee told the Associated Press at the time.

Years later, Leonsis reflected on making Ovechkin the first pick overall, and the centerpiece for the new rebuilding project. "There's a saying I love, which is 'I believe in miracles, I just don't believe in planning for them.' We knew we would get a high pick; we weren't a very good team. We jumped a couple of spots and we got the first pick in the draft.

"There were two really great players available. They've proven to be two of the best players in the league in Alex Ovechkin and [Evgeni] Malkin. Malkin was very highly regarded, and he was a center. Ovechkin was more highly regarded, but he's a wing. During the interviews, George felt [Ovechkin] was more outgoing, charismatic and so we're blessed and lucky and drafted Alex Ovechkin."

Besides Ovechkin, the Capitals had two other first-round selections thanks to the flurry of deals from the previous season.

They took Calgary Hitmen defenseman Jeff Schultz with the 27th overall selection they had collected from the Bruins in the Sergei Gonchar deal, then two picks later, took another blueliner, Mike Green, with the pick they had acquired from Detroit in the Robert Lang trade.

Washington also took Chris Bourque, son of the Hall of Fame defenseman Ray Bourque, out of Cushing Academy in Massachusetts; the forward had tons of potential and was headed to Boston University. In all, the Capitals made four picks in the top 33 selections of the draft.

The team was happy with what they had achieved in terms of restocking itself with prospects, especially knowing these young players likely would get extra time to mature in junior or the minors because the NHL season was very much in doubt.

"We have a lot of young talent, probably as much if not more than any team in the league," McPhee told the *Washington Times*' venerable Hall of Fame writer Dave Fay. "But we have to be patient and let them grow up together. We can't hand them experience pills. They need a little time to develop. We'll be smart about it and build a real good team. But the foundation is there."

"I think [the fans] already understand [rebuilding will not be an overnight process]," McPhee added. "I think they understand what we did last year, accept what we're doing now and are thrilled by what we did. We just need to have the collective bargaining agreement settled, and then we'll do what's in the best interest of the club once we know what the landscape is."

Ovechkin was certainly unlike any other player the Capitals had ever drafted before.

"They've had that high-pick defenseman before, Scott Stevens comes to mind, with the fifth-overall pick [in 1982]," Ed Frankovic recalled years later. "But this franchise had built around defense with [Scott] Stevens, Rod Langway, Larry Murphy, Brian Engblom, Kevin Hatcher, Calle Johansson . . .

"To get that superstar forward they never really had — Peter Bondra, Mike Gartner and Bobby Carpenter were the closest that they had. But nothing like having a first-overall pick like Alexander Ovechkin. To get him, that was key, but it still took a while, and because of those bad drafts [in years before], they had nothing."

Even armed with a potential superstar, there was uncertainty about when Ovechkin would actually put on a Capitals jersey for a game.

Most experts believed the entire 2004–05 NHL season was in serious jeopardy: the owners were pushing to install a hard salary cap and were adamant about not backing down. The Capitals were banking on it quietly; the team retained relatively few contracts and would sign players once the dust settled. If there was a 2004–05 season — truncated or otherwise — there were real questions about what kind of roster the Capitals would be able to field.

"We know where everybody is going," McPhee told the *Washington Times* on the eve of the lockout. "The college kids are going back to college, certain kids are going back to junior and the rest of them are going to the American [Hockey] League, and we'll be able to watch them all season there."

With the uncertainty surrounding the NHL — and no transfer agreement in place with the International Ice Hockey Federation — Ovechkin opted to remain in Russia and skate for Dynamo, meaning he wouldn't cross over the Atlantic even if the NHL resumed play. That didn't mean Ovechkin was absent from NHL rinks that fall, as he skated for Russia in the 2004 World Cup of Hockey, the youngest player in the tournament at the age of 19.

Although a scratch in Russia's first two tournament games, he got a chance to play at Toronto's Air Canada Centre against Slovakia on September 5. He gave the press a glimpse of what he would bring to the NHL, scoring a goal in Russia's 5–2 win.

"Ovechkin looked like your typical overeager teenager when he fell flat on his keester while twisting to receive a pass in the first period," *Toronto Star* columnist Damien Cox wrote. "But by the third he was one of his team's most dangerous-looking attackers . . . He scored a terrific goal, nearly added another and meted out several heavy bodychecks to Slovak players who have probably already had quite enough of this World Cup without having to play Canada one more time.

"Seven minutes into the third period . . . Ovechkin hit the ice with Artem Chubarov and Dmitry Afanasenkov. Afanasenkov carried the puck halfway into the Slovak zone and spun, flipping a blind pass into the slot. Ovechkin got there first. In an instant he shifted slightly to his left and then whipped a backhander past the Slovak goalie. Replays elicited oohs and aahs from the otherwise sedate crowd."

Two days later, Ovechkin got a chance to skate in St. Paul's Xcel Energy Center in the tournament's quarterfinals against the United States. The Russian squad was eliminated by the Americans, ending Ovechkin's brief North American tour — at least until he joined the Capitals the following year.

In the meantime, however, the hockey landscape was preparing for major change, with the future centerpiece of the Capitals playing in Russia. While the league's owners and the NHLPA battled over hockey's future off the ice, no one knew when the game would return.

THE NHL'S
LANDSCAPE CHANGES

As if the NHL lockout wasn't bad enough, there were other developments that further pushed the Washington Capitals down the ladder of the city's crowding sports scene.

Shortly after the NHL's work stoppage officially began in September 2004, Major League Baseball announced the Montreal Expos would play at RFK Stadium in the 2005 season, meaning the District would have baseball back for the first time since the Washington Senators departed for Arlington, Texas, after the 1971 season.

Up the Baltimore/Washington Parkway, the Orioles, who had largely been Washington's de facto baseball team of choice in the Senators' absence, finished near the .500 mark, led by new superstar shortstop Miguel Tejada's 150 RBI season. While Baltimore had floundered since its last playoff appearance in 1997, there was hope the team would soon return to contention.

The NBA's Washington Wizards — long a league doormat that, the year before, had suffered a nasty breakup with the game's biggest star, Michael Jordan — managed to play respectable basketball during the 2004–05 campaign and even won its first playoff series since 1982, besting the Chicago Bulls.

The NFL's Redskins — who dominate the city's sports landscape both by being a part of the most beloved professional league in the United States and as the city's longest-tenured team, having arrived from Boston in 1937 — grabbed headlines early in 2004 by luring Hall of Fame coach Joe Gibbs out of retirement to try to add to the three Super Bowl trophies he won with the team during the 1980s and 1990s.

And so the Capitals — the second-most popular team in town during the heyday of the 1980s, with four future Hall-of-Famers on the roster in Rod Langway, Scott Stevens, Mike Gartner and Larry Murphy — were now staring up at not only the Redskins, but also the resurgent Wizards and the newly minted Nationals in the city's pecking order.

"Having a new team [the Nationals] coming in while we're in the midst of a lockout, it's really the worst of all worlds for us," Ted Leonsis told the *Washington Times*' Eric Fisher. "It's terrible."

Even in a wealthy market like Washington, there is only so much disposable income to go around. The Major League Baseball team's audience demographic is similar to the Capitals' affluent, suburban fan base, meaning the Capitals would have even more work to do once the NHL actually returned to action.

"[The Capitals] were pretty far down there," former *Washington Times* sports business reporter Tim Lemke recalled. "When I took over the beat in October of 2005, the first conversation I had with Mark Hartsell, the sports editor at the time, was if we should do a story if the Capitals could even survive in Washington, or if Washington was a hockey town. It was really that bad. We weren't joking about it. There was a legitimate question of whether the franchise could even survive.

"Ted Leonsis was hemorrhaging tens of millions of dollars, and there wasn't a lot of interest in the team. The attendance was down . . . but there would be 10,000 and change at games, and there's an unwritten rule around the NHL that you don't go below 10,000 — you find a way to keep it above 10,000 by giving away tickets or fudging numbers. Look at the history of hockey, there aren't many teams going below that number, but always 10,000 and a couple dozen."

Because Leonsis did not have complete control of MCI Center — team founder Abe Pollin still had controlling interest in the arena and drew the full revenue from building-related aspects — the Capitals could not draw from the luxury boxes, club seats, concessions and other moneymaking ventures the arena provided despite his group holding a 44 percent stake in the building.

As a result, Leonsis wrote on the team's website that he would lose less money by not playing than actually undergoing a season. "We lost more than $100 million during the five years we have owned the Capitals. This clearly is not a sustainable business model and one that we are committed to righting as soon as possible," he wrote. "No one likes losing money and no one wants the league to miss games. But this stark fact remains: the Caps will lose less money by not playing."

The lack of games on the NHL level didn't mean the organization was completely silent, however. Many of the team's young draft picks gathered in Portland, Maine, for an American Hockey League season that was certain to be unlike any other, with several top prospects who would otherwise be in the NHL skating one rung below the top league.

"This is a unique situation," George McPhee told the *Washington Times'* Dave Fay while watching his future players at Portland's Cumberland County Civic Center. "The guys here, they're starting their pro careers at the same time, so we hope they develop some chemistry that carries over down the road.

"I don't think you've ever seen an expansion team with eight first-round picks on their farm team roster at one time, and that's how many we have on the ice right now. These guys, along with a number of other players we've acquired or drafted, give us a core in terms of depth that most teams don't have, and expansion teams never have.

"You add in the players who aren't here [Alexander Ovechkin and Alexander Semin were in Russia], sprinkle in a few veterans that we have in Washington, and we could be a very competitive and a fun team to watch in a hurry."

For the young players and prospects, it was a chance to bond.

Brian Willsie, who skated for that Pirates team that year, recalled, "The whole American League was totally stacked with players. If you look at the names of players that year, all their NHL teams used that opportunity to develop their prospects. All the prospects that they had scouted the season before were all playing, with Shaone Morrisonn and [Tomas] Fleischmann and all those guys, so it was an opportunity for all of us to play together, get to know each other and try and develop that way.

"There was no chance to get called up, but it was an enjoyable year, a competitive year, and we were all excited for the 2005–06 season to get underway."

While it was understandable that draft pick Ovechkin was biding his time in the Russian Superleague, the fact that Alexander Semin was also staying in Russia — despite having spent the previous two seasons in Washington as the 2002 first-round pick — was becoming an increasingly frustration problem.

"Unfortunately, [Semin] decided not to report to Portland, and the Russian team he is playing for [Lada Togliatti] does not respect our contract," McPhee told Fay. "In the absence of an agreement between the NHL and the International Ice Hockey Federation, neither entity has been able to remedy this issue with the Russian federation as quickly as we would like to."

Without a valid CBA, there was a roadblock for Russian players who wanted to head to North America without a transfer agreement — which was an issue that would complicate Ovechkin's eventual arrival. Semin, instead of playing in Maine for $90,000 under his NHL two-way contract, elected to skate for $300,000 tax-free dollars in his native Russia.

As the months rolled by and National Hockey League arenas remained quiet, little progress was made in the labor talks. The owners were determined to institute a hard cap to control costs while the players were fighting the move.

There was a last-ditch effort to save the 2004–05 season in mid-February, as there was hope the two sides could reach a compromise in order to at least play a truncated season before it was too late to start a new campaign. But a potential last-minute deal collapsed, and the NHL became the first North American professional sports league to cancel a season due to a labor dispute.

For the first time since an influenza epidemic canceled the 1919 Stanley Cup Finals between Seattle and Montreal, hockey's Holy Grail wouldn't be awarded in the spring.

WNST's Ed Frankovic said the silver lining of the lost year for the Capitals was the extra year Ovechkin spent in his native country. "It's never good to have a lockout, but I think for the Caps it actually worked out well," Frankovic recalled. "Ovechkin was big and knew he was going to be a number one pick, and I talked to scouts, they said even at 16 he'd be ready for the NHL.

"But he got to play one more full year in Russia and play against some quality players . . . and get to mature over there. That year made him more NHL-ready when the lockout was over. George actually had a great draft in 2004, and some of those guys got to play in the AHL, and that was a big factor as well."

Russian-American journalist Dmitry Chesnokov, who works for Canada's TSN network and Yahoo!, said, "Initially the reaction [in Russia] was that they were hoping he'd stay home longer, play longer there. But it was kind of obvious that he'd been playing with the big boys since he was 16.

"I think the lockout sort of helped because he came in [to the NHL] later when he was more mature. Being drafted number one, people saw the kind of player he was and the expectations were high. But even [in Russia], everybody was covering Sid Crosby, and they were saying [Crosby] would be the next Gretzky. People were rooting for [Ovechkin] as the underdog to come out and prove that without the hype, he could do the talking on the ice."

But the Capitals' owner was keeping one eye on the bottom line and the other on the future — whenever it would come. "This is a dark day and a necessary day, but ironically we're in the best financial position we've been in since I've owned the team," Ted Leonsis told the *Washington Times* after the season was scrapped. "Our ownership group is committed, we have lots of money in the bank and we will have a young, talented team whenever we get back on the ice. When this thing does get solved, I really believe we will be a turnaround story."

Of course, before a feel-good story could be written, both the league and the Caps would have to undo the PR damage the work stoppage had created.

Washington had the extra burden of dealing with a double dose of bad news between the rebuilding project and the lockout, as the team's season ticket base had dropped from a height of 12,000 when the team picked up Jagr to around 8,000 during the work stoppage.

"When the game reopens, we have a lot of work to do," Leonsis told the paper. "The game is about more than a [collective bargaining agreement]. We have to re-engage the fan base, and I'm obviously going to get out and be more public again. I've long said that we have great fans but not enough of them. That hasn't changed."

While the Capitals were firmly in the background of the city sports scene, the Wizards advanced to the second round of the NBA playoffs, and the Nationals began play in Washington, capping an improbable first half of the season that saw the team take the lead in the National League East for a good portion of the summer.

While hockey fans in Washington missed the game, the Capitals had mostly faded from the casual sports fan's radar as the NHL sorted out its business.

Eventually, in July 2005, the NHL and its players neared a deal, raising hopes that the 2005–06 season would begin on time. Although the deal had yet to be ratified as the window for Ovechkin to opt out of his contract with Dynamo was closing, the star took a leap of faith to jump to the NHL.

Ovechkin opted out of his contract with Dynamo on July 20, two days before the NHL deal was ratified. He signed a three-year entry-level contract with the Capitals, worth a base salary of $984,200 per season — with incentives — on August 5, 2005.

While the league was slowly coming back to life after months of dormancy, the Capitals were still in rough shape.

"I sat down with Ted [Leonsis] that fall and things were not good," Lemke recalled years later. "Really what they had to do is essentially start over, not only on the ice but completely taking a look at everything they were doing.

"They lucked out in a sense that they got the two number-one draft picks and the new collective bargaining agreement helped a lot since it meant that they couldn't spend above a certain amount and they weren't going to be outspent during the rebuilding project.

"They did a good job recognizing they had some good young talent and marketing the team appropriately."

Ovechkin arrived in September for his first National Hockey League training camp, along with a core of young prospects and high draft picks to try to restore the team to a playoff-caliber club.

The Capitals changed their AHL affiliation in April, severing ties with the Portland Pirates — with whom the team had remained affiliated for a dozen years after the franchise moved out of Baltimore in 1993–94 — to partner with the Hershey Bears, who were a much shorter distance from the nation's capital, sitting just a two-hour drive north of Washington.

To lead the Bears, the Capitals hired Bruce Boudreau, who had led the Los Angeles Kings' top affiliate, the Manchester Monarchs, to a 51-win season in 2004–05. For Hershey, it was a welcome relief after a tough marriage with the Colorado Avalanche, who didn't put as much of an emphasis on winning as the locals had hoped.

"The geography of [Hershey's] affiliation with Colorado was tough," former Bears and current Capitals play-by-play voice John Walton recalled. "The biggest change, probably right off the bat, was that we were two hours away. But the geography was a small part of it what makes things so positive between Washington and Hershey.

"I was able to see the relationship work as [Bears general manager] Doug Yingst's right-hand guy . . . I know he and George are on the same page and talk all the time. Doug has nothing but wonderful things to say about working with George, and that means a lot. Just from a player personnel standpoint, they rely on each other. Doug sees a lot at the AHL level; it was just a beautiful partnership from the beginning.

"That said, I don't think anyone could have seen in 2006 that [Hershey] would go from missing the playoffs for two straight years to winning a Calder Cup. But it was a great ride.

"The spring and summer of 2005, when Bruce was hired, it took off from there. And Bruce had as much to do with it as anybody."

Leonsis said years later that the decision to affiliate with nearby Hershey was a key element of the team's rebuilding project, as was the hiring of Boudreau to guide the club's AHL team. "We knew there would be some kind of labor action — either a strike or lockout — and that our players were getting older. There were lots and lots of discussions.

"It's interesting; I just got off the phone with an NBA owner [following that league's lockout in 2011]. He called me because he's in a similar position where the Caps were [in 2003–04]. He said he's going through a planning session right now and wanted my take and advice on it, where I have a good team, not a great team, I maybe have one or two more years left with this core. Do I go for it or do I deconstruct? What's the cost associated with each [option], and what's the risk?

"Many, many times when you're in the middle, you face difficult discussions. We used that offseason and that year we didn't play to become students of what would make for a return plan and relaunch of the Caps, and we were very, very thoughtful in it. Once we decided to go for it, there was no turning back. We said there would be three legs of the stool.

"First, we were going to rebuild the team and all of our trades would be for prospects and picks, and so we would have a really young team — so we had better create a fantastic relationship with an AHL franchise. We used to be in Portland, far away and remote, so next we made the decision to go to Hershey, which was very, very important to us. That was let's spend a lot of time being tight with our AHL affiliate — we're paying for it, might as well stock them with players — and let's get a system in place that the young kids can learn and play in the system and [learn] the vernacular. So we hired Bruce.

"Immediately, George and Bruce and Doug and Glen Hanlon, at the time, kicked off and established a really good relationship. We all spent a lot of time in Hershey. I would go to games, George was there all the time . . . Play the young kids. Let's see what we got.

"There was the three-pronged stool. [In the AHL,] let's create an environment where the young kids could play and bond, and want to play, and [build a] practice and training facility and office facility that's integrated. In the past, practice was in Piney Orchard, the front office was [in an office building on 9th Street] in D.C., Kettler Capitals Iceplex was a key part of the overall rebuild. And there was the rebuild itself."

Tim Leone, who covers the Bears for Harrisburg's *Patriot-News*, said the affiliation worked well and was boosted by the relationship between McPhee and Yingst: "Well, certainly historically and logistically it made a lot of sense. If it's not going to be the Flyers around here, the Caps make a lot of sense. [The Capitals and Bears] had won a [Calder] Cup together in 1980 so there is that part of it.

"The biggest part of it — the heart of the relationship — is George McPhee and Doug Yingst. There seems to be a lot of compatibility and like-minded thinking there. The Caps are a team willing to sign more veteran-type AHL guys because they believe their kids are better served by having to earn playing time and the Bears are the marquis franchise in this league. As an independently owned team, [the Bears] want to have that kind of model. They make a good point that over the long run, the kids have a chance to develop better with the long-term playoff success they've had.

"In the first five years of the affiliation, they've almost played a full season's worth of playoff games. The best laboratory outside the NHL is the AHL playoffs."

While the Capitals and their fans had endured the darkest days of the franchise with the team that closed out the 2003–04 season, things were about to get a whole lot more electric.

OVECHKIN
ARRIVES

After spending the lockout year in Russia, in 2005 Alexander Ovechkin finally arrived to play for the Capitals. Fans were eager to see how much of the soon-to-be-20-year-old's promise would be put on display at MCI Center.

For a public relations staff looking to put the Caps back on the map, the post-lockout return was a challenge.

"I think the big thing was coming back," Nate Ewell, Washington's former director of media relations, recalled. "We saw that as more of a challenge than anything else. Once you turn the corner from the purge, the rebuild was pretty easy. You had a big piece in place by the fall of 2005. As long as you had Alex, you could see things were moving in the right direction."

Not only was the Russian a talented hockey player, he also had a personality that quickly made him a fan favorite, not only in Washington, but well beyond the region. "Good city, good country and good people," Ovechkin told reporters at his first press conference after signing a three-year, entry-level contract in August 2005. "I'm looking forward to my career. Right now, we have one goal: to win the Stanley Cup. I will try to play how I can. I will try to play good."

Still, Ovechkin was certainly aware of the massive rebuilding project in front of the team, and that it would take time to be a contender. "As a sportsman, of course, I want to win games," Ovechkin said. "But we are a young team."

"The Caps are playing a preseason game in Hershey, and if you're looking for a place to go in Hershey for a beer after the game, we don't have many options," former Bears play-by-play voice John Walton recalled. "[Ovechkin, Ewell and I] are all at the same place, and at the time [Ovechkin] had yet to play an NHL game. We're standing at Shakey's and [Ewell] says, 'I want to introduce you to Alex. Alex, this is John Walton, he's the PR director and radio voice of the Bears. Don't worry, you're never going to see him again.' And the rest of the night, Ovi, when I caught his eye, he said, 'I never see you again!'

"The funny thing is we had to give him a ride to the hotel that night."

Despite the massive promise of Ovechkin's talent, his arrival did not instantly translate into box-office success. In fact, for his first official appearance at MCI Center, a preseason game against the Buffalo Sabres on September 21, although 10,129 tickets were distributed, an estimated 4,500 fans showed up.

The Capitals were blanked by the Sabres in the game, but those in attendance did get a taste of Ovechkin's talent when he beat Buffalo goaltender Ryan Miller in the shootout exhibition that took place after the contest — a demonstration meant to introduce fans to the new tie-breaking system implanted after the lockout.

While 2005's top draft pick, Canadian phenom Sidney Crosby, had more talent to work with in his new NHL home as the Penguins were more aggressive in signing free agents out of the lockout, the Capitals were still largely a work in progress, opting for a more patient rebuilding approach.

During the offseason, Washington had picked up some depth, acquiring Chris Clark from the 2004 Stanley Cup finalist Calgary

Flames, as well signing former Penguin Matt Bradley and David Steckel out of the Kings system, but they were still largely a thin club, without much NHL experience.

When Washington returned to action on October 2, 2005, a respectable crowd of 16,325 showed up and earned the right to say they saw Ovechkin's regular-season NHL debut. The fans were shown flashes of the top pick's raw offensive talent, as the Russian became the first Capital to score a pair of goals in his first career game, lighting the lamp twice against the Columbus Blue Jackets in a 3–2 win.

And he didn't just score: he also broke a glass stanchion behind the Blue Jackets' net with a fierce check on Radoslav Suchy just 40 seconds in — much to the delight of the crowd, who roared its approval.

"The first check he threw to start the game, I said, 'That's my boy. That's what we want," Leonsis told the Associated Press afterward. "We want our star players to work hard and be a part of the team. Every time we got down, he answered, and that's what superstars do."

His first-ever NHL point was a goal, as Jeff Halpern drove behind the net and fed Dainius Zubrus, who curled around the corner, then found Ovechkin between the circles. The rookie made no mistake with the centering pass, blasting the puck past netminder Pascal Leclaire after less than 28 minutes in the league.

Following the goal, Ovechkin pointed upward and then admired his handiwork on the arena's video board, even reacting to his own goal.

Less than five minutes later, he had his first power play goal, after Halpern took a rebound from in front of Leclaire, then fed the streaking winger. Ovechkin celebrated by diving to one knee and sliding, truly giving the crowd returning from the lockout something to celebrate.

"He was worth the admission tonight," Columbus coach Gerard Gallant told AP afterward. "He was real good."

While not a sellout, the attendance — and atmosphere — was a far cry from the team's dwindling fortunes as 2003–04 wound down. As the final horn sounded, Ovechkin and coach Glen Hanlon embraced on the bench to celebrate, before Ovechkin congratulated his teammates on the ice.

"It feels very good," Ovechkin told reporters. "I must thank my [teammates] for giving me two excellent passes. It was just a shot. I must only shoot and I score two goals. It's my first game in the NHL, we win and I score two goals. It's a nice start."

Ovechkin also flashed his personality for the crowd, as he got a large cheer after he playfully stuck out his tongue — à la Michael Jordan — when shown on the arena's video board before breaking into a large smile.

"It was exciting for us, we didn't know what to expect," Brian Willsie recalled later. "Alex was a terrific talent, but the first game he had two goals and he had a couple of great hits, and we were like, 'Oh, wow.' He's ready to play now, there's no feeling-out process. He was ready to play in the NHL from day one."

Ovechkin had help adapting to the North American way of life; his family came over to help him adjust. He got help from the club as well, even being a houseguest of general manager George McPhee when he first arrived.

"I think he adapted well. I think it helped him to have his family here, his brother here, to help the transition," TSN's Dmitry Chesnokov said. "He was surrounded by people who were trying to help him. From the get-go, he didn't have to be worried about being sent to the minors or finding a place to stay or getting his own house. As soon as he came over, the only thing he had to concentrate on was the game. His mind wasn't taken away from playing hockey. It was just hockey, hockey, hockey."

Ovechkin tried to speak English rather than rely on a Russian translator. "It was very easy; he was very cooperative," says Nate Ewell, who helped Ovechkin acclimate to his media responsibilities. "He did everything that was asked. Fairly quickly, it was evident that things would have to be reeled in for him, because he didn't say no to anything. He had a lot on his plate and handled it very well, and he tackled speaking English as much as possible and didn't want to get stuck using a translator or anything like that. He was eager and that helps a lot."

"It was surprising, but it was kind of cool he was getting ready for it," Chesnokov said of Ovechkin's desire to do English-language interviews early on. "He came from an athletic family with his mother [a Russian Olympic basketball star], and he knew from the get-go what kind of attention he would get if he could get to the level that everyone thought he was going to get to. It was good that he was getting ready for it, obviously."

Ovechkin was also paired with the Canadian-born Brian Willsie on the road, who helped the youngster learn North American culture. "The part about Alex being my roommate, I don't know how that came about," Willsie said. "The first road trip of the year we got matched up, and we got along great. There were things about the North American lifestyle — not hockey, but things off-the-ice, like walking around and finding a Starbucks before the game, and visiting cities, being at meetings on time and wearing proper attire for games, those are things I helped out with. It was just a start but he caught on pretty quick."

Even when he was offered a sizeable gift certificate from the team's PR department for being patient and cooperative with numerous interview requests, Ovechkin turned it down. "If somebody ask me to give interview, I must not say no because it is my job and you must work and I must help," Ovechkin told the *Washington Times'* Dave Fay in November 2005. "If I don't give interview, maybe you be sorry and interview somebody else [from another team]. I don't want [to be] paid money for interview. When you give me [gift certificate], I say why? It was nice but it was not necessary."

According to Willsie, Ovechkin was excited to play in some of the Canadian cities, recalling the rookie's first visit to Toronto's Air Canada Centre in November. "In our division, we'd go to Tampa, Atlanta and Florida, maybe a little more mellow, and we'd come up [to Canada] and his eyes would light up and he'd say, 'Wills, will it be sold out tonight? What's the arena like?' And I'd say it's a lot different than Atlanta or someplace like that, it's going to be fun. Those were the games he really got excited for.

"Coming to Toronto . . . he went for a walk, he walked the whole afternoon and was so excited to play. He came back; we got dressed at

4 p.m. in our suits and walked to the arena. He was that excited to play that there was no pregame nap."

While the Capitals weren't a whole lot better in the standings than they were two years before, the presence of the Russian helped give a spark of hope to a fan base that had largely burned out through the lockout year.

Despite the arrival of their budding superstar, however, some things still weren't going well for the Capitals. Through six home games, the Capitals were last in the league in average attendance at 12,312 — nearly 5,000 off what other teams were averaging coming out of the lockout.

"They didn't resonate the first year, except for the fact that they had Ovechkin, a player you could latch onto and everyone knew was very special," Tim Lemke recalled. "That was it. There was something. You had [Washington Wizards star] Gilbert [Arenas], but [Ovechkin] was the best athlete in town, and so you can latch onto that.

"I remember a part of that, covering sports here, some people were excited for the team right off the bat, even if they weren't good right away. They knew that something interesting could be happening and that there was a plan. But it didn't translate immediately into ticket sales. There's a lag with that."

Washington had its legal woes as well, as they looked to get another young Russian back in the fold. The team had to go through the court system to try to pry Alexander Semin out of the Russian Superleague and back to playing under his NHL contract, which had two years left. Semin had begun the 2005–06 season with one Russian team, Lada Togliatti, but that club was going through financial issues and subsequently dealt him to another club, Khimik.

The Capitals still had the prospect's rights and wanted him to honor his valid North American contract, but the Russian hadn't reported to the team since ignoring his assignment to Portland for the 2004–05 AHL season and being suspended for his absence.

Despite the off-ice issues, the focus that season really was the rapid progress of the young Russian who *was* wearing the Capitals sweater, as Ovechkin was making a strong case to be the Calder Trophy winner as the NHL's top rookie. He won Rookie of the Month in December, and despite being just a first-year player, he was in the league's top 10 in scoring as the calendar flipped to 2006.

On New Year's Day, Ovechkin scored his 24th goal of the season in a 5–2 loss to Atlanta in front of a small crowd of 11,533 at MCI Center, extending a personal scoring streak to six games. It was the beginning of a terrific month for the young star, and one that would land him on highlight reels across North America with a spectacular goal in Arizona.

"I came up there for the Thrashers game in Washington around New Year's Day, and I went out to Bowie [in suburban Maryland] when they had a practice there to do an Ovechkin story for the *Atlanta Journal-Constitution*," former Thrashers beat writer John Manasso recalled. "The amount of people to watch practice was unbelievable. They weren't out at Piney Orchard because of a problem with the building, and the [Bowie Ice Arena] just couldn't handle the amount of people.

"You could start to sense the excitement there. You could just see he was unique with the ferocity he played with, and the skill."

Despite his relative anonymity in Washington, Ovechkin quickly had become a known quantity around the league, and he did his best to connect with his fans when he could. "When I see a little boy, I remember when I was little and I used to stand and wait for some guy I would go to after a game," he told the *Washington Times'* Dave Fay. "Right now I feel I must sign because I am like this. When I was little, I had signatures from players on Spartak. I had a stick from Alexei Zhamnov. I have a signature picture of [Slava] Fetisov. I was crazy about him. I was a fan of everybody."

A two-game trip to the West certainly put the rookie on the NHL map. On January 13, 2006, Ovechkin recorded his first-ever hat trick, scoring all three of Washington's goals in a 3–2 overtime win in Anaheim. After beating Mighty Ducks netminder Jean-Sebastien Giguere with a wrist shot for his 30th goal of his rookie season to end the contest, he celebrated by "swimming" on the ice at Arrowhead Pond.

"That road trip was one for the ages," former teammate Brent

Johnson recalled. "Him getting a hat trick — I know he'll have many more in his career, hopefully not against me [laughing] — it's something to see. When you go on the road out West, those aren't really easy games out there with the travel and the time difference and whatnot. He had a fantastic game [in Anaheim], and it kept going that whole trip."

Three days later, he scored what simply became known as "The Goal." With Washington holding a 5–1 lead over the Coyotes in the third period, Ovechkin broke in one-on-one on Phoenix defenseman Paul Mara, being brought down in the process. Despite twisting downward with his back hitting the ice, Ovechkin managed to get his stick, which was extended over his head, on the puck and put enough mustard on it to slide it past Coyotes netminder Brian Boucher for an improbable goal from an impossible angle.

"The Caps played a beautiful game that night cover-to-cover, I do remember that, and I do remember where 'The Goal' fell in the run of it," said Joe Beninati, who called the game that night for Comcast SportsNet. "Any time Ovechkin touches the puck, you always had to focus, because there is something special that could happen. But was I anticipating what he did that night? No. Nobody could. I don't think I'll ever see anything like that again.

"Knowing the circumstances in a 5–1 game, I was pleased I was able to take that call up-ice and he's the star in that situation, and what he does is so extraordinary, and to this day, it's simply sensational. It really is."

It was a goal that even left the legendary Wayne Gretzky in awe, as cameras caught the Coyotes coach checking out the replay in disbelief on the Jobing.com Arena video board.

"I remember fans hitting themselves in the forehead, slapping themselves, not believing their eyes," Beninati recalled. "I remember Wayne Gretzky, the greatest player of all time, behind the Coyotes bench, taking at least two or three crooked-neck looks at the scoreboard — sort of like a dog hearing a whistle. This is Wayne Gretzky going, 'How in the world did he do that?' Those are the images I remember:

the shocked looks and dismay of the defenders for Phoenix that couldn't believe that this had occurred.

"I don't know how he contorted himself that way and I think I will never see anything like that again. His entire rookie year was just jaw-dropping."

As Washington's netminder that night, Brent Johnson had a unique vantage point for the tally, standing in the opposite crease as Boucher became forever linked with the improbable tally. "Everybody was just in shock," Johnson recalled years later. "I couldn't show it too much since we still had a game to play, but it was one of those things where everyone afterward was like, 'Are you kidding me?' One of those kind of deals.

"How did he have the presence of mind to flip that behind his back, on the ice, and then you can see with the goalie, and Brian Boucher and the defensemen saying, 'Are you kidding me?' No fault to Brian Boucher, he's thinking the puck's going in the corner with the body, thinking the play's dead, and the next thing you know the puck's in the back of the net."

Asked if that kind of play is a goalie's worst nightmare, Johnson replied simply, "Yeah, it definitely is. You never want to see something like that happen against you. Things like that happen in hockey, and when they do, for a goalie, you just have to put your hands together for him and say good job."

"That was pretty sweet," Gretzky told reporters after the game. "You know, he's a phenomenal player, and he's been a tremendous influence in the game. It's great to see, because he is that good."

"The best goal I ever scored," Ovechkin told the Associated Press afterward. "I just went down and shot."

With the emergence of new media — and in this case, especially YouTube — the highlight quickly went viral and became one of the hottest topics of the sports world.

"The phenomenon of that goal really cemented his national status in terms of hockey," Nate Ewell recalled. "He was already looking like the guy who would win the Calder, but that really locked it in. I think it had a big effect in D.C. as well, in terms of getting people interested.

"I think there was a sense of here is something special that we really ought to be keeping an eye on. It was two weeks after the Redskins were done and he'd already had enough of a body of work that showed he was something good, and that [play] showed he was something special."

While hockey interest in Washington traditionally picks up once the Redskins' season ends, the highlight certainly helped bring attention to a team that badly needed a boost.

"The biggest thing you remember [of Ovechkin's rookie year] was the goal on Martin Luther King Day in Phoenix," Ed Frankovic recalled. "I remember there wasn't a whole lot to watch about this team until they got Ovechkin. A couple of days earlier against Anaheim . . . he took over a hockey game and the Caps beat the Ducks. He had three goals and his famous swimming-on-the-ice-type move, and later on in the same trip he had 'The Goal.' From then on out, it was worth watching because it was Alex Ovechkin; he had a chance to do something special every night, every shift he was on the ice. The team still wasn't very good; there wasn't much around him. But he was worth watching every night."

Frankovic also noted that having hockey's most famous name caught on tape reacting to the tally certainly helped. "It didn't hurt that it was against the Coyotes with Wayne Gretzky on the bench. The cameras caught his reaction," he said. "The greatest player ever has that kind of expression on his face, you know it's going to get airplay all across Canada and all across the U.S.

"It was definitely a turning point for the Caps."

Ovechkin scored 11 goals and 10 assists in January, earning him both another Rookie of the Month honor, as well as the NHL's Offensive Player of the Month honor — only the third time in league history a player was able to accomplish both.

"[I remember] just how sensational he was [in his rookie year]," *Tampa Tribune* writer Erik Erlendsson recalled. "Obviously, it was Sidney Crosby's rookie year, and [Crosby] was a hyped player, and for good reason the league was pushing Crosby.

"After [Ovechkin] scored that goal in Phoenix from his back, I went to Jay Feaster, who was the [Lightning] general manager at the time, and asked him about Alex Ovechkin. He said, 'I love Alex Ovechkin, but I wish he wasn't in the same division so we didn't have to see him six times a year.'"

Erlendsson also noted that Ovechkin didn't fit the stereotype of a Russian player: he liked to hit, showed a lot of emotion and was more an individual talent than some of the great players that had come out of the old Soviet Union. "It was so weird because Russian players have these stigmas attached to them from the 1980 U.S. Olympic team — the lack of passion they would have when they scored a goal. They had no emotion, they would skate back to the bench with congratulations and pats on the back.

"And here, in 2005, comes this Russian player who is just filled with emotion, filled with passion; you could just see he loves to play the game. It electrified a lot of people. Here's this 20-year-old Russian kid who plays the game like North Americans. I think that was the thing that turned a lot of people on to Alex, the way that he plays."

"There was a buzz every time he touched the puck," Yahoo!'s Greg Wyshynski recalled. "And the way he played back then — which is not the way he plays today — it was like watching a comet coming through the zone. He got the puck and it was like vintage Jagr, he'd come down through the neutral zone into the offensive zone, and it was an unstoppable force. He'd shoot the puck on the rush.

"The electricity in this place every time he touched the puck was palpable. And it might be because the rest of the team was so terrible, but that's what you'd look for. People were starting to show up to see this guy. That was the real first pillar for what they eventually built here fan base wise."

Despite the newfound appeal, the face of the Capitals franchise was still just a 20-year-old Russian in North America. Brian Willsie fondly recalled Ovechkin's excitement over being named the cover athlete for Electronic Arts' *NHL 07* video game. "He got the call and was really excited," Willsie said. "It was kind of like Christmas for us. He was like,

'Willsie, you can't tell anybody. It's not coming out for another month, but I just got the word.' Those things were exciting for him, and it was neat for me to be part of that with him."

Despite Ovechkin's vast skill, the Capitals were not surrounding the rookie with a whole lot of talent, meaning opponents began to concentrate on defending the budding star and concede a point or two to him per night, knowing the rest of the Washington lineup was beatable. You'd even see an unusual formation during Washington's power plays; teams would use their four defenders to essentially surround Ovechkin, daring the rookie to pass to one of the other wide-open Caps who clearly didn't have the Russian's scoring touch.

As the Capitals started to see more attention paid to their superstar, with the anticipation of what he would do whenever he touched the puck, his presence made the Capitals a great gate attraction around the league.

"As far as that was concerned, one thing I remember of that year was Ovi, and he came in and was impact all the way," Jeff Halpern said later. "I actually remember telling a story to Steven Stamkos, because I said the same thing about him after my last year in Tampa. When Ovi got the puck, even in his own zone, you could just feel the excitement grow in the crowd."

"He's the best player in the world, so obviously it's a challenge to play against him," Florida Panthers forward Matt Bradley said later of his former teammate. "You can only hope to contain a guy like that, when they're that good, it's tough to keep him off the board. If you can contain him and keep him at bay, that's the best you can do."

"Well, obviously everyone knows what a tremendous talent he is," the Penguins' Brent Johnson said of his former teammate. "What impressed me the most about Alex to start was his just wanting to win; it was never ever really about himself. Obviously, he got excited when he scored, but he also got excited when his teammates scored, and that even shows now. He gets really pumped up. Outside of that, he's a tremendous talent and can do wonders with the puck, and he can also run through guys, and his strength and speed are just fantastic.

"It was great facing him in practice because you knew you were going to get his best out there every day. It's a great challenge for us goalies."

Despite the extra attention, Ovechkin finished with 52 goals and 106 points, which earned him the Calder Trophy for the league's best rookie. He finished the season with the third-most goals by a Capital in a single campaign and the second-highest point total in franchise history.

"It's not very often that a top athlete comes in with so much hype and lives up to every ounce of it and actually surpasses it," Joe Beninati said. "For everything we had heard Alex was supposed to be, he was that and more.

"For someone who is in the broadcast television industry, who has to describe world-class athletes, what he was doing night after night completely challenged my powers of description . . . The thing I always remember is that they hyped and trumped him up so much, [calling him] the player of a generation, and boy, did he prove it that first year with something special. Very rarely did he let anyone down."

When asked what fans might not know about the star player, Dmitry Chesnokov explained that it's a competitive spirit that really drives Ovechkin. "He's a winner, and in terms even when he was young, he was playing hockey, whether it was pond hockey or some other kind of hockey . . . as much as players say it's just another game, he takes every game seriously. Every little bit. I think it transforms into other things on the ice as well. He wants to be the first, he wants to be the leader, he wants to be the winner, and people around him are helping him to become that."

While the bulk of the hockey media's attention coming out of the lockout surrounded the arrival of Ovechkin and Crosby, Washington and Pittsburgh weren't as successful in the standings.

Washington gained 11 points from their previous campaign, but still were last in the Southeast Division, 14th in the Eastern Conference. The only team behind them were the Penguins, who finished with the exact same point total as in 2003–04, just 58.

"I don't know if [the arrival of Crosby and Ovechkin] helped [the league] as much right out of the lockout, because honestly, as much as it got played up, the teams weren't competing," Nate Ewell recalled. "I think it certainly helps having two young stars, but it didn't really ramp up until both teams were good at the same time. I know that they both measured themselves against each other, so there was the individual rivalry, but I don't think it was the same in the first two years."

Despite the Capitals' overall lack of success, they were able to finish their home season by exacting a bit of revenge on one of their divisional opponents that had gotten under their skin all year.

On April 17, the Atlanta Thrashers — and former Capital Peter Bondra — came to town needing a win to keep their playoff hopes alive.

"The Thrashers had dominated the Capitals all year . . . but the Capitals knocked them out of the playoff [race]," John Manasso recalled. "Coming down the stretch, [Atlanta] had to win almost every game and they were winning almost every game. Carolina won the Stanley Cup that year, but the Thrashers were dominating them, beating them 5–0 in Carolina down the stretch, so had they made the playoffs, they would have done some damage.

"Bobby Holik scored 11 seconds into the game and it looked like they were going to win . . . but the Caps hated the Thrashers. [Former Atlanta coach] Bob Hartley inspires a lot of enemity in their opponents for the style that they play.

"[The Capitals] really wanted to win that game and put Atlanta out of it, and they did."

Washington erased a 4–3 deficit in the third. Ovechkin scored his 52nd and final goal of the year for the equalizer, then helped out on a Brian Willsie go-ahead goal that held up as the game-winner.

Afterward, the Capitals weren't exactly shy: they were happy to play the role as spoiler.

"We hate that team," Kolzig told reporters. "I think it started at the beginning of the year. I'm not going to say they're dirty, but they push the limits in how hard they play. They spanked us a few times earlier in the year. It was sweet revenge. We got the last laugh."

"I remember playing that game, and wishing it was more of a

playoff feel," Jeff Halpern said later. "You wanted to move on and not just knock that team out.

"There were a lot of good pieces and really good personalities in that room; a couple years later [the Capitals] turned around with a couple of those pieces. It was a really good group of guys; they [just] needed some things so that they wouldn't need so much from each player."

The 2005–06 season ultimately showed there was a long way to go for the franchise — both on and off the ice.

"We had a really hard-working team, but we just weren't in those meaningful games and games that seem like it's the end of the world if you lose them," said Halpern, who left the club in the following offseason to sign with Dallas. "We were just sputtering along. To be in the prime of my career and not able to be in those games was the hardest part."

Ovechkin still remembers his rookie season fondly. "Of course, you can see the fans in the city and how they were excited," he said. "My first year was a great experience, and it was a good memory."

Washington was 22 points behind the eighth-seeded Tampa Bay Lightning for the East's final playoff spot, closer to the basement than to the playoffs. Attendance-wise, they'd actually sunk: with just a 13,095 average they were the third worst in the National Hockey League — ahead of just the Islanders and Blackhawks and down from the 14,720 figure the team had posted heading into the lockout. Of course, a number of those tickets had been sold based on the team's playoff appearance in 2002–03, before the rebuilding effort had damaged the team's standing in Washington.

Even though the Capitals' season was done, the team's prospects weren't quite finished for the year. The Hershey Bears, which featured a number of future Washington players and even their future coach, were able to gain a bit of extra playoff experience at the American Hockey League level as they started the Calder Cup playoffs.

CHAPTER 5

GREENER PASTURES IN HERSHEY

While Alexander Ovechkin received the lion's share of the attention after being picked first overall in the 2004 NHL draft, another young Washington draft pick was doing some damage in the American Hockey League.

Mike Green, a 20-year-old defenseman out of Calgary, was the team's third and final pick in the first round of that draft, and he was becoming an offensive weapon with the Bears. Although he had split time between Washington and Hershey during the regular season, he became a force in the Calder Cup playoffs.

"I think with anybody at the AHL level you see make it . . . if they weren't a high pick, nothing came easy to them," John Walton recalled. "With Greenie, he obviously had high credentials and was hugely important. There are some guys, you see it when you see them; you know they're just going places."

In 56 games with the Bears, Green had nine goals and 34 assists. He was even better in the postseason, recording 18 points in 21 games.

"He was a force, especially on the power play, someone who could really direct traffic and make things happen from the blue line," Walton said. "I think he made life hard on opposing penalty kills more often than not.

"The thing I remember the most about him that year was how good he made everyone else around him — and not only getting the puck to the folks around him. With the man advantage, he was super."

Part of Green's success came thanks to Bears coach Bruce Boudreau's willingness to let him take chances with the puck.

"I think at the very beginning he was stay-at-home, but it didn't take him long to really develop," Walton recalled. "It was something we had seen before when he came into his own in D.C. . . . He was a man among boys at the AHL level. We knew it was only a matter of time before he stuck [with Washington] permanently. He really ran things."

Although the Capitals' farm system had been stocked — Green was drafted thanks to Detroit's first-round pick that was acquired in the Robert Lang deal — the team didn't have a whole lot of success in its final year in Portland in 2004–05, missing out on the Calder Cup playoffs altogether.

When the team's prospects moved from Maine to central Pennsylvania in 2005–06, the Capitals hired Boudreau from the Manchester Monarchs to guide them. John Walton says Boudreau brought a culture of winning from New Hampshire. "From an attitude perspective, there was a feeling of we're going to elevate what we do here," Walton recalled. "It was mental as much as it was Xs and Os. The players who had come [down from Portland] had no playoff success. The Bears didn't even make the playoffs in 2003–04. All these guys coming in — I remember Lawrence Nycholat coming in after we were done after the [Calder Cup win]. When he was signed with the Caps, he told his wife he'd probably be done early since [Portland] didn't make the playoffs and the Bears didn't make it either. He said, 'Boy, was I wrong.'

"But that was the mentality of a lot of guys coming in. They had no success, and Bruce came in making them believe. For me, being around that every day, that positive vibe from Bruce that spread to the whole team, and for that team even in the regular season to finish second was something we hadn't come close to in three years.

"That was my fourth year [in Hershey], we made the playoffs and were out in the first round in the first year and missed the next two — even for me going to the rink every day, there wasn't a philosophy of success.

"Bruce made everyone believe."

The Bears finished second in their division and opened the playoffs with four straight wins in a sweep of the Norfolk Admirals. In the next round, Hershey took care of the team that finished first in their division, the Wilkes-Barre/Scranton Penguins, in another sweep.

"They had a 10-game winning streak in the playoffs and were plus-32 in goal differential," *Patriot-News* writer Tim Leone recalled. "It was overwhelming."

Facing the Pirates in the Eastern Conference Finals — Portland affiliated with Anaheim after Washington left town — was the most memorable series of the season for Walton.

"The number one memory I have of that — and it sounds strange — is the Eastern Conference Final rather than the Calder Cup Final," he recalled. "It was a series that had everything, on the ice, off the ice, a big lead in the series. It was a strange series too, because even though Hershey was the lower seed, they got Game 7 at home because of ice issues in both buildings. The Bears played Games 3, 4 and 7 at home and then everything else was in Portland. It meant a lot of bus travel, and after four games it looked like the Bears were going to win easily.

"They had a 3–1 lead and had to go to Portland and just win one more, but it didn't happen.

"I remember Al Coates, who was GM of Anaheim at the time, sitting in the press box just down from us, and Tim Leone comes down and says, 'Just so you know, if Portland wins this game, it's not going to be pretty in Game 7, because the Three Horsemen of [Ryan] Getzlaf, [Corey] Perry and [Dustin] Penner are coming.'

"So you almost have this feeling of doom as Portland has a lead in Game 6 and they're going tie the series. Even though you're going home, there's a five-day layoff before Game 7, because the circus was in town — which was only appropriate with the way the series had gone.

"Sure enough, with practices back at Hersheypark Arena, [Pirates coach] Kevin Dineen on one side, Bruce on another, they made a few waves with some of the banter back and forth, so the stage was set for Game 7. Now you see Penner, Perry and Getzlaf coming out on the ice, and even the fan base was like, 'Oh, boy, we'll see.'

"Penner had two goals, but [Bears winger] Graham Mink tied it and [Hershey forward] Eric Fehr [scored] the biggest goal I've ever seen in my life in person to win it — after Getzlaf hits the post three minutes into overtime, thinking we were done then and there. And we were on to the Finals for the first time."

"They did have the classic series against Portland, which was the best series I've ever covered in this league," Leone recalled. "Game 7 is still the best game I've ever covered. Ironically the way things have worked out with Bruce [becoming Anaheim's coach in 2011], with Getzlaf and Penner along with Dustin Penner [in Portland] . . . they were gone most of the second half of the season [to the NHL], but Anaheim was eliminated and made it back for Game 7.

"They took Milwaukee in the Finals in six games. Overwhelming size and power in the forwards . . . They were just able to dominate in the offensive zone and make it tough for opponents to get the puck out. And that top line of Flash [Tomas Fleischmann], [Kris] Beech and Mink was just overwhelming and Flash was unbelievable in the playoff run."

"It's nice; a group of guys came together at the end of the season and we made a good push in the playoffs. Everything went well and the first two rounds we didn't lose a game," Bears left winger Chris Bourque recalled. "We had the tough series against Portland and won Game 7 in overtime, then played Milwaukee in the Finals and beat them. It was really exciting and very fun to be a part of."

The Calder Cup win over the Milwaukee Admirals was the icing on the cake for several Capitals prospects; Mike Green recorded 15 assists during the postseason to help fuel the Bears' first Calder Cup championship since 1996–97 — and the first for a Washington Capitals affiliate since the Pirates won the Cup in their first year in Portland in 1993–94.

Green was a key member of the Bears' title team, moving the puck effectively and helping quarterback the team's power play, roles he would later assume in Washington. He later earned a pair of Norris Trophy nominations and an All-Star appearance in Washington — with his game certainly getting a boost once Boudreau joined him at the NHL level in November 2007.

When asked to recall his best memory of that playoff run, Boudreau remembers Green, although not in a game situation. "The first thing that jumps into my mind was Mike Green sliding along tables in Gatorade after we won the Cup," the former Bears coach said, laughing. "That's the first thing that comes into my mind, the jubilation and the kids crying in the room. The second thing I remember is telling Graham Mink, 'You're up,' and he responded, 'I can't go, my legs won't move' in the third period of Game 6 [in Milwaukee].

"But they were good guys, and we had a really good team. When we wanted to play, we were hard to beat. We could have won without losing a playoff game, and we did in the first two series against Norfolk and Wilkes-Barre — two really good teams, by the way — and the first two games against Portland.

"We should have won Game 3 — we had a 3–1 lead in Game 3, then won Game 4, and we sort of thought, 'This is easy.' Then, they ended up winning Games 5 and 6 and then got Getzlaf, Perry and Penner back, but we won Game 7. The regular season is kind of a blur. Wilkes-Barre got off to a great start, they were 20–1–1 after 22 games, but they couldn't shake us, because we were 18–4. It was a great year."

Tomas Fleischmann added 32 points in 20 games for Hershey, and remembered how it was a benefit playing for Boudreau there. "He took me from the minor leagues to the NHL and gave me the opportunity," Fleischmann said later as a member of the Florida Panthers. "He was probably the best coach I ever had."

Brooks Laich had an unusual season, splitting between the NHL and AHL by first playing 73 regular season games with Washington, then appearing in 21 postseason games in Chocolatetown.

"That was a terrific year," Laich recalled. "First, you win a Calder

Cup. It might not be a Stanley Cup, but it's still a championship. Mike Green was on that team with six or seven guys off that team who ended up playing here. Bruce was the coach, obviously, and that gave us a good relationship. You go through something like that and win something like that, it gives you a good basis for the relationship.

"After that year was over, when I was leaving Hershey, I talked to Bruce and looked back on the year and said, 'I averaged 11 minutes in the NHL, and then won a Calder Cup championship, so it was a pretty good year.' It was a development year, to get your first taste of the NHL and a taste of winning a championship in the minors, so it was a very good development year, and a springboard for myself."

Boudreau had turned what had been a struggling AHL affiliate into a champion in his first season.

"Bruce did a fabulous job," Tim Leone said. "He was well-positioned, because he coached in Manchester against Portland a whole lot as division rivals, so he was really familiar with the [Capitals'] personnel. When he came in here, he thought they had talent but they were lacking confidence. The first thing he [said was] 'You're good, and we're going for the championship.' The guys thrived on that, bought in, and did it."

Chris Bourque agreed. "It was awesome, he's one of the best coaches I've ever played with. I've learned so much from Bruce, and his record shows how good a coach he is. He's a fun coach to play for, very easy to play for, and keeps you honest. It's fun coming to the rink every day when you're playing for someone like that."

Years later, that Calder Cup championship experience helped carry forward several Capitals.

"I think even the players themselves say that's a huge thing to be able to go through four rounds," the *Washington Examiner*'s Brian McNally said of the Bears' 2006 Calder Cup run. "The Calder Cup isn't like winning the Stanley Cup, but you're beat up after that. It's a brutal run. It's playoff hockey almost at its best, and for them to do that and be using a lot of the same players was a huge development and spoke to their trust in Bruce and what he's doing.

"There's a reason Brooks Laich defends [Boudreau] at any time. I think that was huge for them. Winning a title means something, even if there's not 18,000 watching you in person and millions on TV, you're still tested and to come through can only help at this level."

After the AHL team's first year in Hershey, the new arrangement seemed to be working out for both teams.

"Over the course of the affiliation, but right from the beginning, Hershey has had a philosophy that winning is as or more important than development, and this for a team that goes back into the 1930s," John Walton says. "It dovetailed nicely that Washington was flush with draft picks . . . a lot of prospects coming in.

"On the surface, you knew it would be good. You just didn't know how good, until it actually happened. I don't think that's really changed. From 2005 to today, [there's] a beautiful blueprint for success. I think especially of the salary-cap age of having that place to develop, what better place than that. Ten thousand fans a night, good veteran players to be around, and it's as NHL a place as you can be without actually being in the NHL from a media standpoint and a playing standpoint.

"It's certainly paid dividends for both teams."

SOPHOMORE STAGNATION

While the 2005–06 season was an improvement on the ice, the next season saw Washington end with the same point total. The perceived progress achieved thanks to Alexander Ovechkin's arrival had been undone by both injuries and a lack of depth.

The Capitals started quickly out of the gate, opening with a 13–10–6 record and looking like the team might make a run at its first playoff berth since 2002–03. But a stunning loss to their biggest rival in December put the team into a tailspin and the club finished the season 15–30–8 for a total of 70 points. Ovechkin had a strong sophomore year, again leading the team with 46 goals and 46 assists, aided by the return of Alexander Semin — who had finally been lured back to the NHL after being suspended by the club and taken to court to fulfill his contract.

The season certainly looked promising — even off the ice — as Ovechkin even added a bit to his growing legend by managing to hit a hole-in-one in a golf outing in suburban Virginia. "This was my first time playing golf," he told the *Washington Times*' Dave Fay. "I guess it's easy.

"Maybe I would do better if I played golf, not hockey," he joked. "It was lucky. I have to play again now, see how I can do."

In October, Ovechkin also got a firsthand taste of some of his global reach on the Capitals' first trip through Western Canada since the lockout, his first ever visit to Alberta and British Columbia.

"He couldn't be more popular than he has been up here," Capitals general manager George McPhee told Fay. "It's amazing. He was on the cover of every newspaper in Vancouver this weekend; his face is on TV so much you'd think he was running for office. That's all people talked about: Ovechkin."

"For want of a better description, [he] seems to be an absolute matinee idol, a rock star, however you want to phrase it," McPhee added. "No one's more popular. Now there's more television exposure and access to athletes that we had in 1994 [when Vancouver played for the Stanley Cup], so now there's even broader appeal.

"He is a kid who always does the right thing. He respects the game. He respects his teammates. He respects the referees."

The trip was also a good one for Washington, taking five out of a possible eight points, and the Caps finished 4–3–4 for the first month — just the second winning month the team had since the lockout.

The team also put the finishing touches on its new practice facility in Arlington, Virginia, as Kettler Capitals Iceplex opened. The new rink in Washington's suburbs put the Capitals much closer to their home city and in the heart of the team's season-ticket base in northern Virginia.

For 15 years, Washington had been practicing at Piney Orchard Ice Arena in Odenton, Maryland, which was actually closer to Baltimore than to the nation's capital. The arrangement made more sense when the Capitals were playing at the Capital Centre in Landover, Maryland, before the move downtown in 1997.

"When we had an American Hockey League team in Baltimore and were flying out of [the Baltimore-Washington airport] and playing in Landover, Piney was perfect," Nate Ewell told the *Baltimore Sun* at the time. "But to connect with fans closer to the Verizon Center and to let our players live in the community where they play, the Ballston location makes a lot of sense."

A new facility made the team more accessible and Metro-friendly to fans around the immediate Washington area. "I think it has this whole aura of first class," Caps owner Ted Leonsis told the *Washington Times'* Tim Lemke. "It will help us market to where our season-ticket base is."

"It's a little more vibrant on this side of the Beltway and closer to D.C.," Kolzig told the paper. "There are a lot of things that attract free agents — money being first and foremost — but next to that it's the community, whether it's a place to raise a family and the training facility. D.C. is a very underrated city. This being closer to the city than our other facility was will have a great effect."

Years later, Lemke thought the move to Arlington was an important part of the team's rebirth as it helped connect the team to its fan base. "They recognized who their fans were and gave them what they wanted," Lemke recalled. "They opened up Kettler, which I think was a big thing because it put a training camp where they knew the fans were. You hear a lot of folks in Baltimore saying, 'We're here too,' but if you look at their ticket base that was going to games, they were in the District of Columbia and northern Virginia.

"You put the training camp in the heart of northern Virginia and make it a nice facility, one that the players wanted to go to since they lived right there. It is close by and state of the art. That changed the culture of what the team was about, that they were going to provide resources to allow the team to compete in terms of facility and weight rooms. It's a nice place."

Five years after Kettler opening, Leonsis reflected on how the facility was one of the team's core rebuild projects. "It's been very meaningful to give our fans access and keep it open and free and be a world-class facility . . . Our city and our arena are world-class. . . . People and their family say this is a place they'd like to live and work, and we haven't had any issue in keeping our people any more or signing free agents. That wasn't the case five years ago."

Leonsis also thought the connection to the city was important, as according to him, a chunk of their fan base was from Maryland when the team moved to downtown Washington. "One of the issues the team faced was the move from USAir Arena to MCI Center 14 years ago. That was a dislocation. The training facility was in Maryland, the fan base came from Baltimore and Annapolis and out that way, and when the building opened in Washington, now it was far to come from Annapolis and Baltimore, and there also was an unknown/fear factor.

"[Washington had the] highest crime rate in the country, the neighborhood wasn't very good, there was a lot of skepticism, and we lost a lot of season-ticket holders. We had to rebuild to Bethesda and northern Virginia and the District. Now that the city's beautiful, we're getting lots of fans from Annapolis and Baltimore and the like, they buy plans and weekend plans and the like. That was a dramatic relocation for the team and took almost a decade to give people the confidence they'd want to come into D.C."

On the ice, the team held serve in November, record-wise. A four-game winning streak after Thanksgiving put the Capitals within reach of the playoffs as they headed into their first date of the season with the Pittsburgh Penguins at the recently renamed Verizon Center.

On December 11, in a game broadcast on national television, the first half belonged to Washington, with the Caps building a 4–0 lead in under 26 minutes. But the game turned south in a hurry, as Pittsburgh's Maxime Talbot answered less than a minute after Brooks Laich's goal gave the Caps the short-lived four-goal edge. The Penguins rallied to erase the deficit, with Evgeni Malkin scoring the equalizer early in the third. He added the winner in the shootout.

After the game, the Caps were at a loss about how they'd let a game that started off so well slip through their fingers.

"It was an unbelievable game to watch," Ovechkin told reporters. "We dominated the first period and 10 minutes of the second period and then just stopped playing. Sometimes that happens. Nothing is a lock, you know? We're just disappointed right now."

"We just lost our focus, got up 4–1 and lost our focus," Glen Hanlon told Fay at the practice the day after the loss. "We're just trying to learn you start at 7 o'clock and play until 9:30.

"It bothered me because it was such a hyped-up game," the coach added. "It was an exciting game. It was such a big stage, playing on national TV, we had the Crosby–Ovechkin situation, it was an exciting game to play and I didn't want to come out on the short end."

The game proved to be a turning point for both teams. The Capitals went 15 games below .500 after its roster was decimated with injuries around Christmas. Washington struggled to regain the composure and success it enjoyed in the first quarter.

For the Penguins, they went 21 games over the .500 mark following the comeback win and earned the team's first playoff berth since 2000–01.

"Yeah, it's disappointing," Kolzig told the *Washington Times* at season's end. "Right up until about Christmas we were in a playoff spot.

"To a lot of people it's not surprising, but to us in the room there's an empty feeling. I think we felt better about ourselves last year, the amount of points we put up, the way we finished after the Olympic break. But for the last month and a half, wins have been hard to come by."

"The next year or so, hopefully, we'll have depth where guys can come in and the guys who are hurt won't necessarily be missed as much so we're able to continue winning instead of going on long losing streaks," Kolzig added. "In my opinion, that's what really killed us this year, the lack of depth . . . Every team goes through it, but when you're a team like us that isn't as deep and the injuries happen, the consequences are severe. Had we had a full lineup for the whole season, I don't know if we would have made it, but we could have been right up there until the last week or so."

"It's kind of hard, I erased that from my memory," now–Penguins goaltender Brent Johnson said years later.

Johnson did mention that, at the time, the Capitals had trouble with the Penguins; Pittsburgh dominated their head-to-head matchups.

"You're never really happy when the next game is against Pittsburgh, because they had Washington's number. It just was one of those things: at Mellon Arena, it's going to be a tough one. Those are sometimes fun, sometimes they get you going, but that can be tough too."

The numbers were flat pretty much across the board; attendance was up an average of just 26 fans.

The team was clearly a work in progress, with a lot of journeymen in its blue and bronze uniforms. But a new crop of youngsters — along with a new logo, colors and jersey design — were on the horizon.

"They still weren't there yet," Ed Frankovic of WNST in Baltimore recalled. "They didn't have the talent that year. You look at that defense, it was pretty bad, with Bryan Muir out there and some guys who flat-out couldn't skate. But when I talked to some of the scouts around the league, they told me how good the team's 2006 draft was, and they still had the 2004 class — Ovechkin, Green and [Jeff] Schultz — and then in 2006 they draft [Semyon] Varlamov, they draft [Michal] Neuvirth, they get [Nicklas] Backstrom at the top of the first round, but he stayed in Sweden.

"You knew there were players coming but they were still a long way away — especially on defense."

A season unlike any other in Capitals history was on tap, however, one that would see a major rebranding effort evoke memories of a more successful era in the franchise's history. Along with it came personnel changes that would result in the team quickly rising up the charts — in the standings and in the stands as well.

RETURN TO THE RED, WHITE AND BLUE

In the summer of 2007, the Capitals unveiled a new identity. They had used a red, white and blue uniform design since its 1974–75 expansion season, but scrapped the scheme and adopted bronze, blue and white after the strike-shortened 1994–95 season. With the team planning to move from the Capital Centre in Landover to the new arena in Washington's Chinatown neighborhood, the team wanted a new identity; a new logo and unfamiliar colors were adopted for the move inside the District of Columbia's city limits.

The blue and bronze jersey helped boost the team's merchandise sales briefly, but the new uniform never really resonated with the fan base — even though the team wore it during their one and only trip to the Stanley Cup Finals in 1998.

Shortly after Ted Leonsis bought the team, numerous fans began requesting a return to the old colors. Leonsis himself reportedly wasn't a fan of the team's blue and bronze look — the colors were shared by the NBA's renamed Washington Wizards — but he was hesitant to change the jerseys so soon after the design overhaul.

Still, for years it was rumored that the Capitals would eventually return to their roots. The team quietly registered a new logo that featured the Capitol Dome and a stylized wordmark with the U.S. Patent and Trademark office in 2000, and worked with Tommy Hilfiger on a design that was leaked in a hockey supply catalog.

After a not-so-positive reaction to the proposed changes, the new logo prototype and the jersey design were abandoned. The team adopted the black third jersey with bronze trim as the team's dark jersey, abandoning the original blue design in 2000; they kept the white swooping eagle and Capitol Dome through the lockout and into Ovechkin's first two seasons in the NHL.

When the league's new jersey manufacturer, Reebok, elected to reengineer the basic uniform design for all 30 teams, introducing a sleeker and sweat-resistant material, the Capitals decided to finally bring back the old colors.

Applying for league approval of a logo and jersey change required time; so did a market testing process. It took two seasons to tweak and refine. Capitals management also recognized that a bit of time needed to pass after the lockout before they dared introduce an expensive new jersey — unlike the Buffalo Sabres, who changed back to a blue and gold color scheme in 2006–07, one year before the rest of the league switched standard jersey designs — so they stuck with their black and bronze uniform through two post-lockout seasons.

When the Reebok Edge jersey was unveiled for all 30 teams before the 2007–08 season, the Capitals debuted a new, stylized version of their old logo, with the wordmark "Capitals" in a more modernized font, and the "t" of Capitals fashioned into a hockey stick — like the team's original logo. The red, white and blue was, of course, a nod to Washington being the capital of the United States; the three stars represented Maryland, the District of Columbia and Virginia, and was also an homage to the team's old stars and stripes. A secondary shoulder logo was designed as well, as a stylized eagle and the outline of the U.S. Capitol Dome blended to resemble a "W" for Washington. Like the team's original jersey, the primary color for the dark uniforms was red, and it looked like a 21st-century version of the team's original sweater.

The new logos and uniforms were unveiled at the team's draft party at Kettler Capitals Iceplex on June 22, 2007; captain Chris Clark, Brian Pothier, Ben Clymer and Jeff Schultz modeled for fans and on Comcast SportsNet.

"I was here the night they unveiled it for the draft party," former Bears play-by-play voice John Walton recalled. "I wasn't a huge fan of the jersey before. I didn't have anything against it. For me, from a lettering standpoint if you can read it from a great distance, I'm pretty good with it. But as soon as you saw the new logo, which was new- and old-school rolled into one, I said that's a winner."

With the NHL adopting the practice of having home teams wear dark jerseys at home in 2003–04 — the team regularly wore white home uniforms before this, other than for a brief half season during the NHL's 75th anniversary in 1991–92 — it was a chance to brand around a bolder color. Bringing back the striking red from the original uniforms struck the right chord with fans.

"They recognized the fans liked the old uniforms and the history of the team," former *Washington Times* sports business reporter Tim Lemke recalled. "It was a way to move on from an era where they didn't get much done. It was a good, crisp, clean look with the uniforms, and coupled with the uniforms was the ability to rebrand around the color red. Everything was red, from the slogans to the marquees to inside the Verizon; everything was around that color. It was a consistent theme with 'Rock the Red,' and it worked well. It got people excited and changed the culture of things. It became fun and cool to come to a hockey game, and it helped that the team was [starting to win]."

The new design — particularly when paired with one of the game's most popular players — quickly became a best-seller; the old design was easily forgotten by many fans.

"It was a brilliant move. There were all the old Caps fans who still had the red, white and blue garb and this is the nation's capital," Ed Frankovic recalled. "I never liked the switch to [the blue and bronze] jerseys. The blue ones were gone quickly and the only good one of the three was perhaps the black one with the Capitol Dome on it. The switch back to the red, white and blue was a great move, and all of a sudden the talent starts coming along . . . and the rest is history."

But while it was the most obvious change, the uniform design wasn't the only new look the Capitals had beginning that summer of 2007. For the first time since signing Robert Lang in 2002, the team took a real leap into the free agent market on July 1, signing defenseman Tom Poti and forward Viktor Kozlov. The next day, former Capital Michael Nylander — who was dealt away in the fire sale of 2003–04 — was brought back in the hopes that he could do for Alexander Ovechkin what he had done with Jaromir Jagr in Washington and New York.

While the Capitals had been deliberately slow in building the team back up as they came out of the lockout, the signings were a clear indication that the team expected to take the next step toward their future in 2007–08, and make a serious run for the playoffs.

Washington was able to do that, but the manner in which it occurred was expected by no one.

BACKSTROM
AND BOUDREAU

The Capitals opened 2007–08 with heightened expectations. The arrival of free agent additions and young Swedish center Nicklas Backstrom made them believe they were ready to make a playoff run.

Backstrom, the team's fourth-overall selection in the '06 draft, elected to stay in Sweden to skate with Byrnäs IF rather than join Washington during the 2006–07 season. The highly touted prospect finally signed an entry level deal in 2007 and got the chance to join the high-powered club as they looked to end the team's playoff drought.

The Capitals once again started well, going 3–0 after wins over the Thrashers, Hurricanes and Islanders. Ovechkin even developed his now-familiar gap-toothed grin, losing one of his front teeth in the season opener in Atlanta. But after the fast start, things quickly started going south.

Over the next 40 days, the Caps went just 3–14–1, quickly plummeting to the bottom of the Eastern Conference.

The low point of the season — eerily similar to the poisoned atmosphere that was prevalent during the team's 2003–04 fire sale — was a home game against the Thrashers the night before Thanksgiving. The ugly 5–1 loss was the team's fifth straight.

The small crowd of 11,669 was agitated by the team's poor play, with fans chanting "Fire Hanlon!" The crowd even mockingly cheered the final minute of the third as the team was easily routed and appeared headed for another year of rebuilding.

"I have never seen a pro sports team under Hanlon those last two weeks play as tight as they did," the *Washington Examiner*'s Brian McNally recalled. "Everything they did on the ice said, 'We are going to find a way to lose.' The first time two goals went in the other way, heads dropped, fans booed and 'Fire Hanlon' chants started. It was not pleasant to watch."

"Obviously it wasn't a perfect world with Glen, and I'm not talking about everything else, just in winning," fellow goaltender Brent Johnson recalled. "Down from the brass, to George, something had to be done."

With the team sitting at just 13 points in the standings and an afternoon game in Philadelphia looming the day after Thanksgiving, Capitals general manager George McPhee decided to shake up the club radically.

"All of our coaches since the new CBA have brought something unique," Leonsis recalled years later. "Glen Hanlon was a teacher, he was very disciplined, he played a defensive style, he was a very honest and thorough player and he demanded respect for the game and discipline, and we were very lucky that he was the first coach that these young players were exposed to, and I thought he did a really good job.

"Then we went out and made investments in free agents. There's something ironic and non-self-reflective by the media, by some fans, some bloggers, because there's always a demand for free agents, for adding veterans to the lineup. There's a comfort in that request, and so that was the year and we spent money for free agents, and we got off to a really, really bad start.

"The fans were howling, the fans were chanting, the media was over the top and we had to deal with all of that. And then George thought after that game against [Atlanta], when he spent time with Glen, that

Glen said some magic words, which were 'I don't know what to do.' For a coach, there is some symbolism in the 'I'm going to press this button, I'm going to change this lineup,' and when you've run out of those, that really is a cry for help."

As a result of the team's poor start and fading playoff hopes, McPhee fired Hanlon and made the call to Hershey to bring up Bears coach Bruce Boudreau on an interim basis in hopes of lighting a fire under his struggling team. Bob Woods stepped in to take over Boudreau's former team.

"The night before Thanksgiving, [the Bears] were playing Bridgeport and the funny thing, [Hershey] got out to a bad start [that year] as well," John Walton recalled. "We had to win that game to get to .500. We were 8–8 out of the blocks.

"I remember doing the scoreboard show that night, and I knew the Caps played Atlanta and I knew the score was 5–1. I remember reading the score — and we can read the papers with the best of them — but what would happen you didn't know.

"I talked with Doug [Yingst] after the game briefly, and he told me briefly as I left, 'You better keep your phone on. Thanksgiving might be canceled — I'll let you know.' At 7:30 the next morning I got the official word.

"That was one of the greatest and hardest press releases I'd ever written. . . . Two-and-a-half years and it's over, literally in the snap of a finger.

"You never know where this business is going to go sometimes. I knew with Woody with what we had, he'd be great, but [Boudreau] was a larger than life personality that touched everybody. It was wonderful. Turkey was served cold that day. There won't be a Thanksgiving that I won't think about him going up that day."

During his tenure in Hershey, Boudreau had won one Calder Cup and reached another Calder Cup Final as the Bears lost to Hamilton in 2007, and he left behind a legacy of success in a short amount of time.

"There's no pretense at all," Walton said of Boudreau. "He is who he is, and that's his top quality in my mind. He's very good at knowing when to apply pressure and when to let off. When I was around him previously, there weren't many times we weren't successful. Even the times where he lost two or three in a row — and he never lost more than three in a row in Hershey — it was 'OK, we're going to get them tomorrow and here's how we're going to do it.' I got to sit at the front of the bus and being around those guys, and it's more intimate than being at [the NHL] level, but that teaches you about that person too."

"He's a genuine guy," said Tim Leone, who wrote *Gabby: Confessions of a Hockey Lifer* with the coach after his promotion. "What you see is what you get. There aren't ulterior motives. The one thing that's misconstrued is he gets labeled as a player's coach. I don't think that's the case. He has a way of needling guys and motivating guys. Although it doesn't burn out the relationship . . . it's not like a [Mike] Keenan where the fuse is a season or two. He's got a way of needling but not alienating; it's something that you have to be behind-the-scenes to see, but labeling him as a pure player's coach isn't accurate."

"That was a good day," a smiling Boudreau said years later when asked about when he found out his long-awaited dream came true to get his first NHL head coaching job. "It was very surprising, but I was 52, and I'd wanted to be back in the NHL for as long as I can remember. I remember my kid jumping on his bed when he heard, and I remember my wife jumping up and down, and I remember forgetting how to get to Kettler. It was a crazy day."

Boudreau wasn't joking about getting lost on his way, as he actually ended up asking for directions to the team's facility for the Thanksgiving Day practice. But it was a rare mistake, as over the next few months he helped resurrect the team's fading playoff hopes and won the Jack Adams Award as the league's top coach — despite being behind the bench for just 61 games.

For the Capitals, the coaching switch meant a quick change in system; the team took a style that better fit the personnel they had, emphasizing speed and skill and an aggressive offensive approach. It also meant the team adopted a big change in attitude.

"I think the biggest thing . . . in the first two years, Glen didn't want to emphasize results because he really couldn't," Nate Ewell explained. "The results weren't going to be very good. The emphasis was on working hard and doing the right things, and you get a pat on the back.

"Then it was difficult for the team [in 2007–08]. I think Glen was able to make the transition [to better players], but maybe it wasn't communicated and didn't trickle down to the players as smoothly as he wanted. We were playing hard the first 21 games but not getting wins, and I think there was a sense of 'Whatever we do, if we work hard, don't worry about what happens.'"

With Boudreau's arrival, the emphasis was on results, not just working hard. "When Bruce came in, it was 'We're going to win. I don't care how it happens, but we just have to win,'" Ewell said. "That changed the emphasis, guys were ready to embrace it, it was the right coach coming in at the right time.

"The pace of play picked up, the new aggressive systems, the things that fit well with the talent that we had, the real emphasis on winning that needed a new voice to really be heard."

Ed Frankovic of Baltimore's WNST Radio believes Boudreau changing the team's system to better fit its personnel was a huge boost.

"He changed the system," Frankovic said. "You can't play that system with the talent they had. [Hanlon]'s trying to play the Minnesota Wild trapping system with world-class skill players. The night before Hanlon got fired, I was watching that Thrashers game, and afterward, seeing the press conference, I was thinking, 'There's no way that guy should coach another game for the Capitals,' and I wrote that night changes need to be made.

"There was talent here, and something needed to be done. In comes Bruce, and he knows a lot of the organization from Hershey. If you go back and look at Mike Green's stats under Hanlon, he was getting 9 to 12 minutes a game. Bruce Boudreau comes in [and Green] is playing 18 to 20 minutes and becomes an All-Star. You had the coach who knew what they had in the system.

"Hanlon was still coaching like he had a bunch of guys that were hurting and trying to win 2–1 games with skilled hockey players. [Firing him] was absolutely the right move and the next turning point for the franchise."

With the new system came an exciting and aggressive style of play that helped make the Capitals a much more entertaining team to watch.

"The system is so aggressive, especially early, as he hadn't translated it yet," McNally recalled. "It was like, throw the puck in the corner and go get that thing. There also was a lot of hitting, and it played to the strengths of this team.

"Glen Hanlon — it wasn't his style anyway — but even if it was, it's such a risk for him to do that. Bruce comes in and says, 'This is my shot.' He didn't have that risk. He could say this is my talent, let's make full use of it. Maybe we'll get burned and won't be an elite defensive team, and leaving the goalies out to dry left and right — which they did a lot that year — but he was in position to take that risk. I don't know if that was part of the plan, but he was able to do those things and fit the personnel. They had a bruising fourth line and could wear the other team down, and it worked and clicked. It isn't any surprise they started winning in the first two weeks of his tenure."

"Bruce is a fantastic coach, and he gets his players and coaches all fired up and on the same page," Johnson said of the change to Boudreau. "Both are really, really nice guys."

It was no surprise that in Boudreau's first game with Washington, an afternoon contest at Philadelphia's Wachovia Center on Black Friday, November 23, Green and Backstrom were among the game's stars in a dramatic 4–3 win. The two young stars blossomed quickly under the new coach.

Backstrom and Green connected for Washington's first goal, with the Swede feeding a nice pass from one faceoff dot to the other, and the defenseman blasting the puck past Flyers netminder Martin Biron just 2:27 in. The goal, Green's first in nearly a month, helped fuel the defenseman's confidence.

Chris Clark put the Capitals up by two 3:39 into the second period, and then Backstrom buzzed around the cage to help set up a 3–0 lead, grabbing the puck from in front of the Flyers net and feeding Shaone Morrisonn at the point. Morrisonn's long drive beat Biron at 5:49.

The Flyers rallied to force overtime, but Backstrom's breakthrough game would end with his third point of the night — and just the second goal of his NHL career.

Just over a minute into extra time, Ovechkin drove down the wing, while drawing the two defenders, and fed Backstrom the puck in front. The Swede held the puck as Biron dropped to cover a low chance, but Backstrom lifted the puck over Biron's pad for the game-winner.

Boudreau jumped behind the bench and pumped his fists following Backstrom's tally as the Capitals earned just their seventh win of the year.

Backstrom later explained that the coaching change was big in helping him start a productive NHL career. "[Bruce] helped me a lot. He was putting me on the power play and giving me more ice time, and after that, I got more confidence, I was put in more important positions than I was before," Backstrom said. "He's been really good to me, and he's the one who put me in the show, I think."

With more of a chance to show his skill, Backstrom quickly developed into an offensive force, finishing with 14 goals and 55 assists in 82 games; 60 of his 69 points came in 61 games under Boudreau.

"[Backstrom] got ice time and more opportunity to play with Ovi, and really, that was big," Ewell recalled. "It was the right change with the right player at the right time. He was probably going to struggle in his first 20 games in the NHL no matter what. But the new guy came in and preached a style that fit him; it was the perfect time and he was ready to get better as a player."

"[Backstrom's start] was tough, he didn't play a lot early in the year," McNally said. "[Hanlon] felt he couldn't have a rookie cost him his job, and that's only natural. I can't blame Glen for that. If you're trying to win games and are not 100 percent sure this 19-year-old from Sweden is ready to handle that, he's going to make mistakes . . . You think, 'I can't afford that right now.'

"Bruce could come in and say he's better than most of the guys on this team. Go play. Put him up top . . . By the end of the season, he got his legs under him. That was a huge part of that team developing."

Another major change came in Mike Green's play; the defenseman was allowed to be more aggressive and carry the puck up-ice — which better suited his talent. Green, who had only three goals in Washington's first 21 games, chipped in 15 under Boudreau to help establish him as one of the league's top blueliners. His 18 goals led all full-time NHL defensemen, although Chicago's Dustin Byfuglien did score 19 as a defense/right-wing hybrid for the Blackhawks.

"I was excited when [Bruce] got named to be the coach; obviously I was very familiar with him, we'd won a Cup together and had some success," Green said years later. "I knew he believed in me, and sometimes in life, as a player, all you need is an opportunity. He gave me my opportunity, and I thank him for that."

With so many players who skated for him in Hershey now in Washington, there was instant familiarity.

"I played with Bruce [in Hershey] for three years and he was a great coach, and when he came up here, it was the same thing: 'I want to win,'" Fleischmann said years later. "He's great, and players can be happy with the coach they [had] here."

The 4–3 win over the Flyers was a relief for a team that had been struggling, and the fresh start and new attitude was noticeable in the locker room.

"I approach it as the start of a new season," Kolzig told the Associated Press after the win. "We're still in a deep hole and we've got a lot of work to do. It's a good start. We beat a pretty good hockey team in their own building."

"It's subtle changes, not like you're revamping the whole thing," Boudreau told reporters after his first win. "I just think the mindset sometimes has got to change, and the culture's got to change. They've got to believe that they're really good players."

The impact was profound, as the Capitals went 9–5–4 to close out the calendar year and begin to climb out of the East's cellar with the new, improved style of play. With the success, the interim tag disappeared from Boudreau's title.

"When Thanksgiving happened, I happened to be in Florida on vacation, and George and [minority owner] Dick [Patrick] called and they said we're going to bring Bruce up on an interim basis and I'll line up some people we can interview and bring you my top two recommendations," Leonsis recalled. "I said that sounds fair.

"I think George just slow-rolled the interviewing and Bruce got off to a great start, and I remember being in the hallway one day with George and said, 'How's the interviewing going?' George said, 'I'm still doing it,' and I said, 'OK.' A week later we had improved even more, and the interviewing petered away and the interim tag petered away.

"He earned it. He did a fantastic job for us."

"[Bruce] let them free, and the ultimate thing, players had already bought in because they had won a [Calder Cup] title under him — a lot of them," McNally said. "They knew he could coach, they knew he could win and they were perfectly willing, and so desperate.

"As much as the tactical aspect helped, how Bruce is as a coach helped clear the slate for those guys. It was a complete new scenario. 'I have a history with this guy, I know the system, I can trust it, let's go play.' It became, let's just play the game. Perhaps we aren't talented enough to make a playoff run this year, but we can at least make something of the season.

"And they did."

CHAPTER 9

THE 124 MILLION DOLLAR MAN: A NEW DAWN

The Capitals' improved play carried into January, and the team was able to reach the .500 mark on the 19th. It was the furthest into a season the team had been at or above .500 since the 2002–03 campaign.

But there were still worries. As the calendar flipped to 2008, a growing concern about whether Alexander Ovechkin would elect to test the market when his entry-level deal expired in the upcoming summer became news. While he would be a restricted free agent and the Capitals could match any offer sheet tendered by another club, it didn't stop rumors that perhaps some of the league's more established teams such as the Toronto Maple Leafs or Montreal Canadiens might make a play to bring the superstar in with a lucrative offer sheet that Washington wouldn't want to match.

But the Capitals were able to take care of business themselves before their superstar could even seriously consider testing the market, signing the Russian to the league's first $100 million deal — a 13-year extension worth $124 million.

"When you read the newspaper and, like, 'Ovechkin can go over there,' 'Ovechkin can be traded,' you feel it," Ovechkin told reporters at the press conference announcing the deal. "But then you try and don't think about it, but you think about it. Right now, I think all about my game."

"I'm happy I stay here," Ovechkin added. "It's my second home. I like the fans. I like the team. I like everything here."

For owner Ted Leonsis, who was burned when he signed Jaromir Jagr to a seven-year, $77 million extension in 2001, another lengthy, long-term, lucrative deal was a worthwhile gamble. "I'm a risk-taker," Leonsis told reporters at the time. "And if you're going to make a long-term investment, who else would you do it with? This takes away any of the issues of how committed we are to winning a Cup, how committed we are to keeping a team together."

The superstar was locked down for the foreseeable future, and with the team's strong play, exciting brand of hockey and star power, the crowds — and media attention — began to swell.

"It was off-the-charts growth," Nate Ewell recalled. "You couldn't even compare it to the 2005–06 season . . . when we had a superstar who was the darling of the National Hockey League on a national and international level and couldn't get coverage locally . . . The thing that tipped it over the scale was Ovi's contract. [Fans] knew we were going to be good for 13 years and he was committed to us. From that point on, as a public-relations staff, we were able to shift gears from trying to attract coverage to managing it."

"To a lot of people in the city, the 13-year deal cemented that they were going to be good for a long time — as long as Ovechkin stays healthy and the team is committed to winning," Ed Frankovic said. "They signed Green in the summer, they had Semin back on the roster, and Backstrom had a great rookie year.

"You just knew this team was going to be good when Ovechkin re-signed, and shortly thereafter, the building was full every night."

Ovechkin, who had 32 goals and 20 assists at the time of the signing, was making a strong case for his first-ever Hart Trophy as league MVP. And the Russian kept up the pace with a strong second half as the Capitals made a playoff push.

On February 1, he had one of the most memorable games of his career against Montreal, scoring four goals, including the game-winner 1:26 into overtime, and picking up another assist. He accomplished this despite not only suffering a broken nose after taking a tough check, but also a cut lip from a high stick to the face.

The night began badly for Ovechkin. He was clipped by Alexei Kovalev just 0:55 in, but he managed to score his 40th goal of the year, dishing the puck off to Milan Jurcina at the far point, who returned the puck for Ovechkin's one-timer past Montreal netminder Cristobal Huet with 6:54 left in the first.

Ovechkin picked up an assist 4:35 into the second, feeding Viktor Kozlov for a 2–0 Washington lead.

The star then suffered a broken nose as a result of a hit by Francis Bouillon right in front of the Washington bench with 12:13 left in the period, but that only motivated the Russian. Just over four minutes after breaking his nose, he gave the Caps a 3–0 lead. He broke in alone thanks to a pass from Kozlov that went between Roman Hamrlik's skates, roofing the puck past Huet with 8:07 left.

With 7:30 to go in regulation, Ovechkin completed his fourth-career hat trick — and his first-ever at home — taking a pass from Kozlov and delivering a wrist shot past both Canadiens defenseman Mark Streit and Huet for a 4–2 lead.

However, the Capitals couldn't hold the lead, and the Canadiens forced overtime with two late goals. But all that Montreal rally did was set up Ovechkin's dramatic overtime winner.

With under two minutes left in OT, Ovechkin broke in to the Canadiens' zone, then lost his balance. Play continued in the Montreal end. The puck wound up on Jeff Schultz's stick, who passed across a centering feed to Ovechkin. Although the star didn't get the pass cleanly — the puck bounced off his first shot attempt into the crease — Ovechkin beat Huet to the puck and tapped it in.

It was Ovechkin's second four-goal game of the season and his second five-point night of his career.

"Today was a special day," Ovechkin told reporters. "I broke my nose, have stitches [and] score four goals. Everything [went] to my face."

"We scored five, and he was in on all five," Boudreau told the press afterward. "So, how can you say enough about him? He's an amazing person."

However, despite the team's improved play, by the end of February, the Capitals were still at 30–27–8 and needing a strong finish to entertain thoughts of making the playoffs. Despite their uncertain playoff fate — Washington was still on the outside of the postseason seeding at the trade deadline — the Capitals gambled and made a splash.

From Columbus, Washington acquired veteran center Sergei Fedorov — who the team hoped would gel with fellow Russians Alexander Ovechkin, Viktor Kozlov and Alexander Semin — as well as goaltender Cristobal Huet from Montreal and agitator Matt Cooke from Vancouver.

"We're sending the right message to everybody," Capitals general manager George McPhee told reporters at the time.

For the team's Russian players, Fedorov was a huge addition to the locker room, particularly with his presence and leadership.

"[Fedorov] had a huge impact, first of all on Alexander Semin," TSN's Dmitry Chesnokov said years later of the trade. "Ever since Fedorov has left, Semin hasn't had a consistent center. And Fedorov was such a wise guy, not only on the ice but off the ice. People have talked to him and gotten to know him; he could be a mentor to almost anyone. I think he was a great leader in the locker room.

"At the time, Chris Clark was the captain, but I think Fedorov was the true captain. He'd been there, won the Hart, won the Cup. Especially for guys like Ovechkin and Semin, to have someone else who's that magnitude of a player who could take that attention away was a big help."

The additions and building playoff push also helped fuel the team's rapidly growing attendance figures.

"It's funny when you think about those early years, as much attention as [Ovechkin] got nationally — the goal and all that stuff — and how much people were drawn to him, it didn't really translate the first couple of years into his recognition around town and in the stands, certainly," McNally said. "Well, in the 2007–08 season there was 13,000 or so fans a game, on a weeknight game maybe 12,000, or even getting the Panthers in on a Tuesday night, only 10,000 or 11,000 fans would be there. It was an odd dynamic where you had an MVP candidate, a former rookie of the year, but he really wasn't capturing the fan base.

"They had to make that leap at the focal point, but also win some games. It took a while, but when it happened, it was like a light switch went on. He had some incredible games and incredible goals after Bruce took over . . . He would do [amazing] things; it was like free advertising for the team. Suddenly, he was pairing the incredible skill with wins, you reeled off five or six in a row, you looked around and suddenly they're playing Minnesota on a Tuesday and there were 17,000 and the local newscast was leading with them instead of blowing them off."

Fueled by the new additions, the Capitals thrived and made a strong push for the final spot, winning 13 of their final 17 games — including 10 of their last 11 games. But Washington was hampered by the fact that the team they were battling for the Southeast Division title and one of the last playoff spots, the Carolina Hurricanes, also had a very solid finish to the season, going 10–4–1 in March and April.

"I haven't seen a stretch like that where you need to win and seen teams who have done that good for that long, but they were in first place and went wire-to-wire," Nate Ewell recalled. "The sense in those last few weeks when you're winning but not gaining ground was a little maddening."

After being nipped by Toronto to start the month of March, Washington pounded Boston 10–2 on national television and traveled to western New York to beat the Sabres in Buffalo.

However, the team's playoff hopes appeared to evaporate with a pair of tough losses on the second weekend of the month, as the Capitals were beaten in Boston on Saturday afternoon and came home and lost in tough fashion to the Penguins. The winning goal was scored as Nicklas Backstrom accidentally put the puck in his own net with 28 seconds left in regulation — costing Washington at least one valuable standings point.

"That was officially heartbreaking," Bruce Boudreau told reporters afterward. "I feel bad for Nick. He was doing everything that he could and ends up shooting it in his own net."

But instead of that miscue spelling the end of the Capitals' season, Washington rallied and put on an impressive run to nab one of the final playoff spots.

"I remember they were so determined, and Cristobal Huet was so matter-of-fact in wanting to put his best foot forward and realized he was taking the place of a franchise-caliber netminder who had authored so many records in Olie Kolzig," Comcast SportsNet play-by-play voice Joe Beninati recalled.

"I remember Cristobal was very focused. And his teammates were incredibly focused on the goal at hand. Did they think that they could do it? I don't know if they would admit they actually could pull off a run like that, but with each passing win, their confidence grew. Their belief in the coach and the system and themselves grew. And they kept ticking off win after win in impressive fashion."

Reduced to almost no margin of error, with the Hurricanes also playing well down the stretch, the Capitals completed the four-game homestand, following the Pittsburgh setback, with wins over Calgary, Atlanta and Boston.

"It looked like we were afraid to make a mistake instead of 'Let's go get them, and play the way we can,'" Boudreau told reporters after the shootout win over the Bruins. "That's the difference between teams that aren't in it, they play loose. A lot of times they're beating the other teams because they're playing loose. We were tight a little bit out there because of the importance of the game."

The pressure wouldn't let up for Washington as they still needed to pile up points, and a six-game road trip loomed for the Caps, leaving town in mid-March two points behind eighth-seeded Philadelphia and five behind Carolina in the race to reach the postseason.

Ovechkin became the first Capital to record two 100-point seasons in a Washington uniform during a win in Nashville on March 18, but that was the least of his concerns. "The most important thing for me is not beating some records," Ovechkin told AP. "Right now it is all about winning games and all about getting two points."

"There is no rest, because it is so close," Boudreau told reporters. "If everything goes as it could possibly go, you could have five or six teams within two or three points of each other by Friday, so we want to be the team that gains the spot."

With virtually no margin for error, the Capitals then suffered a 5–0 shutout loss to Chicago, which Boudreau termed a "stinker." But it turned out that was the last loss Washington suffered in the regular season, as the team improbably reeled off a seven-game winning streak to finish the year.

Huet took over the goaltending duties for good after Kolzig took the loss in Chicago, and the team visited the rest of the Southeast Division to finish the trip, winning in Atlanta, grabbing a huge shootout win in Raleigh to gain a point in the divisional race, and getting four points in a two-game trip through Florida with a victory in Tampa and then a shutout win in Sunrise against the Panthers.

Washington wrapped up the month with 88 points and just three games left — all at home — in the regular season.

"It was very challenging to go six straight," Cristobal Huet told AP after a 3–0 shutout against Florida gave Washington 40 victories for the first time since 2000–01. "We're 5–1, we're very happy. We have a couple of days to charge the batteries. It doesn't mean it's going to be easy playing at home, but we look forward to the next game."

"I know if we keep winning, something good will happen," Bruce Boudreau told reporters. "We can only do what we can do and if it takes 95 points to make the playoffs, so be it. I believe if we continue to play like we play, somebody is going to falter once and we'll be there to jump on them."

Despite the winning streak, the gap in the Southeast Division race hadn't really lessened: Washington trailed Carolina by two points after the win over the Panthers, and they also were three points behind Philadelphia. There was concern that the run would be for naught.

With the Capitals sprinting to qualify for the playoffs, the crowds and atmosphere at home had taken a dramatic change that hadn't been seen before at Verizon Center, even during the team's Stanley Cup Finals run in 1998.

"It was shocking," former Capitals captain Jeff Halpern recalled. "I think when it really took off, I had just got traded from Dallas to Tampa, and we played Washington the second-to-last game of the season and they needed to beat Tampa to have a chance to still make the playoffs. I couldn't believe how big the crowds had gotten, how into the team they were here. I was definitely jealous to see the turnaround, but at the same time, it was a credit to the local hockey community to see the team grow."

With a sold-out crowd — many wearing the team's new red jerseys — the Capitals pulled into a first-place tie with the Hurricanes on April Fool's Day. Ovechkin scored his 63rd goal of the season and heard chants of "M-V-P!" during a 4–1 win over Carolina. "All the guys played well today," he said afterward. "We're playing for something right now."

"You could tell what was at stake," Boudreau told reporters. "If this is what it's like in the playoffs in the NHL, no wonder it's an exciting game. The NHL knew what they were doing when they put the schedule together. If they wanted tight races, they got it."

Two nights later, when Halpern's Lightning came to town, Ovechkin broke the NHL's scoring record for a left winger with his 64th and 65th goals of the season. The Capitals had their first six-game win streak since 2000 with the victory.

"It's a good time for us right now," Ovechkin said. "We have a chance, and we have to keep it going."

Washington sold out its last four games — more than the team had sold out in an entire season since 2002–03 — and got a huge break before their final contest when the Hurricanes dropped their season finale to the Panthers, meaning the Capitals could clinch the Southeast title and third seed in the playoffs with a win.

In honor of the old "white outs" that were held at the Capital Centre during the team's playoff runs in the 1980s, the team held a "red out" for the last game against Florida, urging all attendees to wear the new team color. Washington was poised to earn a Southeast Division title with a win, but could still miss the playoffs if they failed to beat the Panthers.

The electricity was palpable at the sold-out Verizon Center, with the red-clad fans urging the Capitals to complete the rally from the opening faceoff.

Tomas Fleischmann gave the fans a reason to celebrate at just 6:19 when he broke in on Florida goaltender Craig Anderson and, after whiffing on his initial shot attempt, deked and beat the diving goaltender as he fell himself.

Florida tied it on a strange sequence with 7:02 gone in the second, as Kamil Kreps put a shot past Cristobal Huet and just inside the post. The puck came out so quickly the referees didn't initially call it a goal. Upon video review, the score was 1–1.

But Washington took the lead for good with 4:57 left in the second frame, as Semin backhanded a pass from just beyond the center red line to Sergei Fedorov, who wound up and beat Anderson with a slap shot.

The Capitals could sense the division title was theirs just 2:21 into the third when Nicklas Backstrom fed Alexander Semin, who wound up and took a shot through traffic. The goal gave Washington a 3–1 lead and resulted in a dog pile celebration along the side boards as the crowd roared its approval.

The crowd gave the team a standing ovation for the game's final 90 seconds, once again cheering "M-V-P!" for Alexander Ovechkin and "Let's go Caps" for the entire team. The crescendo built until the final horn, when the players poured onto the ice to mob Huet. The team was heading to the playoffs for the first time in five years. For many Caps — including Ovechkin, Backstrom and Mike Green — it would be the first taste of the postseason.

Washington's improbable run, from being in the NHL's basement when Bruce Boudreau took over on Thanksgiving Day and sitting in 14th in the East as late as the season's halfway point, was nothing short of remarkable.

"I've been around this game a long time, I can't remember a stretch like that," Frankovic recalled. "When Backstrom put the puck in his own net against the Penguins, I remember thinking, 'They're done.' They couldn't afford to lose that game.

"Then they got on a roll — their only loss after that was in Chicago, and that wasn't Olie [Kolzig]'s fault, the team was just terrible that night — but they were going to do whatever it took. Then when Carolina lost to Florida [in their season finale], the door was wide open.

"It was an amazing run, I've never seen anything like it."

For the team too, the playoff drive built big crowds, and the team averaged 15,274 in the regular season — more than 1,500 better than the previous season.

"That was a big turning point," former *Washington Times* sports business reporter Tim Lemke recalled. "I remember sitting down with people that season, and there was a sense that the team was starting to be good, they weren't terrible, and maybe this was the year they had a chance at the playoffs. I think that was part of Ted's plan all along. 'We're going to be bad the first couple of years, make the playoffs by year three, and then the next year compete for a conference title, and then after that we could contend for the Cup,' that type of progression.

"There were people in the beginning of that year saying, 'They could make the playoffs' — then they didn't start so well. But they made that unbelievable run in the second half when Boudreau came in. There was a lot of excitement after that."

And the excitement from that playoff surge would carry the team for years to come.

"You could just get the sense that Verizon Center was going to be a raucous-type arena for many, many years because that team finally took a stronghold and said we're going to do it, we're going to rally and beat Carolina down the stretch," Joe Beninati recalled. "The offensive production was incredible and I know I did a bunch of Capitals games on both Versus and Comcast SportsNet.

"They were terrific to watch. They seemed like they were destiny's team at that time, and I wish they would have gotten a bit further in the playoffs that spring."

According to Elias Sports Bureau, the 2007–08 Capitals were the first NHL team since the 1924–25 Hamilton Tigers to win a division after being in last place three consecutive seasons. And no team had ever qualified for the playoffs when being in 14th or 15th place at the halfway point of the regular season.

"There's a little bit of destiny in this team," Ted Leonsis told reporters after the regular-season finale. "They're very confident. It might be that they're young and that they don't know history. They don't know about anything but looking forward."

First-year Boudreau certainly was making a case for the Jack Adams Award for coach of the year — despite being behind the bench for just 61 games — by guiding the team to a 37–17–7 mark.

"There was never a word of 'We couldn't' or 'We won't' or 'We can't,'" Boudreau said after the win over Florida. "It was always pushing through and believing in ourselves. I just hope I wake up tomorrow and look and we are in. This whole season's been a dream."

Ovechkin was a strong favorite to win the league's Hart Trophy with a team-record 65 goals and also a franchise second-best 112 total points. The Russian found himself in elite company by leading the league in both goals and points, joining Wayne Gretzky, Mario Lemieux, Jarome Iginla and Guy Lafleur as the only players who had done so since the Caps entered the league in 1974.

"Oh, yeah, this is one of my dreams," Ovechkin told AP. "Now we're there. It's only one step. Now we can think about playoff games."

George McPhee summed up the status of the rebuild nicely after the win. "We've been telling people, 'Be patient and we'll wake up one morning and have a good team.' And I think that morning is tomorrow morning."

BITTERSWEET
FINISH TO SEASON

The 2008 Stanley Cup playoffs matched the Capitals with the Philadelphia Flyers in the first round, and the team was set to play its first playoff game since the fateful overtime loss to Tampa Bay in 2003. This time around, the Verizon Center had a much different atmosphere.

The Flyers were a team that traditionally brought a lot of fans to Washington — considering the proximity of Philadelphia to Washington and the number of the area's natives that settle in the nation's capital — but the crowd was largely clad in red, and the tickets for the game were snapped up as soon as they went on sale.

"That was when the team did a good job and did some things to make sure people who bought the tickets were from the area," Tim Lemke recalled. "But you never would have had that a few years before, people would have been selling their tickets. You might have had people who bought tickets who were Capitals fans and then sell them to Flyers fans at a premium. But at that point, it became a game you want to be at because you don't want to miss this particular game. Not because you didn't want to turn a profit, but you wanted to see something special. The level of intensity was off the charts.

"There was a confluence of things that happened. Kettler opened, the new brand was there, the blogosphere was very positive, the media was very positive, you could sense the rebuild was working, that the young players were going to be very talented and that we had a generationally great player in Alex Ovechkin. The combination of all of that and this run to make the playoffs on the last day was really something."

Leonsis realized his team was beginning to hit it big once the puck dropped in the series — and the arena was awash in red. "When you go into Kettler [now], by where they play ping-pong, there's a big picture there of our first home game against the Flyers. And there's a really heartwarming story behind the picture. We didn't know we were going to qualify for the playoffs and make it right away, and we had a short period of time to sell it, and then we didn't have as many season ticket holders, so we had a short period of time to sell a lot of tickets to our fans.

"So our CMO at the time, Tim McDermott, asked if I would do an outbound telemarketing call, a robocall. It went out I think two days before the game. We sent it out, and I ad-libbed at the end, I said, 'Let's Rock the Red. Wear red tonight.'

"And after I hung up and calls started to go out, Tim comes in and said, 'I wish I had known you were going to say that. We could have pre-ordered and gotten a sponsor to give away T-shirts.' That's what teams usually do for a white-out or red-out. Philadelphia has orange T-shirts, they gave them away. And we started the game, and that picture of the game, if there's 100 people not wearing red in the audience that would be shocking. That was the first indicator that, wow, everyone wore red, and we didn't give them anything. It was of their own volition, something big was happening."

Thanks to the newly minted "Rock the Red" slogan inscribed along the dasher boards and sold on T-shirts and hats — smoke machines were installed in the rink's corners and a red glow was created by a string of lights placed along the top of the boards — what had four years earlier been a mostly empty and lifeless venue had been transformed into one of the loudest buildings in the league.

Just 3:16 into the series opener on April 11, the Capitals got a goal from an unlikely new playoff hero, as enforcer Donald Brashear snagged a strange deflection near the cage and beat Martin Biron for a goal. The tough guy did a bit of a leap behind the net after scoring.

Philadelphia tied the game with 11:43 left in what was ultimately a tentative first period.

David Steckel scored with 4:08 gone in the second, taking a feed from Matt Bradley and then beating Biron from just outside the faceoff dot for his first-ever playoff marker.

The Flyers, however, took control in the last nine minutes of the second, starting with a Daniel Briere goal. As the forward left the penalty box, he snuck behind the Washington defense and broke in alone, beating Cristobal Huet with 8:14 left.

Just 33 seconds later, Vinny Prospal scored, taking a Kimmo Timonen pass and beating Huet. Briere then made Washington pay for a Matt Cooke penalty, scoring his second goal in less than four minutes as he took a pass from Mike Richards.

Three goals in a 3:36 span deflated the Capitals, but between periods, Bruce Boudreau told reporters he implored his troops, "Don't give up. Don't give up. Just keep pushing."

Two of the team's young stars responded in the third period.

Mike Green scored his first career playoff goal less than two minutes in, sneaking down from the point and taking a Sergei Fedorov backhand pass. He leapt over Biron as the puck went in to cut the deficit to one.

With under 14 minutes to play in regulation, Green wound up from the point and hit Flyers defensemen Patrick Thoresen in the groin, injuring the blueliner. Despite Thoresen writhing in pain, play was allowed to continue. Ovechkin collected the puck and fed Green, who wound up and beat Biron for the equalizer with 13:34 left. The crowd roared its approval as the team did a dog pile celebration at center ice.

Then it was Ovechkin's turn.

The Capitals star, who had been held without a shot until late in the game, took over in the dying minutes, stealing the puck after an errant Lasse Kukkonen pass deep in the Flyers end. Ovechkin muscled his way to the loose biscuit, sliding it past Biron with 4:32 left. He celebrated by slamming himself into the glass and the 18,277 in attendance roared their approval with more shouts of "M-V-P!"

With the tally, Ovechkin became only the fourth player since 1990 to score a game-winner in the last five minutes of regulation or overtime of his first career playoff game. Washington had a 1–0 series lead.

"They held him in check pretty good," Bruce Boudreau said afterward, "but he's one of the guys that needs one chance."

Sergei Fedorov remarked on the star's calm demeanor despite being frustrated most of the night by the Flyers. "A pretty veteran move," Fedorov told AP. "It's not easy: so much talk about everything and such a great season. Playoffs is a little different. I'm actually surprised — really amazed — that he kept himself so together, so cool in the final moments of the game."

Two days later, the Capitals — who had won 12 out of their last 13 and hadn't dropped one at home since Nicklas Backstrom's ill-fated own goal against the Penguins — began to show a bit of fatigue. They were simply flat in a 2–0 loss to the Flyers in Game 2.

Philadelphia scored a pair in the first 15:17 of the contest and were able to make them hold up by keeping Ovechkin in check. Martin Biron recorded a 24-save shutout.

"I didn't like how much [Ovechkin] played," Boudreau told reporters afterward. "He stayed on too long. It's hard when it's Alex. He wants to go so badly. He gets it in his head, 'I can do it,' and most nights he can. He looked a little tired, but he looked a little frustrated as well. He wasn't getting the puck, and they were all on him when he did touch the puck."

Things wouldn't get much better for the Capitals when they headed up Interstate 95. The Philly fans were clearly going to try to intimidate the playoff-inexperienced Caps when they arrived in the city.

"It got the Flyers fans riled up. They started to recognize there was this other team in the Eastern Conference, and all you have to do is look at YouTube and see the Flyers fans chant 'Ovechkin sucks,'" Lemke recalled.

Briere scored a pair of goals in Game 3. Ovechkin continued to struggle and was held to just an assist and four shots in 24:51 of ice time. Philadelphia collected a 6–3 win. The Flyers were able to generate too many good chances on Christobal Huet, and the lack of experienced depth on the Capitals' blueline began to show.

Two nights later, Flyers forward Mike Knuble scored the biggest goal of his career, breaking a tie in double-overtime to give the Flyers a commanding 3–1 series lead. Ovechkin was held off the scoreboard for the third straight game.

It appeared the Capitals' dream run would end with a whimper, but a somber Ovechkin simply told reporters, "It's not over," following the tough Game 4 loss.

Back home on Saturday afternoon, April 19, the Capitals were able to take command of Game 5 early, as Nicklas Backstrom scored just 7:31 into the contest and Sergei Fedorov added another goal just 95 seconds into the second. Huet was able to hold off the Flyers in the 3–2 win. Philadelphia's series lead was cut to 3–2, and the series traveled back up north.

Although Ovechkin was held without a goal for the fourth straight contest, he did make an impact by depositing the Flyers' Jim Dowd into the bench in part of what was a much more physical effort by the Capitals.

The Capitals continued to flex their muscle in Game 6, two nights later. Ovechkin returned to vintage form late in the contest, breaking a 2–2 tie in the third to notch his second career playoff game-winner and an insurance marker. Washington had forced a Game 7, scheduled for the next night back at Verizon Center. The momentum was with the Capitals.

"The stars, it seems to happen around them, whether it's John Elway and 'The Drive' or great baseball players getting the last at-bat," Bruce Boudreau told reporters. "[Ovechkin] was getting frustrated because they did such a good job on him, but he persevered and came through."

In Game 7, the Capitals broke on top when Backstrom scored 5:42

into regulation, but the Flyers were able to stay close thanks to a strong effort by Martin Biron, tying the game before the first period ended. The Flyers took their first lead near the halfway mark of the second, but Ovechkin notched his fourth goal of the series with 4:31 left in the frame to even the score.

The two teams fought to a scoreless third period. It was an amazing run, but, like five years earlier against the Lightning, the Capitals' season came to an end while trying to kill a power play in extra time.

Tom Poti was called for a trip at 4:15 of extra time, and although the Capitals were able to kill off most of the infraction, Joffrey Lupul became Philadelphia's unlikely hero, sliding the puck past Huet with just nine seconds left on the minor. Poti was naturally upset, telling reporters, "To have the referee decide the series like that, with two teams battling like that, is tough to swallow. I definitely didn't think it was a penalty." He added, "It's tough to beat the officials as well as the Flyers."

"It was a great series, pretty intense," recalled Knuble, who joined the Capitals in 2009. "A lot of fun to play in . . . I remember Game 7 in Washington like it was yesterday, and it was pretty exciting."

After the bitter sting of defeat faded, the Capitals could take pride in what they'd accomplished both on and off the ice. They picked up 24 points over back-to-back 70-point campaigns and had emerged as the team to beat in the Southeast Division. They were blessed with both youth and talent.

Off the ice, they'd gone from a team that had struggled to move tickets early in the year — twice having crowds of less than 12,000 early on — to one of the city's hottest attractions. What had been an ugly atmosphere in Glen Hanlon's final games had become the buzzing Verizon Center of the playoffs.

The fans had embraced a star who was locked into a 13-year extension, arriving at their seats in new red jerseys. There was an entirely new feeling inside the arena.

"You point to a number of turning points, but . . . it was turning into a hockey town," Lemke said of the season. "They recognized what they had, and they embraced it. A lot of these people are on the bandwagon — but there's nothing wrong with that if they're showing up."

Thanks to his spectacular year, Ovechkin was honored with the league's Hart Trophy as the most valuable player, as well as the Lester B. Pearson Award, the MVP award as voted on by the players. It was the first time a Washington athlete had won a league MVP award since Redskins quarterback Joe Theismann was honored as the NFL's most valuable player in 1983.

In a special press conference with Washington mayor Adrian Fenty following the Hart Trophy win, Ovechkin showed his playful nature. "Today is a big day," he said from the front steps of Washington's city hall. "I have a key for the city. And I'm the president this day in the city, so everybody have fun — and no speed limit."

The post-award celebration would be one of the lasting memories for Nate Ewell, who had helped Ovechkin build a media strategy during his years with the Capitals.

"We flew back from Toronto and an event with the mayor was planned . . . We had a couple of media people — NHL.com came down and followed him every step of the way, along with Eric Adelson, for what ended up being an *ESPN: The Magazine* cover story.

"That night we had a fancy cocktail party at a restaurant downtown for VIPs . . . The excitement of that and coming off the day before — where you kind of knew it was going to happen, he'd win that year, it was pretty much a lock — that was a lot of fun, and I thought that and the speed limit line really captured who he was. He was having a good time.

"It was a tiring day after a couple of tiring days, but he kept going. It showed a lot of who he was."

CHAPTER II

DOOR OPENS TO NEW MEDIA

During the nadir of their rebuild, emerging from the lockout that scrubbed the entire 2004–05 season, the Capitals were looking to generate publicity wherever they could. The team was aggressively looking to new media outlets to give fans more in-depth coverage than the city's two newspapers and televisions stations offered in a crowded sports marketplace.

No stranger to the power of the web, considering his role with AOL, Capitals owner Ted Leonsis was open to welcoming new media to the press box soon after acquiring the team. In fact, he welcomed web-based writers to MCI Center to cover games as early as the 1999–2000 season when Rivals.com was accredited for both the regular season and the playoffs.

With space in the press box atop MCI Center largely going unused coming out of the lockout, the team turned an eye to the emerging blogosphere.

The novel effort to court blog writers started innocently enough in October 2005, when Off Wing Opinion's Eric McErlain crafted a piece contrasting Alexander Ovechkin and Sidney Crosby. The post explained why, although Ovechkin had a better statistical start to his rookie season, Crosby had earned the initial Rookie of the Week honors — in part because the league wanted him to succeed and become its face as it looked to rebuild its product.

"At the beginning of Ovechkin's rookie year, they had the NHL Rookie of the Week Award, and they named Sidney Crosby the winner instead of Alex, even though Alex had scored more goals," McErlain recalled. "I wrote a piece saying, 'Look, the league has decided to hitch its marketing horse to Sidney Crosby. It doesn't really matter that Alex had a better week, it's about what the league thinks would be better to promote their product, and promoting a kid from the Maritimes rather than a kid from Moscow makes more sense to them — that's just the way it is.'"

That piece earned the attention of Leonsis, who contacted McErlain and invited him to watch a game from the owner's box.

"I was in the box for a game against the Lightning. We sat and talked. It was a normal conversation, and he was gracious, as I was a guest of his — like everyone else in the box. He's a big fan, very, very excited; you could see he lives and dies with this team.

"He explained to me what the plan was, and he was direct with me in what had gone wrong. In particular, he made it very clear that when they acquired [Jaromir] Jagr, [Capitals President] Dick Patrick and George McPhee were both against it, and he overruled them. He was the one that said, 'Let's sign him up to the big extension,' and so forth.

"That was his entire responsibility, and he learned his lesson. What had to happen next was strip down, build with youth, with speed and with skill, and see where it led. He was very direct, very open with me, answered any questions I had and was clear, but you could see he was excited about that team, and they won 3–2.

"It was a textbook example of how the team had to win. Olie Kolzig had to keep the team close going into the third period, and you could see they had a chance to win a game. They didn't win a whole lot of games that year . . . it was pretty brutal.

"But the blueprint was there, and Alex was an exciting player. I remember saying, 'You have to go out and see this kid, and [fans] will.'"

Shortly after his visit to the owner's box, McErlain was offered press credentials for games. He sat down with Leonsis and the team's director of media relations, Nate Ewell, to set up guidelines for bloggers to cover games alongside the more traditional media — something that was a first in the National Hockey League.

"I'm a big believer that fans want as much information as they can get to digest their team," Ewell later recalled. "When I'm at work, I want to read Michigan State football stuff, and if there's one paper, that's not going to do it. I want to read more, I want different perspectives.

"So our feeling, and certainly Ted and Eric articulated it very well, but I'm more of the 'I want more coverage' [type] than either of them were. Ted's sort of like, 'Let's open the doors, media is media.' To me it served the goal of trying to fill the appetite of fans who weren't getting it from the newspapers."

Leonsis felt that the emergence of blogs and other new media was important to embrace, and so he took great care to craft a document on what was expected for those credentialed to cover games. "At the time, not many people in professional sports understood interactivity and what a blogger was, so for the most part, bloggers were looked at as fanboys," he said. "They have another job, they can write what they want, and I think there was a sneering that they just wanted to write so they could get free tickets.

"I obviously didn't feel that way, so I thought we should embrace it as a league. We had the most wired audience, and we should have the most wired community. But I knew there would be a lot of consternation around it. So the concept of working on the blogger bill of rights and what was expected — that was a lot of work, and Eric and I worked on that very, very diligently because if we didn't get it right, it would hurt. Now the bloggers are accepted everywhere."

In the beginning, McErlain joined what was a small press corps covering Capitals games. "Back in 2005–06, no one bothered to go to training camp since it was still in Piney Orchard," he recalled. "I also went to Ashburn [in suburban Virginia] — they had a pretty good crowd the one year they held it there [in 2007].

"But the games were a graveyard. It was never a problem getting a seat in the press box. I remember we used to do the post-game press conferences with Glen Hanlon, and it was held in a phone-booth type of room near the Capitals locker room. Now we have had to switch to the press lounge with rows of seats and cameras in the back of the room. [Regional cable sports network] Comcast [SportsNet] used to be the only camera, and perhaps the out-of-town network would be there with their cameras."

"Ted brought the blogs in because the local papers weren't covering the team," Yahoo!'s Greg Wyshynski recalled. "They specifically weren't covering the team because they didn't think there was an audience for it. So Ted opens the door to this latent, sort of alternative media and says, 'Here, come and cover our team. Spread the word through the various blogs and places on the internet.'

"And a wonderful thing happened . . . He created an amateur press corps. A lot of people learn on the job. I know the first time I showed up here in a polo shirt and looked over at [*Washington Post* reporter] Tarik [El-Bashir] and he's dressed like Johnny Cochran. You learn."

The strategy to court blogs for coverage was a successful one, according to Tim Lemke, who covered sports business for the *Washington Times*.

"It helped a lot because Ted recognized that most of the blogs were written by fans, so the coverage was going to be pretty positive most of the time, and that helps," Lemke said. "There is a lot of passion, and a lot of those guys are pretty prolific and knowledgeable and it helped fill a void where coverage of the team was lacking.

"The *Times* had one hockey writer, the *Post* had one, and you look at the traditional print outlets covering the Stanley Cup Finals, it's dwindling. People weren't traveling to road games. Ted's a pretty tech-savvy guy, and, frankly, they had room in the press box. I think other cities have struggled with it more since it's a logistical thing, since you're literally taking seats from a traditional media entity to house a blogger."

The experiment took off, and in a technology-driven region like Washington, several key blogs began to gain traction as an alternative news source for those who wanted more than what the daily news-papers offered — particularly during the times when the two dailies were busy covering other sports.

"It means there's a constant buzz about the team 365 days a year, and all these folks talk to one another, listen to one another and have conversations about the team," McErlain said. "Doesn't it make sense in business, if you're a hockey team or if you make widgets, if people care about your success, want to see you succeed and are supportive of your business, doesn't it make business sense to talk to them? Basically, they're evangelizing your product. So why don't you want to talk to them? Why don't you want to be friends with them? Why don't you want to invite them into the press box if that's appropriate? Why don't you want to have a relationship with them? You'd be crazy not to want to. You'd be crazy not to have those people there."

"What happened over time, as the team got better, and the coverage online stayed consistent and in depth, the local papers had to up their games," Wyshynski said. "Now all of a sudden the *Washington Post* had a blog. All of a sudden the *Washington Times* had a blog. And all of a sudden they're dedicating more space to the team.

"I really believe that were it not for the coverage and ingenuity that was coming from the blogs, from the lockout to three years after, the coverage of this team wouldn't have changed as dramatically as it did.

"I also think the blogs help foster the communal thing that hap-pened within the fan base. Now all of the sudden you have a 24/7 outlet and you can feel part of that community. When you come here, you feel part of the community. The success part of this is they all feel like they're part of something. They wear the same color, they all know the same chants, they do the same stuff on the JumboTron. The blogs really contributed to that in giving the fans a place to congregate and learn the same jokes. No newspaper can ever do that."

According to Lemke, the non-traditional media is also one of the reasons that Alex Ovechkin's popularity surged so quickly.

"His popularity coincided with a lot of additional coverage, maybe not a lot from traditional media, but a lot with the blogs. Around that time that you started to see a lot of Caps blogs pop up.

"You see people like Dan Steinberg of D.C. Sports Blog pop up. He was able to kind of cover [the] popularity and say, 'You've got this guy, he's really special.' They were getting media attention in an untraditional way — and to their credit, they embraced that.

"True hockey fans know what they had. It probably took a couple years for other sports fans and non-sports fans in D.C. to catch up in bigger hockey markets like Toronto and other NHL cities."

It also helped the Capitals sell the hopeful message of the rebuild.

"It certainly helped," Nate Ewell said. "Especially early in the rebuild . . . It really helped to communicate . . . what it meant and what they were trying to accomplish and the progress that they were making.

"Both from internal sites, things like Ted's Owner's Corner, to blogs on what's happening in Hershey, from prospects and who's out there. Generate excitement about drafting a Nick Backstrom–type of player. The depth of coverage there was hard-core, it kept [fans'] interest. It helped reassure them that there were better times coming."

By the time the Capitals had become a playoff team, the press box was beginning to get crowded.

"It used to be a ghost town, and now you can't get a seat; people are fighting to get in the press box," Eric McErlain said. "It's become kind of a problem in the locker room because the scrum is so big. It might not be the way it is in Toronto or Montreal, but to have a presence like this in what was a minor American [hockey] market is pretty incredible."

"I think we were trendsetters there," Ted Leonsis said. "I believe that this media is where the future is. The blogosphere has been very, very important to us."

"What I can vividly remember the first [Capitals] game I covered," said NBC Washington's Jim Iovino, one of the pioneers of internet hockey coverage with the popular LCS Hockey site in the 1990s. "I looked at the rundown in the press box. It was like, *wow*, from when I first started covering hockey 15 years ago.

"When you see all the bloggers that are on the list and all the outlets that are covering the games now and have access to the team, it's a far, far cry from what I started out with in this business. It was an eye-opening experience. It got even more eye-opening when you get down to the locker room and see the crowd surrounding the players, and it's just a little bit crazy to think about that."

Other NHL teams have tried limited credentialing of bloggers. The New York Islanders introduced the "Blog Box," with limited access to the home team only; the Buffalo Sabres now allow up to five bloggers in the First Niagara Center press box, only granting access to the coach's postgame press conference. But the Capitals' experiment allowed bloggers the same access that traditional print and broadcast media had.

League-wide, other non-traditional outlets started to get credentialed to such NHL events as the draft and the Winter Classic, and several Capitals blogs got access to the 2011 game in Pittsburgh through the league itself.

It isn't an arrangement that would work for every team, Eric McErlain concedes. "It's going to depend on the market," he said. "In New York, they are never ever going to have to, or even have the space to, accommodate all those who want to cover the Rangers. It's just impossible. There's just not enough room. Will they work with them? I'm sure at some point, the PR people have talked to them and might work with them, but it's going to depend on need.

"I'm sure a market like Carolina or Colorado when their fortunes are not so good, or Dallas, you're going to be able to find some space for someone with some smarts and industry to come in and do as good a job as someone who's paid to get to do it for a living."

And, according to Ted Leonsis, the team may also have to adapt to the growing number of bloggers covering the team.

"The biggest issue right now is I don't have more seats to sell, or more seats in the press box," he said. "To be blunt, I never thought it would take off the way it has. We're going to do our best to continue accessibility, but I don't know what I'm going to do when there are

1,000 bloggers covering it — and we're on our way to that. But we're going to need a better way to manage through all that."

Leonsis said having the Capitals' blogosphere explode certainly is a good problem, although it is creating a logjam. "Now we have a different issue, there are too many bloggers. That wasn't expected. We have a press box. We've reached capacity on press box. We have lines of people to get in. There is a pecking order. Comcast pays us a lot of money for our rights, and they should have some preferential treatment. Then after that, it's kind of who writes the most, who has the most audience. But we've tried to remain true and ecumenical."

While in recent years the league has restricted access to certain visiting teams due to complaints, Nate Ewell explained he was more concerned with the Capitals' benefit than what other teams were doing.

"I don't care if the Rangers are going to say the bloggers can't come in their locker room. Frankly I'd rather them come in our locker room," he said. "I didn't worry too much about the way other PR staffs were doing their job, I wanted to do a good job ourselves."

There are certain individuals in the traditional media who also haven't been pleased with the influx of bloggers, and McErlain said part of it is that the old order in hockey media is slowly evolving to a more online and video-heavy future. "I only see the role increasing . . . There are people who don't want them in there — and I've run into plenty of those folks . . . Some writers and reporters consider it to be an affront, and it's because, let's be honest, they're invested in what was, and they're annoyed that all they've invested in is deteriorating. And all the new people, they're not invested in that. It's only going to grow in acceptance.

"I'm wondering if something like we do will eventually go away as well because everyone has a camera in their hand and everybody's got a video recorder. You don't need a press pass to do any of this. You can aggressively cover the Capitals and never walk inside the wire.

"It's going to keep blending and building . . . I only see good things, and there are so many smart people covering and writing about this team. And the team benefits enormously. We talk about what happens with Google results, and there are reams and reams of positive stuff about this franchise and it's going to be paying off for years.

"They've done it the right way and are reaping the benefits."

"They got the right idea on it," said Jim Iovino. "There's no question about it. I'm never going to say bloggers shouldn't have access because of my background. This is where things are going; many of the blogs aren't just your average fans, and these are knowledgeable hockey people living here in Washington.

"They deserve to be able to access these players in some way . . . Even if you're not here every day, going to practices, you give them an outlet that they can actually come and feel like they're covering the team and getting that inside knowledge."

"I think it's great," Capitals radio voice John Walton — who was Hershey's public relations director during his days with the Bears — said of the emergence of the team's blogosphere. "I know there are some varying opinions out there about that, but the Capitals have done it, in my mind, as well as any team could have.

"There's a time and place for following and rules to live by and establishing parameters up front. It's so timely, a lot of the content generated online is turned around fast and it's so well done by so many people here. I find myself going there easily as much as traditional media . . . When I was in Hershey, when I wanted to know what was going on in Washington, you'd go to the *Post* and the *Times*, but I'd go to On Frozen Blog, I go to Japers' Rink, all of those. Everyone does something that is in-depth, and provides links and services where everything is.

"I think it's fantastic. I followed in Nate [Ewell]'s footsteps as much as I could in Hershey. I even had Penguin bloggers — who weren't even interested in our team — out at Giant Center; I spelled out what our expectations are and let them in. Other teams are more hesitant to do that. But I've never been hesitant to do that."

Ewell, who left the team in February 2011 to work for College Hockey Inc. in suburban Boston, is happy with what the six-year effort has created. "I'm proud of how good [the coverage by the blogs] is, how good the quality is. That's more a reflection of the quality of people writing it than anything we did, but the access helps produce better quality stuff. In that regard I'm proud of it."

The energence of other social media, like Twitter, is also a game changer. Now it's not just the media that's a conduit, players and fans actually interact.

Capitals like Alex Ovechkin and Mike Green are on Twitter, but according to Ewell, the biggest beneficiaries of the medium were the more anonymous guys, players like Eric Fehr.

"I think Eric Fehr was the best example we had of that. He embraced that pretty early and was able to show his personality," Ewell said. "He got a bigger following than you think he would have. He's a talented guy, but he got a bigger following than his talent would normally allow for. He made that connection in a community like Washington that was leaning heavily on digital media for Capitals news. It helped a lot."

For Walton, another lesser-known player stands out for his Twitter presence: former Capitals farmhand and Hershey Bear Andrew Gordon has excelled in the social media world. "From a player stand-point, Andrew Gordon was one of the best I'd ever seen," Walton said. "John Carlson's fantastic. You have guys who truly like it and embrace it, and it comes off like they do. Karl Alzner does it too. I think it's important.

"But for a guy who doesn't play that much in the NHL to break through like that? Holy cow. He's locked on to something, and hockey player or not hockey player, he's one of the best I ever seen. I know when Graham Mink came back to Hershey, he said he wanted to catch Andrew in Twitter followers. I said good luck with that, you have 900, he has 10,000. You're going to need help from him directly, nobody can help you get to that."

Ewell said it was tougher for the game's bigger stars, since they would be lightning rods for criticism on a very public forum. "It's tough for a guy like Mike Green. I was worried about Ovi at first since he takes criticism to heart and I knew he'd get a lot. So the first thing we tell people is don't reply to anybody that isn't a fan, and block whenever you can," Ewell said. "Take the satisfaction you've blocked him rather than writing something you're going to regret."

Ovechkin stopped using Twitter for an extended period of time. Nate Ewell discovered the scope of the phenomenon first hand when the star decided to begin tweeting again in March 2011. "I was actually here at my office in Boston and I got a text from him asking, 'What's my password?' I told him . . . and I didn't think anything of it, I just thought he was checking it out. Later that night, my phone started buzzing, and it was because he sent something out and it still had my e-mail address set up as the account. I got 8,000 [notifications] in the course of a day. So I was able to go in and switch that e-mail," he said, laughing.

Of course, the tweeters aren't just the players. John Walton developed a following while calling games for the Bears, and he brought his following to Washington when he became the Capitals' radio voice.

"It's something that we all learn as we go," Walton said. "It was something that I latched onto two or three years ago. I still marvel that 3,000 people would care what I have to say on anything, but it really is nice to go back and forth at whatever pace you want to.

"More than 10 years ago, it used to be fans had their opinion, but there wasn't that ability to go back and forth. Now it's here to stay, I think. I think with the selling of hockey especially — or any other sport — you have a lot of entertainment options, you can do anything . . . We have to be on guard as an organization whether any team or any sport. You need to be interactive and know what your fans are saying. Maybe what you hear isn't what you want to hear, but it'll teach you.

"From a radio perspective, it interacts with fans, builds loyalty with radio listeners. Fans think, 'Not only can I listen to John, I can interact with him. I like hearing what goes on with his life outside the hockey rink.' Once people know who you are, they tend to like you better. Like anything else, there's value to that."

The medium has also changed the way the game has been covered, as media members are quick to tweet news before it even gets written in blog form.

"I'll say this about Twitter: [Verizon Center] was the first place I realized it was a powerful medium," Wyshynski said. "The reason why is in the [2009 playoff] game where Sid and Ovechkin had the double hat tricks, that was the night that Sid said that it took them too long to clean up the hats. At this time, Twitter was not all that huge, but I was on it and had my phone with me and I sent a text message to Twitter about Sid saying the thing about the hats.

"When we got done with the press conferences, I get back to the media room, and I fire up the laptop, and there are literally 200 comments off that comment, and most of them are like, 'This is a joke, right?' And it dawned on me, 'This is out there before anyone else has written it, before it's been on television, before it's been on radio, before it's been in a newspaper.' The immediacy of that medium became really apparent."

According to Wyshynski, Twitter still has some kinks, particularly when some go overboard with in-game coverage. "As far as how it's changed things, it's really annoying that you can't go on a hockey night without someone doing play-by-play from the press box. Sometimes that's fun, but most of the time, it's incredibly annoying. I don't understand why people don't tell me about the things that are happening around but not necessarily where the camera is. You can tell me what's happening behind the play; I can't see it, I'm at home. So do that. I don't need shot-by-shot, play-by-play."

But overall, Wyshynski, one of the biggest names in internet coverage of the sport, thinks Twitter is a positive step forward. "It's opened up some doors for fans' relationships with players; it's opened up relationships with media; and in some cases, media has recoiled because they don't like how accessible things are, when they can look at their timeline and see 'you suck' and they have to read it. They don't have a moderator to remove it. But it's only been a good thing in building bonds between fans and media and teams."

CHAPTER 12

RISING TO CONTENDER

After the drama of 2007–08, it's probably no surprise the Capitals quietly settled into the role of a true Stanley Cup contender.

There were changes, however, most notably in goal. Cristobal Huet elected to sign a four-year, $22.5 million deal with Chicago despite his successful stretch run, forcing the Caps into their fallback plan: signing former Colorado Avalanche and Montreal Canadiens goaltender Jose Theodore to take the starting role until prospects Semyon Varlamov and Michal Neuvirth were ready to play full-time in the NHL.

Olaf Kolzig, who had been on the bench after taking the team's final regular-season loss in Chicago back on March 19, left as well, signing with the Tampa Bay Lightning. The last connection to the team's only trip to the Stanley Cup Finals, in 1998, was cut — and not on the best of terms.

Washington stumbled in their season opener, with their new goaltender Theodore getting pulled in the 7–4 loss to the Thrashers. But the Capitals bounced back in their home opener against Chicago.

For the team's first meaningful game since bowing out to the Flyers in the playoffs, the sellout crowd of 18,277 arrived early and was loud, cheering as the team raised the 2007–08 Southeast Division banner to the rafters of Verizon Center. That celebratory mood was put on hold early, however, as Theodore allowed a goal just 26 seconds into the game.

But Alex Ovechkin showed his flash, collecting the puck at center ice early in the second and blasting it past Chicago netminder Nikolai Khabibulin to erase a 2–0 Blackhawks lead. Alexander Semin and Ovechkin scored in the game's waning minutes to give Washington a 4–2 win, with the crowd once again chanting "M-V-P" after Ovechkin's second of the night.

"Showed our character," Ovechkin said afterward. "We know we can come back. It doesn't matter what the score is."

"Fabulous," Boudreau said of the crowd. "They were ready to rock right from the beginning, and I'm glad at the end we gave them something to cheer about."

Washington heated up as the season progressed. After a 5–3–1 October, the team went on a seven-game stretch without a regulation loss en route to an 8–5–2 month. December was even better, with an 11–3–0 stretch helping to author the best first half in team history.

The team's on-ice success was matched by its quickly growing fan base. The 41st game of the year, against the team that knocked them out of the playoffs, was the Capital's 10th sellout of the season, one better than the year before, and more than they had in the 2003–04, 2005–06 and 2006–07 seasons combined.

In front of near-full or capacity houses every night, the players thrived, amassing an impressive 18–1–1 record. The press box was also nearing capacity, and at one point Bruce Boudreau joked that it must be a slow sports day with all the reporters in attendance.

The coach also noticed a change in the team's mentality. After the breakneck chase to get into the postseason the year before, there was little question the Capitals would qualify this time. Instead of just looking to crash the party, Washington would have to adjust to the role of being one of the targets once there.

"It's one thing to get there; it's another thing to stay," Boudreau said after the Flyers game. "We like it up there. And I think the guys like it up there, and they want to be known as one of the better teams. So it's not a question of 'OK, we got here, let's relax.' We're going to push the envelope as far as we can push it and see where it takes us. And hopefully it'll take us far."

Boudreau also mentioned that in his 33 years of being around the game, he couldn't remember a streak of 20 home games with just one regulation loss.

The emergence of the Capitals as one of the Eastern Conference powers had also fueled a war of words with the Flyers, as the two teams carried over some of the bad blood from the previous playoff series.

"Enough has been said about the 'war' between Philly and Washington, and we felt this was a business day," Boudreau said. "We wanted to be like machines and go out there and do what we're capable of doing. It was a 50–50 game right to the end, and that's what happens when two real good teams play."

Washington was making a run at the East's top seed, on the heels of the Boston Bruins, who had also enjoyed a tremendous first half.

A week after the Flyers game, on January 13, 2009, the Capitals dropped a 5–2 decision to Edmonton. While not particularly memorable for what occured on the ice, it did prove to be the last non-sellout at Verizon Center for years — a major accomplishment for a team that had struggled to fill seats just a season before.

As January turned to February, Alexander Ovechkin began to heat up, notching five goals in just three periods, including a two-goal outburst against the Red Wings in a Saturday afternoon matinee. A hat trick against the Senators the following afternoon capped the unusual back-to-back home weekend.

Ovechkin joked afterward that he was "usually sleeping" by early afternoon, but felt better as the weekend progressed.

"I go to bed a little bit early, like 8, and wake up again 6:30 and go back again to sleep, so I kind of feel pretty good today," he told reporters.

Mike Green also was playing well, as he too scored in both weekend games, extending his own goal-scoring streak to three games. Green then scored in a win over the Devils and a loss to the Kings. By the time the Florida Panthers arrived to town on February 7, he'd notched another pair to set a career-high with 19, as well as setting a franchise record for a defenseman by scoring in six straight games.

Green scored again in a loss to the Rangers, and then broke the NHL mark for goals in consecutive games by a defenseman — set by former Bruins defenseman Mike O'Connell in 1983–84 — on Valentine's Day against Tampa Bay, beating Lightning goaltender Kari Ramo for a tally in his eighth straight game.

The team got permission from the league to leave the bench to celebrate the record-setting night with the defenseman, and Green's father was on the trip as part of the club's annual fathers' weekend.

"I got a shot and [Matt Pettinger] made a good block," Green said during an interview with Comcast SportsNet during the intermission. "I went right behind him, and I was just waiting for it to drop. I was in the slot, and I just put it five-hole."

Although Green's streak came to an end the next night in Florida, unlike the previous season, the Capitals were comfortably in control of the Southeast Division.

On February 22, the Capitals matched up with the Penguins in a nationally televised game at Verizon Center. Things quickly turned nasty.

Although Sidney Crosby and the Penguins had dominated the first nine times the two superstars met — with the Capitals going 1–7–1 — Washington had matched up much better since Boudreau took over, establishing a 3–1–1 record against the Pens under the coach's watch. They'd already won the first two meetings of the year.

Ovechkin tallied his league-leading 43rd goal before the two Hart Trophy winners collided late in the second period. Crosby unsuccessfully tried to deposit Ovechkin into the Washington bench and had to be restrained by the linesman.

Ovechkin gave Sid the Kid a derisive wave as the two yelled at each other in front of the team benches.

"[Crosby] started it," Boudreau said after the game. "Sidney was jawing at everybody . . . You see our bench talking to him, him talking to our bench, and I think he was getting frustrated because he wasn't getting the freedom he had in this building before."

"What I can say about him?" Ovechkin said. "He is a good player, but he talks too much."

"Like it or lump it, that [physical play is] what he does," Crosby said of Ovechkin down the hall in the visitors' dressing room. "Some people like it, some people don't. Personally, I don't like it. I was just skating to the bench and he pushed me from behind. So I just gave him a shot back. That's hockey, and he likes to run around these days, so that was it."

"I play hard," Ovechkin responded. "If he wants to do something like hit me again, try to hit me again — and I'll talk to you guys who plays dirty. That's my game. It's not cheap shots, it's a game moment. But he doesn't like it, it's his problem."

The two rivals were certainly going in opposite directions at that point, as Washington held a 13-point lead over Florida in the Southeast Division race, while Pittsburgh was four points out of a playoff spot. But like the Capitals did the year before, the Penguins soon made a coaching change and promoted their AHL bench boss to the NHL, and that move eventually set the two teams on a collision course toward what would be an epic playoff series.

Although the Capitals made a run at Boston for the top seed in the East, a four-game losing streak to open March put them instead in a race with the New Jersey Devils for the second seed, as the Bruins pulled away.

Ovechkin generated some controversy after scoring his 50th on March 20 in Tampa, dropping his stick and standing over it, warming his hands like it was on fire.

The "hot stick" celebration drew notice from both coaches, as well as some media who thought the stunt was excessive.

"I think he's a terrific player. He went down a notch in my books after that," Lightning interim coach Rick Tocchet told the Associated Press. "It's not something I like. It's hard for me to accept, to see something like that in our building."

"He has never done that with me that I've seen," Bruce Boudreau told reporters. "He celebrates, but I think that was a little planned out."

With the Capitals' star looking like he was going to earn a second straight Hart Trophy, everything the Russian did was gaining notice — both good and bad. The celebration, which might be more accepted in the NFL and NBA, was certainly out of character for an NHL player.

Washington wrapped up its second straight playoff berth on March 25 with seven games left in the season. It was the first time since 1999–2000 and 2000–01 that the Caps made the playoffs in successive seasons, a long time for a team that once went 14 straight years with a playoff berth (1982–83 to 1995–96).

They wrapped the Southeast Division title up on April 3 in what Bruce Boudreau called a "bittersweet" moment. The title was theirs after a 6–5 overtime loss to the Buffalo Sabres.

The game also set the Capitals' single-season attendance mark — with one home game still left to play — and also gave them 102 points, the second-best total in franchise history.

Washington finished the year with 741,992 fans going through the turnstiles in the regular season, an average attendance of 18,097 — the first time the team had ever finished north of the 18,000 mark in per-game attendance.

Unlike previous years, when it wasn't known if the final home game would mark the end of the campaign, as the team vacated Verizon Center for the sold-out 2009 Frozen Four to decide the NCAA's men's ice hockey champion, everyone knew there would be playoff games in Washington.

Ovechkin's popularity continued to grow in some unusual circles. The star even earned an unusual endorsement, making *Time*'s 100 List after Hollywood producer Jerry Bruckheimer nominated him. Bruckheimer wrote, "At 23, Alexander Ovechkin is already the Iron Man of the NHL, having played in 203 consecutive games. The leading goal scorer last year, Ovechkin has revitalized hockey in our nation's capital. What makes him great is his pure, heroic genius on the rink."

Back home in Washington, the Boston University Terriers talked about the reverence for the Capitals during the Frozen Four. As the NCAA's top seeded team, they were able to use the Capitals' dressing room and were thrilled mainly because it was where Ovechkin prepared for games.

Washington secured the second seed in the conference in the second-to-last game of the season with a six-game season sweep of Tampa Bay, although Ovechkin did lose out on the Art Ross Trophy to the Russian who was picked right behind him in 2004 — Pittsburgh's Evgeni Malkin. The team earned its 50th win for just the third time in franchise history, and also set a single-season franchise mark with 108 points.

But despite all the regular-season records, the team's focus had changed. Just making the playoffs wasn't good enough: they were intent on doing some damage when they got there. First up for the Capitals was the New York Rangers: a defense-first club that would try to keep scores low by frustrating their opponents with close checking and solid goaltending from Henrik Lundqvist.

New York had started the season strongly, but had slowly slid down the ladder to finish seventh, just two points ahead of ninth-place Florida. Still, the Rangers opened the series on April 15 with a win in Game 1 at Verizon Center. Lundqvist was able to outplay his counterpart Theodore in the 4–3 victory, serving notice that the team from NYC would not be an easy out.

Jose Theodore stopped just 17 of 21 shots in the game, leaving both the goaltender and his coach riled. "I'm not happy with my game," Theodore said afterward. "I wasn't good enough. But in the playoffs, you bounce back and that's it — you have to turn the page."

Boudreau didn't disagree, saying Theodore "didn't make the save when we needed it," adding that Semyon Varlamov, who had just six games of NHL experience under his belt, might be used in the playoffs. The words became prophetic — a lot sooner than expected.

Still Boudreau was hopeful that the Capitals would be able to at least split on home ice before the series headed north to MSG.

"We won the first game last year, and that didn't do us any good," Boudreau said. "New York is confident that they stole one here, and we're confident that we're a pretty good team and we'll play well on Saturday."

Varlamov — who had not yet turned 21 — replaced Theodore for Game 2 of the series, and while he allowed just one goal on 24 shots, Lundqvist was mistake-free, blanking the Capitals for a 2–0 Rangers lead in the series. Ryan Callahan's goal 7:44 into the contest held up over the entire game, as the Swedish netminder frustrated the Capitals, and the rest of the Rangers limited Washington's scoring chances.

"If you don't score," Ovechkin told reporters afterward, "you lose."

"You can say he's a great goalie, but we're good players too," he added, "and we have to score goals."

Two nights later, the Capitals got a shutout of their own to climb back in the series, as Varlamov made 33 saves to earn his first NHL playoff win, 4–0, at Madison Square Garden.

"He's played in the finals of the Russian elite league, which to him is probably like our Stanley Cup," Bruce Boudreau told reporters afterward. "He's played in the world championship, and the fact that he doesn't understand a word we're saying probably really helps."

Alexander Semin scored a pair of first-period goals to put the Capitals in control early, and although Ovechkin was held scoreless for the third straight game, he did chip in a pair of important assists.

"It was an important game, but it's over," Ovechkin told AP. "It's done. It's history. And we have to battle next game."

The urgency that helped the Capitals in Game 3 vanished two nights later, with the result being a tightly fought New York win that pushed Washington to the brink of elimination for the second straight year.

Like the year before, Ovechkin promised the series wasn't over, despite the long odds for Washington. But unlike a year earlier, the Capitals were able to complete the turnaround.

"It's not done yet," Ovechkin told reporters. "We were in this situation last year and we came back. We got that experience and it was good experience. We know how to come back."

While the Rangers had been successful in slowing down the Caps in the first four games, things became unglued for them in Game 5. Sean Avery, who had been effective in the series, took two bad penalties late in Game 4 and was benched by Rangers coach John Tortorella.

During Game 5, Tortorella squirted water and threw a plastic drinking bottle at a fan behind the New York bench and was suspended by the NHL for Game 6 for his actions.

Washington was able to force the series back north with their effort in the must-win Game 5, besting Tortorella's squad 4–0.

Unlikely hero Matt Bradley scored a pair of goals, and Varlamov recorded a 20-save shutout — his second in three games — as the Capitals closed the series gap to 3–2.

Despite the win, Boudreau said the team hadn't earned a thing except staving off elimination. "They only have to win one. We have to win two. The pressure's all on us," he told reporters. "You look at the odds, the odds definitely don't favor us."

On a clear blue April Sunday afternoon in midtown Manhattan, the Capitals once again rose to the occasion; the 5–3 win in Game 6 wasn't as close as the score indicated.

Washington chased Lundqvist from the net after scoring five times on just 20 shots, grabbing a 5–1 lead before the Rangers made the final score look cosmetically better in the third. The rout took place with Tortorella watching from high up in MSG, serving his one-game suspension.

"[Lundqvist] can't play every game like a god," Ovechkin said. "He can't save the game all the time. When we play our game, we play simple. We play hard and nobody can stop us."

"When you're down 3–1, there is no pressure on you," Boudreau told reporters. "They expect you to lose. Now we see how they can handle it when they're expected to win."

All of this set up — for the second straight year — a winner-take-all Game 7. A trip to the second round was on the line at Verizon Center.

Despite Washington holding the momentum, both teams were tentative at the outset of the rubber match. The Capitals fell behind 5:35 in when Nik Antropov deposited the rebound from a Brandon

Dubinsky shot past a diving Semyon Varlamov. The early lead allowed the Rangers to ply their defense-first style: sit back and let the Capitals attack, and rely on Lundqvist.

The Capitals finally tied the game with 4:26 left in the first. Mike Green was coming out of the penalty box, and Washington had a 3-on-2 break. Nicklas Backstrom dropped a pass to Alexander Semin, whose shot was partially blocked by Ryan Callahan. The Rangers defenseman actually changed the direction of the puck with a double-deflection off both his stick and body. It fluttered past Lundqvist for a strange goal.

Despite Semin's equalizer, the Capitals remained overly cautious and sat back with the score tied. At one point, the timid style of play was even booed by the home crowd.

In the end, it was one of Washington's veterans — a player who'd scored a game-winning goal during the only Stanley Cup Finals the Caps had been involved in — who broke the tension. This time, instead of scoring for the visiting Red Wings, who paraded hockey's Holy Grail around this same ice 11 years earlier, Sergei Fedorov helped the home team advance.

With just under five minutes left in regulation, the Russian veteran collected the puck off a Matt Bradley feed in the Caps end and broke into the Rangers zone, then slammed on the brakes in the faceoff circle in front of Rangers defenseman Wade Redden. Fedorov then delivered a wrist shot that beat Lundqvist for his 52nd career playoff goal. He'd have no bigger marker as a Capital — and it turned out to be his last for Washington.

"There was not much going on," Fedorov simply said afterward of his game-winning goal, "so I decided to shoot the puck."

"Experience sometimes pays off. He knew what he had to do, when to do it," said Boudreau. "That's what makes him one of the greatest players ever."

The goal sent the crowd into a frenzy, causing the building's upper deck to literally shake. The fans were roaring for the game's final 4:59, standing most of the way as the Capitals advanced to the second round.

"I don't know what Chicago is like [with the "Star-Spangled

Banner"] . . . but that was the loudest five minutes after we scored,"
Boudreau said. "They never sat down. They never stopped cheering. If
you look at the energy we had in checking, the fans brought that out of
us. They wouldn't let us not continue skating, not continue anything.
It was really a thing to watch."

As Boudreau's post-game press conference took place underneath
the stands on the Washington Wizards' practice court, reporters were
keeping tabs on the action from New Jersey. The Game 7 duel between
the Devils and Hurricanes would decide Washington's second-round
opponent.

New Jersey held a late lead, and the Devils would have been the
Capitals' second-round opponent had the score held. But legendary
New Jersey goaltender Martin Brodeur had an uncharacteristic melt-
down in the final 80 seconds to allow both the equalizer and the series-
deciding goal. The win went to the Hurricanes — all the action taking
place as Boudreau addressed the media.

The dramatic win meant the Hurricanes would move on to face
top-seeded Boston — and Washington would draw Pittsburgh instead
of New Jersey. The playoff matchup the NHL had hoped for since
Ovechkin and Crosby entered the league would finally take place.

OLD RIVALRY, NEW HEIGHTS

Black-and-gold uniformed postseason opponents were nothing new. The Caps had met the Penguins in the Stanley Cup playoffs seven times before. Almost always, they'd wound up on the wrong side of the ledger, winning just one series back in 1993–94.

Pre-lockout, the rivalry between the two teams was also a sharp contrast of two cities: Pittsburgh was the blue-collar town, but the Capitals were the blue-collar team, looking to outwork their opponent but usually falling short to their opponent's vast wealth of talent.

"It's tough; in a way it wasn't a rivalry before. Penguins fans would say, well, when one side wins, it's not a rivalry," the *Washington Examiner*'s Brian McNally recalled. "But in the early 1990s, those series were hellacious. The Capitals won one under [former coach Jim] Schoenfeld, but they came close to upending some of those Cup teams. It just didn't happen — it probably should have — but whatever that little boost that gets you from a 3–1 lead to a quick series win wasn't there.

"The Penguins . . . cemented the identity of the Capitals being playoff disappointments. The Cubs had an identity. The Red Sox had an identity.

The Capitals after those Lemieux series became a team that you expected to lose. After that, they just didn't have the talent to compete. It was a rivalry — you can't tell me any different, and the teams hated each other — although at some point you have to win those games and series."

The rivalry became stranger as the new millennium arrived, when the Capitals and Penguins were forced to play an unconventional first-round series in 2000. A "Burn the Floor" dance show was scheduled for Pittsburgh's Mellon Arena; as a result, Washington hosted Games 1, 4, 5 and 7, while the Penguins got Games 2, 3 and 6.

Once the Penguins took a critical Game 1 in the Caps' building, they took advantage of their two home games.

"Jeff Halpern used the term 'chaos' for that series; he said it was the craziest thing he's ever been involved in," McNally said.

"That was kind of indicative of how the Caps were run back then, complete second-banana status, and that never should have happened. Those two years, they had 100-point seasons but went out in the first round. It set the stage [for the rebuild]; they missed the playoffs [in 2002] and retooled and lost to Tampa [in 2003].

"The rivalry became what it was. The Penguins were the better team and the Capitals were like Wile E. Coyote — always chasing and couldn't finish."

But the 2009 series had a different complexion.

"The great part about 2009 for Caps fans is it put the two teams on even footing," McNally said. "It wasn't Lemieux and Jagr, where one side had the elite talent and the other team was the blue-collar, hoping-we-can-knock-you-off team. It became toe-to-toe, like a boxing match. You got a hat trick? I got a hat trick.

"It was as good as sporting theater as I've ever seen."

The Capitals-Penguins regular-season meetings had already become intense: the series shaped up to be unique.

"It was great," Nate Ewell recalled of the rivalry. "Eighty-two-game seasons are pretty long and there's not a lot that breaks it up — most games just feel like most games. And really, maybe I'm not making enough of it, they were still special in 2005, but even more so in 2008–09. The intensity around those games was something special."

But it wouldn't be a vintage Capitals-Penguins playoff series without a scheduling quirk. In 2009, the Capitals and Penguins were forced to play Games 4 and 5 on back-to-back nights to allow Mellon Arena to host a concert by pan flute star Yanni.

"The playoffs are very intense and physical, and players need time to recoup," Leonsis wrote on his blog, Ted's Take. "No one is advantaged by playing back-to-back games so no one can complain, but it is unfortunate that the Yanni concert takes precedence over high-quality NHL playoff hockey."

The series began on May 2 at Verizon Center, with Semyon Varlamov making his mark — and an incredible save on Crosby — to help give the Capitals an early series lead.

Crosby opened the scoring at 4:09, but the Capitals roared back to take the lead when David Steckel and Ovechkin put the Caps ahead going into the first intermission.

Pittsburgh surged late in the second period, with Mark Eaton tying the score with 7:06 left. The Penguins missed a golden chance to take the lead going into the third when Crosby took a Chris Kunitz pass in front of a wide open net with just over two minutes to play.

Varlamov lunged across the crease, just catching the puck with his paddle before it crossed the line to keep the game tied.

"It was a great save," Boudreau said. "There's no doubt. Goalies are taught never to give up. You look at all the great goalies that are in hockey. No matter where the play, they never give up. You keep fighting. And that's the only way the [Martin] Brodeurs, the Tim Thomases and the [Roberto] Luongos make great saves, it's because they never quit on the puck . . . It was obviously a turning point because they would have had the lead and we would have had to play catch-up."

"I was out of position, there was really nothing I could do, so I lunged with the stick, and it just so happened the puck hit it right on the line," Varlamov said through a translator.

"It was kind of a desperation save," Crosby explained. "You don't want to waste those opportunities."

Lifted by his goalie's play late in the second, Tomas Fleischmann scored 1:46 into the final period, converting a feed from Nicklas Backstrom for the eventual game-winner.

"I just went to the net, stopped and chipped it over," Fleischmann told reporters. "When your top guys have a lot of pressure on them, you have to take it away with secondary guys, like we are, and try to put it in."

With the Caps holding a 1–0 series advantage, Game 2 proved to be one of the best playoff games in recent NHL history. Both team's superstars struck for their first career playoff hat tricks — with Ovechkin's Capitals getting the best of Crosby's Pens in the 4–3 win.

Crosby scored the only goal of the first at 6:38. Semyon Varlamov couldn't handle all of a Sergei Gonchar shot, and the Penguins star was parked at the doorstep.

Ovechkin answered 2:18 into the second, after Sergei Fedorov spun along the boards inside the Penguins' zone and fed Viktor Kozlov in the middle. Kozlov dished it over to the Caps' star, and he blasted one past Fleury.

Crosby struck next, giving Pittsburgh the lead again just past the halfway point, taking a Bill Guerin rebound and beating Mike Green in front of the net to poke the puck past Varlamov.

Steckel evened things up with 4:11 left in the frame, taking a deflected Tyler Sloan shot at the side of net and beating Fleury to send the game into the intermission tied at two.

Late in the third period, Ovechkin took over.

Just four seconds after Malkin was sent to the penalty box for a trip, Washington got the go-ahead goal. Nicklas Backstrom won the faceoff back to Green, who fed the Russian star. Ovi's one-timer ripped past Fleury — and sent the crowd into a frenzy.

The din grew when Ovechkin completed his first career playoff hat trick with 4:38 left, breaking in on Gonchar in the Penguins zone, then unleashing a wrist shot past Fleury's glove.

Caps rained down on the ice in celebration; Crosby was irked.

"People kept throwing hats," Crosby said at the press conference podium after the game. "And I was just asking if he could make an announcement to ask them to stop."

Despite his annoyance, Crosby wasn't done producing himself. He scored with Fleury on the bench for an extra attacker with just 31 seconds left.

When the dust settled, it was David Steckel's marker, not the six by Ovechkin and Crosby, that proved to be the difference. Washington had its fifth straight playoff win — a team record — and the Capitals had a 2–0 series lead as the series shifted north.

"Sick game. Sick three goals by me and Crosby," said Ovechkin. "It's unbelievable to see how fans react, how fans go crazy. The atmosphere right now, it's unbelievable. You see all the red, and — probably I'm afraid to go home right now."

"It's nice to score," Crosby said. "But it's better to win . . . I'm sure it's entertaining for people to watch, if I were to look at it from a fan's point of view. As a player, you don't like when the guy on the other team gets a hat trick. That's usually not a good sign."

"When you build up hype about superstars playing against each other, and then the superstars play like superstars, it's a neat thing," Bruce Boudreau said.

Despite that, the coach realized the Capitals hadn't accomplished anything. "If this was a game of tennis, we've held serve," he told reporters.

While the Capitals headed to western Pennsylvania with the series lead, problems had emerged with their play. The Penguins had seemingly found a weakness in Varlamov's game: shots right under the crossbar. At the same time, the Washington defense was struggling to contain Sid the Kid — simply by parking himself beside their net the Penguins star would get his chances.

Despite the opportunity to take a 3–0 stranglehold, the Capitals failed to deliver a solid effort in Game 3. Still they had a chance to win thanks to their young Russian netminder. Semyon Varlamov made 39 saves — many of the stellar variety — but was undone on a Kris Letang shot that deflected off Shaone Morrisonn's skate in overtime.

Ovechkin started things off on the right foot for the Caps, scoring just 1:23 in, but after that, the team seemed content to rely on its netminder, putting only 23 shots on Fleury in more than 70 minutes.

Pittsburgh solved Varlamov 9:29 into the second, when Ruslan Fedotenko squared the game. Washington was outshot 15–4 in the middle frame, and fortunate to be tied at 1–1.

Evgeni Malkin, who had been quiet through the series, appeared to have given the Penguins the win with 4:59 left by netting a power play maker, but Nicklas Backstrom forced overtime with his own power play tally at with just 110 seconds left. Regulation time ended with the Capitals being outshot by a 34–18 margin.

Then, after killing off an early Brian Pothier minor in overtime — Washington's seventh penalty of the night — it was only a matter of time before the Penguins ended the contest. The game ended on Pittsburgh's 42nd shot of the night.

"When you get a goaltending effort like that, you have to win," Bruce Boudreau told reporters. "I think we might have deserved the penalties, but they sure as hell deserved a few more than they got [two]."

The loss snapped Washington's five-game streak, and with back-to-back games — and travel between Games 4 and 5 — the next contest in Pittsburgh would prove critical.

Again things started well. Backstrom gave the Capitals an early lead, just 36 seconds in. But the rest of the first was all Pittsburgh. The Pens took a 3–1 lead they would never relinquish into the intermission. Varlamov was beginning to show his youth and inexperience: stoppable shots began getting through.

"There were four soft goals out of the five," Boudreau said later. "But he'll bounce back. He's a real competitive guy."

Ovechkin was held off the scoreboard for the first time in the series, while Crosby's league-leading ninth of the playoffs proved to be the game-winner.

"They were desperate," Boudreau said. "Alex is only human; he can't be unbelievable every night. He's a great player; he just had one of those nights where he's not going to get three goals."

For his part, Ovechkin didn't make himself any more popular in western Pennsylvania. A hit on Sergei Gonchar knocked his fellow Russian out of the game.

"Yeah, it probably was knee-on-knee — I tried to hit him with my shoulder and he just moved left [into] the same spot," Ovechkin said afterward.

With the short turnaround, Washington had little time to regroup. They were once again pushed to the brink of elimination. And for the second time in the series, Pittsburgh's game-winner came off a Washington player.

Jordan Staal put the Penguins up 5:17 into Game 5, but Ovechkin tied Crosby for the playoff scoring lead with his ninth 59 seconds later. Backstrom put the Capitals up with 5:25 left in the frame.

After Ruslan Fedotenko scored at 0:51 of the second, and former Capitals rental Matt Cooke scored six and a half minutes later, the Penguins were back on top.

Ovechkin evened the score with his 10th of the playoffs with just 4:08 left in the period, and then the teams played a scoreless third. They went back to their rooms to prepare for the second overtime of the series.

David Steckel had a golden chance to end things quickly, but missed an open net just 19 seconds into the extra frame. The miss proved costly. Milan Jurcina was whistled for tripping Malkin 1:29 into overtime.

In the dying seconds of the penalty, Malkin was on a 2-on-1, with Tom Poti backing up. The other great Russian's centering feed deflected off the Capitals' D-man's stick and into the net. Pittsburgh had its third straight win — and Washington's back was against the wall.

"First shift, Stecks missed an empty net," Ovechkin said afterward. "I said, 'Jesus, where is our luck?' The puck was bouncing, and next they got a power play and scored a goal."

"It's Malkin, so you can't give him too much time and space," Poti told reporters. "It became a 2-on-1 and I tried to go down to take the pass away and take away his angle coming to the net. He tried to make the pass and it ended up going off my glove and my stick or something. An unfortunate bounce."

After arriving in Pittsburgh just days before with a 2–0 lead, the Capitals were going to have to win at Mellon Arena to keep their season alive.

"We've been in this position before," Boudreau said. "It's a tough hill to climb, but you've just got to think of it as one game."

One thing the Capitals proved over this playoff run was they were nothing if not resilient. And in Game 6, Steckel wouldn't miss another open net.

Bill Guerin put the Penguins up in the first period, but Kozlov and Fleischmann gave Washington a lead in the second. It almost held up going into the third, but Eaton scored a power play goal with just 34 seconds left.

Stoked by the late marker, the Penguins got another on the power play, when Letang scored 4:40 into the third. But then the Caps were given a power play of their own, and Brooks Laich answered 58 seconds later. Viktor Kozlov then put the Capitals ahead 29 seconds after that.

Crosby was able to force another extra session, however, recording his tenth goal of the playoffs, and his sixth of the series, by beating Varlamov with 4:18 left.

Once again, the Penguins dominated the shot clock, holding a 39–20 edge through 60 minutes of play.

In a moment of redemption, Steckel was able to force a deciding game back at Verizon Center, rushing to the net after winning a face-off and deflecting a Laich shot past Fleury with 6:22 gone in overtime. The Capitals had the 5–4 decision.

"I told myself if I had a chance again, I wouldn't miss," Steckel told AP. "I was in the right place at the right time. I personally didn't know where it went or anything.

"It was the biggest goal of my career so I didn't know what to do. I just jumped around."

Ovechkin had already notched 13 points in the series, and both the team's stars were shining bright in what was already an epic war.

"They're incredible, both of them, and Malkin is just as incredible," Boudreau told reporters. "They play at a level other people can't attain."

"I think it's going to be great game," Ovechkin said. "I think the league wants us to play Game 7."

After a roller-coaster ride of emotion for fans in both cities, and while the Capitals had played two thrilling Game 7s in the previous two years, this Game 7 turned out to be a disappointment for Washington.

Gonchar returned to the lineup for Pittsburgh, and it proved to be an emotional lift. The Penguins rolled to the easiest win of the series.

Fleury stopped Ovechkin on a breakaway less than three minutes in and the Penguins assumed control.

Crosby notched his 11th goal of the series with 7:24 left in the first on a power play, and just eight seconds later, Craig Adams made it 2–0 for the white-clad Penguins, who outshot the Capitals 16–5 in the first frame.

While the Caps had shown resilience all spring, the team had simply run out of gas after 14 tough playoff games. They yielded another goal to Guerin 28 ticks into the second. Letang added a fourth 2:12 in to chase Semyon Varlamov. Jose Theodore saw his first action since Game 1 — with the Penguins holding a commanding 4–0 lead.

Jordan Staal beat the new netminder to push the lead to five. Ovechkin scored his own 11th goal of the playoffs with 1:51 left in the second, but he barely celebrated, knowing Washington's season was winding down.

Laich was called for a double-minor for high-sticking Crosby early in the third, and the Pens' star answered by scoring his 12th on the power play. Laich managed to redeem himself at 6:26, but the game was all but decided. It would end as a 6–2 Pittsburgh victory.

The loss was tough for the Capitals, and a strange end to a series that featured three overtime games. There was never more than a one-goal difference for 92 percent of the play in the first six games — and no team established a three-goal lead until early in the second period of Game 7.

After the game, the two stars shook hands at center ice. The Penguins were advancing to the Eastern Conference Finals and would eventually get past the Hurricanes and the Red Wings to raise their first Stanley Cup since 1992. Ovechkin's Capitals had to settle for the bitter consolation of progress: reaching the second round and pushing the eventual champions to the limit.

"I just wished him good luck," Ovechkin said of facing Crosby in the handshake line, "and told him to win the Stanley Cup."

The postseason had taken its toll. Ovechkin later told Dmitry Chesnokov he personally played every game on painkillers despite putting up solid stats.

Mike Green had an injured shoulder, one that limited his ability to check Crosby and clear him away from the net, giving the defenseman a −5 rating for the series — including a −3 before being benched in the second period of Game 7. "He wasn't very good," Boudreau later said. Poti, who had the unfortunate deflection in Game 5, played the series with a broken foot, while Semin was playing with an injured thumb.

The long grind of an 82-game season, with 14 games in the playoffs, had taken its toll.

For Brian McNally, however, this series wasn't like Washington's other losses to the Penguins. This time the Capitals had held their own.

"You get downtrodden as fans . . . I distinctly remember one of the early playoff series, when the Penguins eliminated the Caps at home," he said. "I remember being on the Metro and the Penguins fans had taken over the subway and were taunting Capitals fans who got in the car. You just saw your team's season end in horrific fashion, half the building is cheering the Penguins, and drunk fans are screaming at you. That had to seep down into every fan's view of their team.

"The 2009 season built off that, at least for the older fans. Finally, skill-wise, this is 50–50 deal. This is a toss-up series. They didn't win it, but it changed the image of the franchise completely, where even in losing, you kind of gain a benefit out of it."

One player who has had a unique view of the rivalry is goaltender Brent

Johnson, who spent extended time in both cities, playing in Washington from 2006 to 2009, then heading north to back up Fleury in Pittsburgh the summer following the Capitals' playoff loss to the Penguins.

"It's been great to be on both sides," Johnson said in 2011. "I think where I'm at right now in Pittsburgh, I'm so fortunate. I'm fortunate that I got to play with Ovechkin first for a few years, and now I get to play with, in my estimation, the best player in the world, Sidney Crosby.

"Seeing the rivalry on both sides has been great. There's not a lot of love for one another . . . Watching [the 2009 Capitals-Penguins series while injured], it was a heck of a series, tough and rugged, and every game seems to be like that now. I think they've had a few games where [Washington has] come to our building and won, and we're definitely not happy about that, and we want to do something about that."

When asked to compare the game's biggest stars, Johnson spelled out each player's strengths. "Sid just has a presence. He has a presence in the dressing room; people know where he is at all times. Every sense of the word, he's a fantastic guy. He's very, very respected around the hockey community as well as around Pittsburgh.

"Alex is happy-go-lucky. He seems to be always smiling unless something's going wrong in a game, always having fun, he's having fun with the guys.

"Two completely different personalities, two fantastic hockey players, and no one's taking anything away from either of those guys."

While the Capitals were knocked out by the Penguins, as the spring went on, the team watched the emergence of a future Capitals goaltender: in Hershey, Michal Neuvirth helped the Bears capture the Calder Cup championship thanks to his solid netminding.

Neuvirth went 16–6 in the postseason, establishing a 1.92 goals-against average and a .932 save percentage while dispatching the Philadelphia Phantoms, Wilkes-Barre/Scranton Penguins, Providence Bruins and Manitoba Moose en route to the team's 10th Calder Cup title. For the second time in four seasons, the Bears skated around with the AHL's hardware.

According to the team's play-by-play voice, Neuvirth was stellar in that playoff, earning the Jack Butterfield Award for the top performer in the AHL postseason.

"In 2009 I think he was somewhat of an unknown," Walton recalled. "When the playoffs started, you knew that team was going to be good, but goaltending was going to take them as far as they could.

"It's funny, you go back to the beginning of the season, Neuvirth wasn't even going to play in North America, let alone for Hershey. And he ended up coming back, but didn't play for us until December, and played sparingly. He didn't have a lot of regular season games, but he was going to be our guy in the playoffs. For Bears fans watching the series, it was like, 'We'll see what this kid can do.' And boy did we find out.

"I saw something from him [while] calling games; he just locks in and it's over. I don't know that I've seen a goalie at an AHL level like that. When the playoffs come around, he's a performer."

Ten days after the Bears took the victory skate in Winnipeg's MTS Centre, the Capitals got a bit of hardware of their own at the NHL Awards ceremony: Ovechkin repeated as the MVP and Pearson winner. Mike Green was nominated for the Norris Trophy, but finished second.

"It's important for me. What I'm doing on the ice, it's working and I don't want to stop," Ovechkin told reporters in Las Vegas. "Right now, I'm the best. But next year everyone will be better."

THE BIG TIME

While the Capitals' recent rise from one of the league's worst teams to one of its top contenders is impressive, so too is the story of the rapid change of hockey culture in Washington.

The city was originally granted an NHL expansion team in 1972, and the first puck dropped in October 1974 at the saddle-shaped Capital Centre right off the Capital Beltway in Landover, Maryland, due east of the U.S. capital. The original Capitals were tasked with trying to assemble a competitive team during an expansion era that saw the league grow from six to 18 teams in just seven short years. At the same time, they had to battle the upstart World Hockey Association for talent.

As a result, the newly minted Capitals struggled mightily. They set the NHL's futility record with just 21 points in 1974–75 and were not a whole lot better over the next few years. Attendance at the Cap Centre reflected the sorry state of on-ice affairs, as the team averaged just 9,835 to 11,800 per game over its first eight seasons.

With the Capitals failing to make the playoffs through the 1981–82 season, team founder Abe Pollin wanted improvement at the gate, and threatened to move the franchise. A merger with the relocating Colorado

Rockies in northern New Jersey — if the team didn't reach a season ticket quota and get the county ticket tax eased — was even contemplated.

A season-ticket campaign in the summer of 1982, labeled "Save the Caps," both helped boost sales and garnered tax breaks from Prince George's County. Pollin backed down.

Not long after, the team's new general manager, David Poile, swung a deal to acquire defenseman Rod Langway from the Montreal Canadiens. The acquisition paid dividends, and the Capitals in 1982–83 qualified for the playoffs for the first time. They wouldn't miss again until 1996–97.

With the new success came a rise in fan interest and the average attendance grew to over 17,000 by the end of the decade. While not nearly as popular as the city's NFL franchise, the Capitals took over second spot in the pecking order, ahead of the floundering Washington Bullets and Baltimore Orioles in the marketplace.

But after years of playoff disappointments — along with a headline-grabbing incident involving a postseason party after the team's longest playoff run in 1990 — the team eventually parted ways with popular players Scott Stevens and Dino Ciccarelli. Interest in the team began to fade.

Passion was rekindled by the team's Stanley Cup Finals run in the spring of 1998, as the Capitals dispatched the Bruins, Senators and Sabres to earn its first-ever championship finals berth. Once there, however, Washington was no match for the defending Stanley Cup champion Red Wings. They fell in four straight to a team that was just too much for them to handle.

During that series, Capitals management sold thousands of tickets to a Detroit travel agency, leading to thousands of Red Wings fans at the MCI Center to celebrate the Cup clincher in Washington — much to the chagrin of Capitals fans who had long awaited a chance to see a Finals game but found a large number of red-clad Detroit fans.

Washington couldn't build upon the momentum of the run; their play for the Cup was followed by an injury-filled season where they missed the postseason completely.

In the summer of 1999, Ted Leonsis purchased the team from Pollin, and the Capitals made an impressive run to their first Southeast Division title in 1999–2000 with a tremendous second half before falling in an unusual series to the Penguins. The Caps repeated as division champs the next year, but fell to Pittsburgh once again in the playoff rematch.

After back-to-back playoff losses to Pittsburgh, Leonsis acquired superstar Jaromir Jagr from the Penguins. They missed the playoffs in the star's first year. Then came the disappointing loss to the Lightning that sparked the rebuild.

Fast forward to the run of success in the late 2000s and the re-emergence of the brand: the city's appetite for hockey had grown exponentially and much faster than ever before.

The average attendance in 2005–06 was 13,905 — the lowest for the team since 1983–84 — but by the end of the 2010–11 season, the average had reached 18,398. By the end of that season, the team compiled a sellout streak of 106 straight that carried over into the new season. In fact the season was expected to sell out completely, with a waiting list for season tickets growing daily.

"This would be considered a growth stock, that's for sure," owner Ted Leonsis said. "We're able to sell out everything we touch, and that shows how wonderful the fan support is. My fondest goal is to build a team that's as good as our fan base."

According to Comcast SportsNet's Joe Beninati, it is something that is a bit hard to fathom for a franchise that once struggled to fill seats. "Could you imagine it? No. Could you wish or dream for it? I don't know you could say with any certainty it was going to occur.

"Piece by piece, you started to see that belief system. It starts with the ownership and management. They believed in the process, and there was a time, there was a spell there, where the drafts weren't as fruitful as they could have been — or should have been — although *should* is a strong word since drafting is such an inexact science. There was a spell that was, there was a miss . . . shucks, we missed on that one.

"Then, as they did this rebuild, it started to hit, in good spots, in first round places — there weren't mistakes made. The people they brought in were solid. Those draft classes were terrific. Those are the building blocks and smart moves . . . the proper free agent, the right trade, and you're building a contender. With that, the belief in the stands came right along. They could see that this team could be a power in the East.

"And it has been, in the regular season, the last three or four years — it has. The building has become an amazing place for hockey fans."

Although the team's built around a superstar, former Capitals goaltender Brent Johnson said that Washington has helped attract fans with the pieces surrounding Ovechkin as well. "From the first year after the lockout, I think people were excited because they had this new face in Alex," he said. "It was one of those things where you weren't going to get the crowds all season. The team wasn't built up so much as it is now. I think as the years progressed and they start finding more guys to back Alex, like Backstrom and Semin and Green — he just stepped up his game — and then they got a lot more keys since."

Brian Willsie, who returned to the Caps organization for the 2010–11 season, playing mostly in Hershey, marveled at the turnaround. "It didn't feel like the same team," he said. "It wasn't a lot like the first time I was there. They had a great falling [in 2003–04], and once they turned the corner with the uniform change and the 'Rock the Red,' and had a competitive team, it was pretty unbelievable to see how everything had flip-flopped. I was kind of in awe.

"They definitely have a home ice advantage comparable to what other of the top teams would have. I don't think we had that when I was there before, when the Red Wings or Maple Leafs would come in. We'd joke that there would be almost as many [visiting fans] as ours. Now they have the home ice advantage — and that's a big thing."

For longtime Washington observers, it's become a little surreal to see how popular hockey — not so long ago considered a niche sport in the city — has become. Part of the opportunity the Capitals have had can be traced to the other teams in the city not capturing the local imagination.

"It's amazing," Brian McNally of the *Washington Examiner* said. "If you think about the Wizards, it's similar. You had [Michael] Jordan and the end of his career, and the [Gilbert] Arenas teams were so unstable. So in D.C., other than the Redskins in their glory days [in the 1980s and early 1990s], we never really had that.

"Anyone who's young doesn't remember the Redskins being an elite level team — and there are more and more of those people every year. There was no baseball here, the hockey team was very, very good but not a championship caliber team and the NBA team was as poorly run as anything I've seen. There was nothing to hang your hat on. This was the first time — and it coincided with the growth of hockey in this area. A perfect storm developed."

"They're fortunate in a number of respects in that none of the other sports teams have done well in the same stretch," former *Washington Times* sports business reporter Tim Lemke said. "The Nationals never really took off and really got off to a bad start as a franchise in D.C. with all the drama of the stadium. The team wasn't winning, even when they opened a new ballpark."

Part of the Caps' appeal is the atmosphere inside Verizon Center, which quickly has become one of the most electric buildings in the league. That has fueled demand, which has made once-available tickets scarce as fans now come both for the experience and entertainment — something the other venues and teams around the city rarely match.

Fans regularly complain about the location of FedEx Field, home of the Redskins, which is ironically just across the Capital Beltway from the site of the old Capital Centre (where a shopping mall now stands). The inconvenient location requires a full-day commitment just to get to a game, and the overall game day experience isn't quite up to par with what fans expect. It's led to the softening of the market for what once was Washington's most sought-after sports ticket.

Nationals Park was completed in 2008 in southeast Washington. The hope was that it would revitalize the Navy Yard area along the Anacostia River the same way Verizon Center has Chinatown. But the whole project has been hit hard by the slumping economy, and several projects planned for the area are still stuck on the drawing board. There isn't a whole lot to do there before or after games as a result.

The Caps' fellow Verizon Center tenant, basketball's Wizards, have suffered from years of poor play. And even though Ted Leonsis, after taking over the club when Pollin died in 2009, took a page out of the Capitals' book by changing the team's uniform back to a red, white and blue color scheme in 2011, any excitement about the change faded with the labor woes that wiped out nearly two months of the NBA season.

The Capitals' on-ice success, paired with Verizon Center's vibrant Gallery Place neighborhood, filled with bars and restaurants and a good game day experience, has been the backbone of the rise of the NHL team.

"[The team was] able to capitalize on this void . . . Here we have this winning franchise. This is the place to be, Verizon Center . . . Ted talks a lot about this, and the location of Verizon Center helps a lot. You can go downtown, get a bite to eat, go to Clyde's [restaurant] or whatever, meet up with some old Georgetown buddies. The area around Gallery Place [surrounding the arena] is amazing.

"I've written a lot in the past about whether stadiums or arenas do anything to help the economy, but the life and vibrancy in that part of the city is amazing, and that speaks to it becoming a place to go, a destination, and almost like appointment viewing. It's a cool place to be.

"I don't know if the Capitals have been able to capture the celebrity factor. There was a lot of talk when Obama became president that you'd see famous people lining the ice or going to Wizards games, but it never really materialized. These are just really good, average hockey fans."

"They can come to games and be really entertained and be part of something remarkable," Capitals general manager George McPhee said. "I've never seen a fan base like this. You come to regular season games where they're sold out for [2010–11] and sold out for [2011–12]. Everybody's wearing a jersey . . . It's a great environment and it's a great experience, and our building is as good as any in all of sports."

And, with the fans' enthusiasm, it makes Washington an attractive destination for players, when not too long ago some asked to leave the franchise for the chance to ply their trade elsewhere.

"This has turned into one of the best places in the league to play," Jeff Halpern said. "The players on the ice have given the people a product and they've responded."

"I started here when hockey wasn't as popular as it is now. It's great to see how far they've come, and now they're one of the top franchises in the league," said Matt Bradley, who spent from 2005 to 2011 with the Capitals before joining the Panthers. "They're selling out every game. It's an unbelievable place to play and an unbelievable building."

Capitals merchandise, which was rare to find at retail stores around town coming out of the lockout — even with one of the game's brightest young stars — has become a staple for local sporting goods retailers, rivaling only Redskins merchandise in availability. The change back to the old color scheme was a hit, and it quickly became difficult to find fans wearing blue and bronze jerseys.

Among the top-selling jerseys at NHL.com, according to *SportsBusiness Daily*, two Capitals were among the top seven best-sellers in 2010–11, with only Ovechkin trailing Sidney Crosby, and Nicklas Backstrom coming in seventh overall in the league. While this popularity is partially due to the retro uniform introduced for the 2011 Winter Classic, Ovechkin was also second the season before in terms of retail sales from the league's official website, according to Yahoo!'s Puck Daddy.

Today, Capitals T-shirts, hats, bumper stickers and license plate holders are much more commonplace. Endorsements featuring members of the team — most notably Ovechkin — have become more prevalent as well.

Ovechkin did national ads for hockey equipment manufacturer CCM, as well as local ads for Capital One Bank and a local chain of car dealers. Mike Green appeared in a national GEICO commercial, and even Bruce Boudreau got in the act during his D.C. tenure with ads for a Mercedes-Benz dealership as well as a copier chain and a carpet cleaner.

Most striking of all, perhaps, the Capitals — a team that had to give away thousands of tickets to try to generate interest for years after the lockout — have finally reached the point where they've had to implement a season ticket waiting list, something that was unheard of for anyone other than the Redskins.

"There's not a dollar to spend, there's not another ticket to sell; it's all up to the organization to be very, very focused and improved upon last year," Leonsis said before the 2011–12 season began. "It's now up to the players and the coaches, and they've internalized that. The fan base is built, the team is rebuilt, and we're ready to go.

"We're sold out, the business is very, very strong and we're grateful for that," he added.

Jeff Halpern, who grew up in suburban Potomac, Maryland, rooting for the Capitals at the old Capital Centre, has noticed the change since returning to the club in the summer of 2011. "It seems like there are more fans and more passion for the team in the area," he said. "Not just the hockey fan, but the casual fan as well. I think the biggest thing is that the product that management's been able to put on the ice is pretty exciting. If you go across the league with the top-end talent like this team has, it makes it easy to support them."

The rise of the team's profile has generated more general interest in the sport, and that has fueled a surge in the growth of youth hockey around the region.

"There's no doubt there's been an effect on new membership [in the area]," said Chris Peters, who tracks USA Hockey membership numbers for the United States of Hockey blog. "The Capitals certainly are playing a role in that. When you look at the growth since before 2003–04, it's been nothing like the growth over the last two years — it's been astronomical.

"Hockey has grown tremendously there since 2004, particularly in Washington D.C. itself. In 2003–04, there were just 192 registered players, and now there are 805 players. When you consider the population of D.C. and the amount of rinks [one in the actual District of Columbia], that's a significant amount of growth. It's gone up every single year since 2003–04, and growth was really stagnant between

1999 and the 2003–04 season. It went up in minor increments, but nothing like how it has grown now.

"When you look at Virginia, it's the same way. It's grown tremendously since 2003–04, and I looked back 20 years, when hockey was not really on the map there at all. Now it's huge. I think the membership in 2010–11 in Virginia was 7,837 and back in 2003–04 was 5,709. That outpaces national growth in a big way.

"The crazy thing is Maryland, which has gone through peaks and valleys over the last few years, has had unprecedented growth. They started 2003–04 with 7,010 players — just players, not coaches or referees — they went down by 300, down another 200, and finally back up, down again, and now the last two years have been insane — up 510 members in 2009–10, and an additional 1,025 in 2010–11. In one year, they doubled the growth and now are at an all-time high of 8,351 members.

"That was among the biggest growth of any state, and it's a pretty important state."

For years ice time was a rare commodity around the capital, but several new rinks have popped up over the past decade, most notably the team's new twin-rink Kettler Capitals Iceplex in Arlington.

"Youth hockey in the area has gotten big, and the number of new rinks in this area is a big part of it," Halpern said. "When you have a team that has done as well as the Caps have, kids want to be more like their role models — you want to be an Ovechkin or a Backstrom instead of a football or baseball player. It's great to see kids want to stay in hockey."

"I went to Gonzaga [High School] and graduated in 1995, and the hockey team when I was there was fighting to [survive]," McNally recalled. "Now, Jeff Halpern told me this, the growth from when he was coming up and with the Caps, compared now to 2001, it's just exploded the number of rinks. It's like a hurricane, it feeds into the growth of the sport, and overall can only help the Caps when Ovechkin isn't here and they'll need something else to sustain it."

The Capitals have also helped to weave themselves into the fabric of the city, fostering a strong interest in the club among the city's political set. *Meet the Press* anchor David Gregory has an Alexander Ovechkin McFarlane action figure on the set of his weekly NBC political show. CNN anchor Wolf Blitzer said he learned of the news of Osama bin Laden's death, in May 2011, while watching a Capitals playoff game. While the most powerful man in the free world — President Barack Obama — was reading a speech to the nation relaying the bin Laden news, the man behind the teleprompter just happened to be wearing a red Ovechkin jersey.

A *Washington Post* poll of residents in the Metro area conducted in August 2011 showed that 61 percent of respondents said they had a favorable view of the Capitals, with only 3 percent having an unfavorable opinion of the team — compared with a 55 percent favorable view of the Redskins and a 34 percent unfavorable opinion. The Capitals also were the favorite team of 72 percent of the people who identified themselves as fan of the sport, by far the highest percentage of any other local team, followed by the Redskins at 48 percent.

The *Washington Post Express* newspaper does an annual survey of its readers for the "Best of D.C.," and the Capitals have won the "Best D.C. Team" three years in a row, being "runaway" winners in 2011. The survey also concedes the title of best athlete in town, calling the voting for the *second-best* athlete its "Athlete Who Isn't Alex Ovechkin" award.

An April 2010 *Washington Post* poll also showed that though the NFL franchise still holds a sizeable lead in number of sports fans from around the region, with 31 percent selecting them as their favorite team, the Capitals came in a strong second with 13 percent, well ahead of the Nationals (8 percent) and Wizards and Major League Soccer franchise D.C. United (5 percent).

The Capitals' growth has even spread northward to Baltimore — a city that normally despises any sports team that calls Washington home.

"With the arrival of Alexander Ovechkin after the NHL lockout there has been a huge uptick in popularity of the Caps in Baltimore," said Ed Frankovic of WNST Radio. "Since Washington started making the playoffs on an annual basis beginning in 2008, the interest has grown exponentially and the television ratings that Comcast reports bear that out. The interest is definitely there and growing. In fact, people routinely call the WNST morning show to talk about the Caps during hockey season, and this is occurring in a very strong Baltimore Ravens market."

"Baltimore has been dragged along with the Washington hockey craze," said Steve Lepore, who tracks the business of hockey on television for Puck the Media. "There is now a legitimate, large, cult following for the Capitals in Charm City."

The Capitals have also pursued a deeper relationship with the city, holding a preseason game in Baltimore in September 2011 at First Mariner Arena, which once housed the Baltimore Skipjacks, the Capitals' former AHL affiliate.

"I think it's important in that you can tell the Washington Capitals brand is expanding; hockey itself in the D.C. area and beyond is becoming relevant," then-Caps Boudreau said on that occasion. "The people in Baltimore are clamoring for the game as well as we are. Hockey in general is becoming more popular."

"It's exposure to a non-traditional hockey market that we're not far away from," Brooks Laich said of Baltimore. "We put a great product on the ice. In D.C., since I've been there, six years, I've seen a big change in the grassroots market with kids and minor hockey programs; if we can start to build that further out from D.C. and turn it into a hockey market, it'd be great."

John Walton has also noticed growth in interest in the team around Pennsylvania's state capital of Harrisburg, not too far from the home of the team's top AHL affiliate in Hershey.

"I think Caps fans in 2005, they existed, but maybe one hockey fan in 10 [followed the Caps around central Pennsylvania]," Walton said. "They were almost the choice if you didn't like one or the other team in the state. You could side with Pittsburgh, because it was easy to see them on TV — and it still is — and the Flyers are everywhere on TV.

"Only half the households in central Pennsylvania get Comcast SportsNet Washington, but [among] those that do, and even those that don't, it's amazing how much [the Capitals are] followed. I firmly believe it's now a third/a third/a third . . .

"Inside Giant Center, it's probably 75 percent Washington, because you get a [Sidney] Crosby Reebok ad that's aired in our building because that's mandated by the league — we had to air it — it gets booed like crazy, every single time. People go nuts. A Flyers score goes on the board, people boo like crazy. Never used to be that way.

"The Flyers were in Hershey for 10 years. There was a little love-hate when they left. There are some who say, 'I'm a Bears fan but I'm a Flyers fan,' you run across them too. I think Bruce Boudreau had a lot to do with leading the flock south. A lot of people [followed] him."

As 2011–12 rolled around, Washington's radio network not only reached stations in the District, Maryland and Virginia, but also into neighboring states of Pennsylvania, West Virginia and North Carolina.

Television ratings in the Washington market have risen nearly four times to what they were just before the lockout, with the average rating for a Capitals game on Comcast SportsNet going from a 0.45 to a 1.78 in the Nielsen Designated Market Area. The numbers have nearly tripled in the last four seasons, from a 0.65 in 2007–08 to where they are now.

"Locally, Comcast SportsNet is thrilled to have the Washington Capitals as one of their flagship properties, the ratings have climbed and increased in such a positive way as the team's improvement on the ice has," Beninati said. "It's that kind of lockstep. Hopefully, someday, Comcast SportsNet is doing a bunch of events, pregame and postgame, as much as they can, around the Stanley Cup champion. That's the goal someday."

"Since the lockout, the growth has been consistent and steady in the D.C. market, as the Capitals now outdraw both the Wizards and the Nationals in their hometown," said Puck the Media's Steve Lepore. "In addition, the team has set playoff [during the series against the Rangers in 2011] and regular season [during the 14-game winning streak in 2010] ratings records in D.C. since the lockout."

And, thanks to the star power the team has now, the Capitals, who rarely got time on national television or on *Hockey Night in Canada* before the lockout, are regularly featured on NBC, CBC and TSN.

"In the year coming out of the lockout, the Capitals appeared six times on OLN [the former name of Versus/NBC Sports Network] and none on NBC," Lepore said. "In 2011–12, the Capitals will appear so many times on Versus/NBC Sports Network — 12 — that they won't even be able to televise all of them in Washington, since the number is over the limit for exclusive appearances by a team. The only other teams with that privilege are Original 6 clubs like Boston and New York, as well as other marquee franchises like Pittsburgh."

According to Lepore, Ovechkin's star power helped make the team more marketable and visible. "Ovechkin made them at least a curiosity for TV networks early on," he said. "But his rise as a bona fide superstar and the rivalry with Crosby has made the Capitals probably the third or fourth most attractive TV team for the networks across America and Canada, behind Pittsburgh, Detroit and Toronto."

"Now they're the darlings of national television," Beninati said. "The NBC Sports group makes sure to take as many games as they're allowed to in their contractual limit. They're wise to do so. It's a fun team.

"They're great theater when they're doing well. It's great theater when they're not doing well. They have that incredible mood swing. NBC cherry picks some of the top games on the Caps schedule for good reason."

For longtime hockey observers, seeing the dramatic transformation of what once was considered a very soft hockey market turn into one of the United States' hottest is nothing short of remarkable.

"I was doing a number of games nationally for Versus, and I'd be in other teams' dressing rooms and I'd be doing a Boston-L.A. game, and all they'd want to talk about was how wild Verizon Center is," Beninati recalled. "They'd recognize me as being connected with the Caps, and they'd say, 'That's a great thing you guys got going there.' And it was genuine. These are star players in the NHL. It was great to be part of, and the fans can take credit for that."

The question is: how permanent will the change be? And while most agree a return to the dark days of 2003–04 is unlikely, the team has to capture at least one Stanley Cup to really cement its place in the marketplace.

"It would help if they would win a Cup," Lemke said. "If they could win multiple Cups, it could reach a point where it would never, ever go back. For a while there, it seems like it was set up where that could have occurred, but they've had some missed opportunities. They hoped they would have been in position to win at least one, and last year they took a step back. [They have to] evaluate how they move forward. They have a bigger window than most teams since they're relatively young."

CHAPTER 15

RECORD-SETTING SEASON
SETS RECORD EXPECTATIONS

In September 2009 the Capitals returned to Kettler with an eye on going the distance. After advancing to the second round of the playoffs in the previous season, there was a sense that the team was ready to take the next step.

There was some turnover in the offseason, as Washington lost one veteran forward and added another. Sergei Fedorov elected to return to Russia, and the Caps signed free agent forward Mike Knuble out of Philadelphia on July 1 to help the team crash the net.

"Washington is everything I wanted," Knuble said the day of the signing. "I think the team is on the verge of something good, something great."

In the aftermath of a playoff series where they were victimized by Penguins forwards who collected dirty goals, Washington wanted a veteran who had a nose for the net and wasn't afraid to battle in front of the cage.

"We needed someone to go to the net," George McPhee explained. "Mike's made his living there."

The veteran had an immediate impact, and the Capitals put on quite a show as the new season progressed, playing an aggressive offensive style that netted them the most goals by any team since 1995–96, just before the neutral zone trap came into vogue after the Devils' 1995 Cup win.

Washington opened the season against the best team in the East from the previous season, the Bruins, and were able to grab a crisp, clean 4–1 away win. Ovechkin had two goals and an assist, and Washington limited the B's to just 19 shots.

"If you could bottle that game up, we'd take it," Bruce Boudreau told AP afterward. "Every night."

The Capitals next beat Toronto in their home opener and then, after stumbling through a 0–2–2 stretch, kicked into gear, winning six straight and finishing 8–2–3 after the first month of play.

Washington put together another six-game win streak after Thanksgiving and were in full control of the Southeast, having an 11-point lead on second-place Atlanta by the time the Capitals blanked Tampa Bay on December 7.

That wasn't to say the team wasn't being tweaked along the way. In the first half of the season, Washington traded captain Chris Clark, whose ice time had somewhat diminished, and Milan Jurcina to Columbus. They received Jason Chimera in return, and the new man added a burst of speed to the lineup.

"It was the right trade for us right now," McPhee told AP after the deal. "We had extra defensemen all year, and it's not a great situation to be in. [Also] we just had too many right wingers and not enough left wingers."

With Clark's departure, the Capitals needed a new captain. Their Russian superstar won a vote for the "C."

"I have a 'C' on my heart, but I'm going to do the same thing," Alex Ovechkin told AP after becoming just the sixth Russian player to captain an NHL team.

"I talked to [Ovechkin] . . . three days ago about it," Boudreau told reporters after Washington's 4–2 win over Montreal. "He said, 'I would accept the responsibility, but only if my teammates want me to.

If they're happy with me as a captain, I'd be glad to be captain.' So he was already thinking about the team rather than thinking about himself, which is what captains do."

When the team named Ovechkin their captain on January 5, the Capitals stood 24–11–6 (the first half of the season ended with a winless two-game trip to California). It was an impressive record but paled in comparison to the second half. After the first week of January the team suffered only four regulation losses. A 30–4–7 mark smashed franchise records for wins and points, and it also allowed the Caps to claim one of the longest win streaks in league history.

Of course, stitching the "C" to Ovechkin's sweater added more pressure on him to perform — and be a true leader.

"When you're named the captain, you've got to do certain things," TSN's Dmitry Chesnokov said. "I think it did add pressure . . . [It's not just] being the captain . . . on the ice but off the ice and with the media. The media expects Ovechkin to be like other leaders, like Steve Yzerman. But Ovechkin is Ovechkin. He's doing it his own way, but I still think the pressure is there."

The team-record win streak started strangely enough, as the Capitals trailed Florida 4–1 halfway through regulation on January 13 in Sunrise, but, thanks to goals by Brian Pothier, Nicklas Backstrom, Ovechkin and a shootout winner by Tomas Fleischmann, Washington rallied for the 5–4 win.

Returning home two nights later, Ovechkin notched a career-high four helpers in a 6–1 win over Toronto. On the 17th, he became the fastest player in NHL history to take 2,000 shots, and he scored his 30th goal of the year on a penalty shot in a 5–3 win over the Flyers.

The Caps finished the homestand with their fourth straight victory, and seventh in eight games, rallying from a 2–1 deficit late to beat the Red Wings.

"That's probably the best I've seen [Jose Theodore]," Boudreau said. "I'm watching him and going, 'This must have been how he won the Vezina and the Hart in Montreal that year.' Without him, it could have very well been 6–0 after the first period."

Washington headed into Pittsburgh on January 21 for their first meeting with the Pens since being ousted by them the year before. They erased a 3–2 deficit with four unanswered goals to push the win streak to five. The team was 20 games above .500.

"We just wanted to win this game, it doesn't matter how," Ovechkin told AP. "All this group was really concentrating. I think we deserved this win."

Two days later, the Capitals beat Phoenix for their third six-game win streak in 51 games then headed up to Long Island on January 26 and pushed it to seven — despite Ovechkin and Mike Green being held off the scoresheet.

The following night at Verizon Center, Washington broke open a 1–1 tie in the third period, tying its longest win streak since 1988–89 with a 5–1 win over Anaheim.

"The guys like what they're doing — and they like winning," Boudreau said afterward. "We talked about it in the dressing room in between periods. We're going to go after them. We've got a good thing going. Let's just take it right to them and see where it leads."

The Capitals were averaging 3.83 goals a game — nearly half a goal better than the next highest scoring team — and were on pace to become the NHL's most prolific offense since the 1992–93 Pittsburgh Penguins.

Washington wasn't as sharp two nights later, but solid netminding from Michal Neuvirth led them to a 4–1 win over Florida, their ninth in a row.

On January 31, the Capitals tied their all-time franchise record with their 10th straight win, beating Tampa Bay on a late goal by Ovechkin to match the mark set in 1983–84. The win also established a franchise record for victories in a single month (13). The Southeast Division title race was all but over, and Washington pulled to within a point of San Jose for the league's best record.

"The number 10 is pretty tough to get," Bruce Boudreau said. "I told the guys it's something that you might go your whole career again without getting 10 [straight wins] again, and so enjoy it."

"It's kind of fun and it's kind of good," Ovechkin said. "But we don't want to stop."

The Caps headed to Boston and beat the slumping Bruins 4–1 on February 2 to set the new franchise mark and establish the longest win streak by any team in the league since 2008. During the stretch, Washington had outgunned their opponents 51–22.

In New York two nights later, the Capitals kept the ball rolling with another rally, erasing a 5–3 deficit with three unanswered goals against the Rangers to make it a dozen straight. Ovechkin potted his 37th goal of the year and became the fifth player to reach the 500-point plateau in just five seasons.

Washington returned to the nation's capital as the city was in the grip of a rare heavy snowfall. And although the Capitals won their 13th straight over an Atlanta team that had recently traded star winger Ilya Kovalchuk to New Jersey, the crowd was rather sparse due to the weather.

The Caps streak was the longest winning run since the Devils went 13 straight in 2001. The stage was set perfectly for the team's next home game: a Sunday afternoon tilt against the Penguins — Pittsburgh's first visit to Verizon Center since eliminating the Caps the previous spring. With the league set to break for the Vancouver Olympics less than a week after the nationally televised contest, the focus was once more on Sid the Kid and Ovechkin, whose national teams were expected to compete for gold in British Columbia.

Two feet of snow on the ground and almost impassable unplowed roads around the area, however, created doubt about whether the game would be held at all. The Penguins were in Montreal the day before, and the airports around Washington had been closed by the storm that had paralyzed the capital with an accumulation of snow rarely recorded in the area. But with the game on national TV and with the Olympics — which also happened to be on NBC — a week away, the Penguins flew into Newark, New Jersey, and then took a bus down to Washington. In the end, the Penguins didn't check into their hotel until well after 2 a.m.

The fans who braved the elements and made it out to the snow-bound Verizon Center certainly saw quite a game, even though the start probably reminded most of the lopsided Game 7 from the year before. Crosby did his part and quickly put the Penguins in front with a pair of goals in the first 9:59 of the contest. Ovechkin answered with one of his own (his 40th of the season) in the second. Then Jordan Staal chipped in two to put Pittsburgh ahead 4–1. It looked insurmountable and inevitable: the Capitals' win streak would come to an end on a cold and blustery Super Bowl Sunday afternoon.

But like the great heavyweight battle that the playoff series had been, the regular-season game still promised more twists and turns. Eric Fehr scored with 2:48 left in the second to pull Washington within two, and then Alex Ovechkin scored his second and third to send the crowd into a frenzy. Mike Knuble capped the Washington comeback, scoring on a power play marker with 2:49 left in overtime to give the team its 14th straight win. The streak had become the league's longest since 1992–93 — a mark set, naturally, by the Penguins.

"It was what people pay to see, when the superstars shine," Bruce Boudreau said afterward. "There's tension, and there's excitement, and there's physical play, and there's passion on both sides. That's what hockey is all about."

"It's always nice to win, especially when you are a little bit frustrated in the first [period]," Ovechkin said. "[The] game [didn't] go well for us right away. It's nice to come back and win in overtime especially."

Ovechkin also noticed the difference of a less-than-capacity crowd — that grew as fans trudged their way to the arena to catch what they could of the game.

"It's the weather," the captain said. "The crowd wasn't getting in during the first period. You can see [them] pushing us in the third . . . and we just keep going, keep going, and it's pretty sick."

Afterward, Crosby remarked, "I think everyone always expects an emotional and intense game when these two teams play each other. It felt like a playoff atmosphere to me. Everyone wants to win these games. These two teams have quite the rivalry now. I think everyone tries to bring out their best here."

Eight times during the fourteen games of the streak, Washington trailed. When their winning form began they rallied from a three-goal deficit. The same thing happened when the streak finally came to an end.

Following the dramatic OT win over the Pens, the Capitals headed out on the three-game road trip that would take them to the Olympic break. In the first game they went head-to-head with the storied Montreal Canadiens at the Bell Centre.

They were clearly sluggish, but it looked like the Capitals would be able to salvage things to grab win number 15. They trailed 5–2 heading into the third, but scored three times to force the extra session. With Jose Theodore off for an extra attacker, Brooks Laich notched a hat trick with 18.4 seconds left in regulation. Montreal's Tomas Plekanec, however, handed Washington its first loss in nearly a month with just eight seconds left in OT.

The next night, the still-sluggish Capitals fell in regulation in Ottawa. The team parted ways for the Olympic break following a shootout loss in St. Louis — its third straight L after 14 consecutive Ws.

Olympic logistics made things tricky for the Capitals. Despite the three defeats, they had points in 16 of 17 games (14–1–2) and were playing strong hockey. The Vancouver games meant shifting gears for Ovechkin: the spotlight shone directly on him and Crosby, and both were expected to lead their respective country to the gold medal. It was something the Capitals star had always dreamed of, especially because his mother had been an Olympic gold medalist in women's basketball in both 1976 and 1980.

Alex Ovechkin was at the center of one of the highlights of the preliminary round, landing a crushing open ice body check on former Capitals captain Jaromir Jagr in a game against the Czech Republic, but the Russian squad was beaten by the eventual gold medal winners, Sid the Kid's Team Canada. In the end, Russia's goaltending and lack of depth was exposed by a stacked host team.

"I think we [were] not ready for first five minutes of game and when we [woke] up it was too late," Ovechkin told the Associated Press. "It was 3–0 and it's pretty hard to come back, especially that game."

For the second time in nine months — even though the Penguins star wasn't particularly a standout for the majority of the tournament — Crosby was in the right place at the right time, and he became a national hero by firing the overtime winner in the gold medal game against the Americans. Once again, Ovechkin's team had fallen victim to Crosby's en route to a championship, and while the Russian had back-to-back Hart Trophies as league MVP, he began to be overshadowed by his Canadian rival once the NHL resumed play.

Soon it appeared the disappointment of failing to medal in Vancouver had a tangible impact on Ovechkin. The star, who was criticized for largely not speaking to the media during the Olympics, was caught on video pushing a fan's camera out of his hand outside Russia House in Vancouver. Certainly it wasn't the image many had seen of the Russian star, who normally was more gregarious and fun-loving. But having seen the Russian team's hopes fall well short of the gold medal, the frustration was evident in the clip that went viral.

For someone who clearly values the importance of an Olympic medal — the star is pushing the league to make sure NHL players are allowed to participate in the 2014 Olympic Winter Games in his native Russia — to go back to Washington empty-handed was very disappointing.

He returned to Washington more serious than people had seen him and had to quickly refocus on trying to claim the silver of the Stanley Cup instead of Olympic gold. "He really fancied the idea of Russia winning in Canada," Yahoo!'s Greg Wyshynski said. "It's always been a thing for him. The fact that Canadians criticized the way he plays hockey and saying he should play the Canadian way, or looking down their nose at him because he's not Canadian. And I think he really enjoyed the idea of winning on their soil. It didn't happen and bombed out in spectacular fashion.

"There was a certain bitterness, because at the same time, all his peers, Sid, [Jonathan] Toews . . . they're all winning. The United States

Washington's loss to the Tampa Bay Lightning in the first round of the 2003 Stanley Cup playoffs became the impetus for a drastic reshaping of the Capitals' roster, which saw the team trade captain Steve Konowalchuk (22) early in the 2003–04 season. (AP PHOTO/STEVE NESIUS)

By the end of the 2003–04 season, the Capitals had shed their most expensive talent via various trades, and the team was relying mostly on journeymen and minor-leaguers to finish the campaign before a lockout would cancel the ensuing season. Goaltender Matthew Yeats, who began the year in the ECHL, got his chance to play and recorded his only career NHL win against the Penguins on March 30, 2004. (ROSS D. FRANKLIN/THE WASHINGTON TIMES)

With the top pick in the 2004 NHL draft, the Capitals selected top Russian prospect Alexander Ovechkin. Once the lockout ended, team owner Ted Leonsis, left, and general manager George McPhee, right, signed Ovechkin for the 2005–06 season and hoped to build around their talented player who had dazzled scouts. (DANIEL ROSENBAUM/*THE WASHINGTON TIMES*)

Bruce Boudreau instilled a more offensive style when he arrived in Washington in November 2007, and he also implanted the belief the team could win on a regular basis. The team responded, as they won four consecutive Southeast Division titles, two top seeds in the East and became a legitimate Stanley Cup contender under his watch. (© ZUMAPRESS.COM/KEYSTONE PRESS)

Mike Green, a defenseman who was one of the keys to the Hershey Bears' success at the AHL level with his scoring prowess, really elevated his game once former Bears coach Bruce Boudreau was hired in November 2007. Green quickly became an offensive threat on the blue line, scoring this overtime game-winner against the Rangers in December 2007. (JOSEPH SILVERMAN/ *THE WASHINGTON TIMES*)

The Capitals finished the 2007–08 regular season winning 11 of their last 12 games, including this overtime victory against Tampa Bay on March 27. Washington earned its first playoff spot since 2002–03 on the final day of the campaign. (© DIRK SHADD/*ST. PETERSBURG TIMES*/ ZUMA PRESS)

Washington won the Presidents' Trophy in 2009–10 for the NHL's top regular-season record, registering 54 wins and 121 points to smash franchise bests. The high point of the campaign was a club-record 14-game win streak in January and February, which was capped off by a comeback overtime win over the rival Pittsburgh Penguins on Super Bowl Sunday. (AP PHOTO/LUIS M. ALVAREZ)

The Capitals signed Alexander Ovechkin to a 13-year, $124-million deal in January 2008, and the Russian star responded by recording back-to-back Hart Trophy–winning seasons in 2007–08 and 2008–09. Ovechkin's long-term deal helped the Capitals become a box-office hit in Washington, and he became one of the game's most dynamic players to watch league-wide. (MICHAEL CONNOR/*THE WASHINGTON TIMES*)

The Capitals were featured in the NHL's Winter Classic on New Year's Day 2011, and it turned out to be a successful trip to Pittsburgh. Eric Fehr scored two goals as the Caps beat the Penguins in front of a sold-out crowd at Heinz Field and a nationwide TV audience. (AP PHOTO/ GENE J. PUSKAR)

After struggling early in the 2011–12 season, the Capitals brought in the team's former captain, Dale Hunter, to coach. Hunter helped Washington qualify for the playoffs for the fifth straight year and eliminate the defending Stanley Cup champions in the first round. (CAL SPORT MEDIA VIA AP IMAGES)

and Canada, they're succeeding and here's Ovechkin going back with his tail between his legs and I think it really kind of affected him."

The Capitals reconvened after the Olympic break in Buffalo on March 3, with 19 games left to play. They'd already accumulated 92 points and were threatening to clinch a division faster than any team in 32 years. A 3–1 win over U.S. Olympic hero Ryan Miller was the result, with Theodore outdueling the Sabres' ace.

"When you play against a guy like Miller, you know he's not going to give up too many goals," Jose Theodore told AP after the game. "It was a real tight hockey game, and I'm really happy with the way we got the win."

Washington picked up gritty forward Scott Walker from the Carolina Hurricanes at the trade deadline, as well as defenseman Joe Corvo. Walker paid immediate dividends, scoring the tying and winning goal in the third period of a 5–4 win over Tampa. It was Washington's 12th straight home ice victory, and it gave the Caps a 24–3–3 mark at Verizon Center.

"Sometimes I caught myself thinking a little bit, but it's a learning process and the guys on the bench . . . [were] awesome," Walker said afterward. "They helped me out a lot because that's what you need when you are the new guy coming to the bench."

"I think they fit in [well]," Nicklas Backstrom said of his new team-mates. "Scott Walker scored two right away. He had a good start . . . We've got a great group of guys. The new players fit in [well,] even if there are a lot of trades going on . . . We're building a good team."

Another of the newest Capitals, Eric Belanger, acquired from Minnesota, scored in a 2–0 win over the Rangers on March 6 as Washington reached 96 points. It was already two more than the 2007–08 squad had amassed in a full 82 games.

With the win the Caps were a full 30 points ahead of Atlanta in the race for the Southeast Division title. They also held a 14-point lead on the Penguins for the top seed in the East, as well as a five-point lead on Chicago and San Jose for the league's best record. They were on pace to obliterate the team's mark for wins and points in a season and also were looking to become the first non–Original 6 team to pass the 120-point mark.

With their trade deadline acquisitions, the coaching staff had plenty of ice time decisions to make. "We've got a lot of players here and people want to keep playing," Bruce Boudreau said. "It's a really difficult decision for coaches when you're consistently winning with different lineups, but everybody in that room is a real competitive player and so they want to play. And when that happens, you usually find a new way to play a little better."

While the play of Walker and Belanger helped the team craft a three-game win streak out of the Olympic break, two of the team's biggest stars — Ovechkin and Backstrom — were sluggish.

"I think if you look at [Backstrom] and Alex [Ovechkin] they're just off by like half a second," Boudreau said. "Their timing since coming back from the Olympics has just been a little off, but you know they're going to catch on and it's going to happen sooner or later.

"I'm not worried about them and it says an awful lot for the rest of the players that they can score while two of your best players are not."

Two nights later, the Caps' home win streak came to an end. Despite pouring 42 shots on Dallas goaltender Marty Turco before the second intermission, Washington gave up a 2–0 lead and fell 4–3 to the Stars in a shootout.

The only real positive was that Ovechkin got his first goal in more than a month, beating Turco for his 43rd of the year on the team's 40th shot.

"You could see it," Boudreau said. "[Ovechkin] looked up at the sky, and he had been frustrated the past few games. I told him this morning, 'You just have to work harder.' I thought he was in a mode where he was waiting for the play to come to him instead of going out and creating the play. But you saw in his first two or three shifts in the game, he was going out and hitting guys and he had his energy back. When he has his energy, he is what he is: the best player in the world."

On March 10, Washington moved to the 99-point mark and within a point of clinching a playoff berth by beating the Carolina Hurricanes in overtime on a Tomas Fleischmann tally.

Mike Green also had a fine offensive effort, scoring twice. But a terrible defensive giveaway led to a Hurricanes goal and a stinging Boudreau quip: "He had two goals and a beautiful assist . . . but the assist was to the other team."

Although they had the next night off, the Caps clinched the Southeast Division with a month left in the regular season when the Thrashers lost in Columbus. It was quickest any team had clinched since the 1977–78 Montreal Canadiens, and it seemed like a good omen — that year the Habs raised the Stanley Cup.

Unlike two years earlier, when the Caps didn't learn their playoff fate until game 82, clinching so quickly presented a bit of a problem: the team wouldn't have a whole lot to play for until the postseason began.

"The playoffs don't start till April [15]," Boudreau said. "As long as we can, and I don't like doing it either, we'll keep rotating guys in and out of the lineup to keep them fresh and sharp. The players don't like it, but they understand it. They have the common goal."

The lack of urgency showed the next night, as Tampa Bay came into Washington and handed the Caps a 3–2 loss, the first time since December 28 they had failed to get at least a point in a home game.

"After the [Olympic] break, it gets a little bit more difficult to score a lot of goals," Mike Knuble explained. "You're not going to blow teams out. They're playing for their lives . . . You have to give [Tampa Bay] credit. They had a gutsy effort.

"I think we thought it was going to be easier than it was tonight, and we've got to give teams, our opponents, a lot more respect than that."

Washington headed to Chicago next. Despite a nice comeback, the Caps suffered a different type of loss: their biggest star was given a two-game suspension after a hit on Blackhawks defenseman Brian Campbell. Ovechkin delivered the check in the first period; Campbell crashed awkwardly into the rear boards, breaking his collarbone. The Capitals captain was assessed a five-minute major and was ejected from the contest.

Without their top gun, Washington fell behind 3–0. They fought back, however, and grabbed a dramatic 4–3 overtime win to crack the 100-point barrier for the second straight year. The Ovechkin hit — and ensuing suspension — caused a firestorm.

While the star had always played a physical game in North America, there were several pundits calling the Russian to task for what they saw as dirty play. It was Ovechkin's second suspension of the season, having been hit with a two-game ban for a knee-on-knee hit on Carolina's Tim Gleason in November, and he was being accused of being a predatory player, looking to hurt his opponents.

"That hurt him . . . the impression that he was trying to hurt people was worse than [the fact] he wasn't scoring goals," said former director for media relations Nate Ewell, who was close to Ovechkin.

"I'm really disappointed for Alex," Caps coach Bruce Boudreau told reporters. "If you're looking at it from our point of view, people keep calling it a reckless hit. To me it was a push from behind that, if he had have gone straight, he would have gone to the ice."

Ewell believed the suspension bothered Ovechkin to the point of making him less effective through the regular season's close. Still, he also believed Ovechkin was in a better place mentally by the time the playoffs rolled around.

Even without their star, the Capitals managed to take three of a possible four points, beating Florida at BankAtlantic Center on March 16 and falling to the Hurricanes in OT two nights later.

Ovechkin returned to action in the fourth and final game of the road trip, a 3–1 win in Tampa, and scored his 45th of the year. "Well, it's always nice to go back and play hockey — and score goals," said a grinning Ovechkin after the game.

Jose Theodore was also solid, withstanding a 34-shot barrage to preserve the victory.

"I thought [Theodore] was outstanding," Boudreau said. "I felt so comfortable with him in the net. It was a really good feeling to have."

Washington returned home and equaled the franchise record for points set a year before — 108 — with a 3–2 shootout win over the

Penguins, not only erasing a 2–1 third-period deficit but, more improbably, a 2–0 deficit in the shootout.

"It's pretty nice when you come back after [being down] 2–0," Ovechkin said. "It's a great thing to do."

As the stakes for Washington diminished, however, a lull set in. The team was lackluster at the end of March, going 0–1–2, but still managed to clinch the top seed in the Eastern Conference for the first time in franchise history.

"I've seen teams that rest their guys, and then they stink in the first game of the playoffs," Boudreau said when asked about the decision to rest players with little to play for in the regular season. "I think last year we didn't put an emphasis on the end of the season . . . We lost the first two games [to the Rangers] until we got into a playoff mode, so I bounce it off both ways all the time, believe me. It's what keeps me up at night."

Washington tied the team record of 50 wins in a season on April 1 against Atlanta.

"We really have to pay attention to details," Green said. "I thought tonight we did that, especially the last seven minutes of the game. We were getting pucks deep. Guys were going hard [to the net]. That's what it's going to take to win in the playoffs."

Two nights later, the Capitals set a new mark; one night after that, they clinched the Presidents' Trophy, awarded to the team with the best record in hockey. "It's nice to set records," Boudreau told reporters after the win in Columbus. "It gives us a goal to shoot for next year."

In the last week of the season, the only question that remained was whether the team could reach 120 points — a barrier no expansion team had ever broken.

At their penultimate home game, on April 5, the Capitals were presented with the Presidents' Trophy. But bowing to hockey tradition to treat hardware other than the Stanley Cup as radioactive, the players were not interested in this particular silver award.

"We'll just wait when bigger things come," Ovechkin said afterward.

Boudreau was a bit more succinct. "It's not [the trophy] we want," he said.

In the game itself, Ovechkin hit the 50-goal mark for the fourth time in five seasons; Nicklas Backstrom hit the 100-point mark for the first time with a helper on his captain's goal.

"I'm just really proud of [Backstrom]," Boudreau said. "He's such a great young man. You like to see great people succeed. I'm sitting there thinking, '[Backstrom] just got his hundredth and [Ovechkin] just got his 50th. Who's picking up the puck [for his plaque]?' It shows that [Backstrom's] one of the elite players in the league and he does it every night. I think that's his third game in a row with three points. He's a good player."

In the locker room, the two were presented the single puck for their accomplishments.

"We're going to split it," Ovechkin joked. "[Fifty is] a pretty big number, especially when you miss a couple games to suspension and get injured. You always want to score 50 goals, but sometimes you don't have luck."

With the win, the Capitals joined the 1977–78 Montreal Canadiens and the 1995–96 and 2005–06 Detroit Red Wings as the only teams to have ever cracked the 120-point barrier.

After a shootout loss to Boston in the season closer, the Capitals prepared to finally play meaningful hockey once more.

"We're really glad [the regular season] is over," Boudreau explained. "We've known for a long time that we were going to be in the playoffs. As much as you want to push them, they are looking forward to a different kind of challenge."

That challenge would be the Montreal Canadiens — a team that finished 33 points behind them in the standings.

SHOCKING UPSET

CHAPTER 16

The Capitals headed into the 2009–10 postseason as Eastern Conference favorites. They'd shown their mettle against some of the league's best teams all year and faced a Montreal club that needed a late season overtime just to qualify for the playoffs. Experts and pundits predicted a fairly easy Washington win.

But there *were* signs that the Canadiens might be able to hang with the Capitals. Montreal was the team that had ended Washington's 14-game winning streak, and the teams split their season series with just a difference of five goals between them. At any rate, this was the NHL, where, come the playoffs, the regular season often means little. All of Washington's regular season accomplishments — the 54 wins and NHL best record, the 313 goals and 121 points — would mean nothing in the postseason. The only advantage they had was a guaranteed extra home game for every round over the duration of the playoffs.

It was an unfamiliar way for the Caps to head into the postseason: the team had pretty much been in a holding pattern since mid-March. Unlike previous years, they could coast, knowing they had a high seed locked up.

"I think there is a bigger target [on us], but at the same time we are just anxious to get going," Bruce Boudreau said. "Once you have clinched stuff in the regular season, this is your next goal — this is the carrot, the thing that is going to drive you."

Washington also had to learn how to deal with not being the underdog for the first time in a long while.

"I think there's been expectations all season," Mike Green said. "We've done a fairly good job of trying to achieve them. The bar's set so high for us now that we have to make sure that we stay intact and reach our goals. Since training camp, our goal has been a Stanley Cup. The real season starts now.

"I think we're more hungry, we're more focused," he added. "And you can really sense that around the dressing room. Guys really want this. It's obviously a different game in the playoffs and we have to adjust."

The task was perhaps made daunting by the fact that they'd be playing in the brightest of spotlights and visiting one of the most hockey-mad cities in North America.

"That's the only game in town," Boudreau told reporters. "They don't have to split it up and have the Nationals on half the page and the Wizards on some of the pages, the Redskins and us. It's Montreal. It's the Canadiens . . . All the TV stations will lead with the stories about the Canadiens, so there is a lot of pressure.

"Everybody in [Montreal] knows who every player is. It's not like in this city, where you know who Alex and Mike and Nicky are and maybe guys like John Carlson can walk around unknown — they know every single [Canadien] from Mathieu Darche to Brian Gionta."

"It's going to be great," Alexander Semin said via Yahoo! Sports' Dmitry Chesnokov. "Playing in Montreal is one of the best experiences ever. A great building."

According to Nate Ewell, the credential requests for the Canadiens series outpaced the matchup with the Penguins the spring before — mostly thanks to the visiting influx of reporters from Quebec.

Things did not go as planned for the Caps once the puck dropped in Game 1 on April 15.

Washington blitzed Habs goalie Jaroslav Halak early and outshot Montreal 19–7 in the first. But they went into the intermission with only a 1–1 tie despite their territorial advantage. Michael Cammalleri scored an early power play goal to put Montreal up before Joe Corvo answered as the period neared a close.

After a scoreless second, Nicklas Backstrom took a Mike Knuble pass to finally put Washington up at just 0:47 of the third. The lead was short-lived. The Canadiens' Scott Gomez tipped a Brian Gionta pass past Jose Theodore with 12:26 left to play in regulation to knot the score at two.

The two teams fought into overtime, and Washington had a golden chance to win the game on a 3-on-1 break, but Backstrom elected to pass rather than shoot.

Not long after, Tomas Plekanec stunned the crowd with 6:41 left in the extra frame. Ultimately, Jaroslav Halak had kept the Canadiens in the game long enough to take a 3–2 overtime win.

Afterward, Boudreau admitted he wasn't too happy with his stars. "[Alex Ovechkin] didn't play [well]," he said. "I mean, they gapped up on him really well, but I don't think Alex played very well. I can't put my finger on it right now, but when you get [47] shots on goal and Ovechkin doesn't get any — and you have four power plays. They took him away pretty good, but I just didn't think he was very good tonight."

"[Montreal's] got a great hockey team," right wing Boyd Gordon said. "They come at you in waves and have good transitions at forward. They're a good, solid team. They're a hard-working team. We know we're in for a tough series."

Nicklas Backstrom earned redemption in Game 2 — although early in the contest it looked like the Capitals were in trouble again.

Brian Gionta put a puck in the net just 60 seconds in, on a play Jose Theodore misplayed badly, and then Andrei Kostitsyn rifled a shot past the Caps netminder at the 7:58 mark. Boudreau had seen enough, and, for the second straight year, Theodore found himself sitting on the bench in the playoffs. After giving up two goals on two shots in the first eight minutes, Semyon Varlamov came on in relief.

Washington responded well. Eric Fehr scored just 2:23 after the switch to cut the deficit to one.

But then the Canadiens got two more, late in the second, both off the stick of Kostitsyn. Washington was trailing 4–1 with 2:16 left in the frame, with boos raining down from its home fans.

"We were a desperate team," Tomas Fleischmann said afterward. "If we got behind two games in the series, it would be really tough for us to come back. We were a desperate team — that was the difference."

Backstrom got Washington to within two again with 1:37 left in the period. "We have that side of our team — we never give up," he later explained. "The second period was kind of embarrassing for us. But we bounced back."

In the third, finally, Ovechkin got on the board. Lunging for a puck with 2:56 gone, he poked one past Halak to cut the deficit to 4–3. Then, with 10:13 left, Backstrom got his second of the night to send the red-clad sellout crowd into a frenzy. The Caps had rallied from three goals down and the momentum seemed to be theirs when Plekanec gave Montreal the lead back with only 5:08 to play.

Once more, however, the Capitals clawed back. John Carlson scored his first-ever playoff goal with 1:21 left in regulation to force overtime.

"It was a last-minute goal so we were all coming in hot," Carlson said. "We just said, 'Relax — get back to our game. Let's not try to do too much.' Certainly it didn't work because we went out like a ball of fire, but it was good."

Nicklas Backstrom, who had passed up a good opportunity to end Game 1, took the shot in Game 2: he fired the puck past Halak just 31 seconds into the overtime session to square the series.

"[I was] a little bit [surprised it went in], but if you are going to score, you have to shoot, right?" he said afterward. "I was trying to get it on the net, and I was lucky it went in."

"[Backstrom] had a good game," Boudreau said. "Nicky's a great player. Great players come to the floor when you need them."

Washington's other criticized star had a much better effort in Game 2 as well. "I feel pretty good today, especially in the first period,"

Alex Ovechkin said. "I got into the game, got some hits, made some shots. I think I played not bad today."

The mood was definitely loose as the teams headed to Canada; Backstrom and Ovechkin even played a pickup basketball game behind the stage set up for Boudreau's postgame press conference on the Wizards practice court.

"We just have to play our game, it doesn't matter how they play. If we play our game, finish checks, shoot the puck, go to the net, it is going to be ours," Ovechkin said. "We're going to win. I think if we are going to play the same way we played in the third period [today], we are going to be successful."

Boudreau, however, pointedly reminded everyone that the series was going to be tight; he was clearly concerned with the team's lackluster effort in stretches of the first two games. "The only way we were going to win tonight was if we decided to go all offense," he said. "By no stretch did we probably deserve to win, but we got lucky and we did. We know we're not out of the woods. There [are] probably a lot of people that are going to say that Montreal outplayed us for two games and they were on the road and now we're in their building and we have to play a whole lot better. We have to tighten up, obviously, if we want to succeed . . . whether it's this series or beyond, but right now we're just worried about winning the next game."

Former Canadiens goalie Theodore heard loud, derisive chants during the warm-up before Game 3 at the Bell Centre, even though Varlamov got the start. The young Russian kept the Capitals in it early, quieting a raucous crowd with a big glove stop on Josh Gorges and then two solid shorthanded saves.

"He was really good early," Boudreau said afterward. "He made two big saves. The one on Gionta, on their penalty kill was a really big. He was very solid in net tonight and he kept us in it."

The game turned Washington's way early in the second, when Boyd Gordon scored a shorthanded goal on a 2-on-1 with Mike Knuble to put the Capitals up. Montreal was obviously deflated.

"To get that first goal, it made us feel good," Ovechkin said.

"We got a huge break on that 5-on-4 and that turned the game around for us," Eric Fehr added.

After killing off the minor, Brooks Laich beat Halak with 4:42 gone in the frame, then Fehr tipped in a rebound of a Laich shot for a 3–0 Washington lead at the 8:33 mark of the second.

Canadiens coach Jacques Martin had seen enough from his goaltender; Halak had allowed three goals on 13 shots, and the Capitals onslaught continued.

Ovechkin got some extra space as Montreal pressed to climb back into it, then beat Carey Price with 6:10 left in the second to give his team a 4–0 lead.

Washington became a bit too content and when Montreal scored early in the third, Boudreau called a timeout to try to halt the momentum shift.

"We were playing not to lose at that point, and allowing them to come on and making afraid passes," Boudreau said. "We had to get back to playing the game. I've seen it happen too many times; you play not to lose, and you end up losing."

The Capitals held on for the 5–1 win.

Despite the win, there was concern for Washington. The team's power play, which was tops in the NHL during the regular season, still looked disorganized and had fallen to 0-for-14 after three games. The Caps also had to deal with the raucous Montreal fans, even if, according to the Washington players, that wasn't really a problem.

"I think the whole team loves to play here, [it's] a good atmosphere," Alex Ovechkin said. "Unbelievable place. They have fans like ours."

"Sometimes you forget how much fun it is when the opposing building is so alive, it makes you want to be a hockey player," Boudreau said.

Ovechkin opened Game 4 with a goal 8:10 in, but then the Canadiens took control and seemed to be coasting, holding a 2–1 lead late in the second. But a shorthanded break for Gordon and Knuble seemingly put a dagger in the Canadiens' chances with just 6.3 seconds left in the frame.

"It was a big boost for us to go in tied 2–2 instead of down one and just kind of reset ourselves," Knuble told AP. "We were getting too many penalties there in the second and getting really on our heels with their power play. It just kind of gave us time and a shot in the arm to refocus for a strong third."

Ovechkin agreed. "I think it was a pretty big goal. Again we played great shorthanded, and Gordo, what can I say about him? He's a hard-working guy, and when he makes a play like this, it means a lot for our team."

The Capitals responded, scoring four times in the third. Jason Chimera and Ovechkin tallied against Price, while Knuble and Backstrom added empty-netters. Game 4 ended as a 6–3 Washington victory, and the series headed back to D.C.

The trip home, however, proved to be an adventure. The team was scheduled to land at Dulles International Airport in Virginia at 1 a.m., but fog made it impossible to land. The alternate airport, Reagan National, was fogged in as well. As a result, the team had to land at Baltimore-Washington International and wait for customs officials to arrive. The players sat on the tarmac for three hours. After that, the team had to find cabs. Most players didn't get into their beds before 5 a.m. The delays caused Thursday's practice to be cancelled. The Canadiens, on the other hand, regrouped at home after Game 4, practicing at their Brossard, Quebec, facility before heading to Washington Thursday afternoon without encountering any problems. The 3–1 series lead perhaps made the Capitals drop their guard. Whatever the cause, the team's focus slipped after two relatively easy wins in Montreal.

Washington started off slowly in Game 5 and never recovered. Montreal was desperate, and the Capitals never matched their intensity. It cost Washington the chance to clinch on home ice. Cammalleri and Travis Moen staked the Canadiens to a 2–0 lead in the first 7:01. That would be all the Canadiens needed for a 2–1 Montreal win.

"We have Game 5 in our building, and we play like crap the first 10 minutes and the game is over," Boudreau said. "We're not getting 20 guys playing. We're getting 13 and 14 guys every night, rather than everybody coming to play. Tonight we had five or six passengers again."

"It didn't happen [tonight]," Caps center Brendan Morrison said. "I thought we applied some pretty good pressure in the second and third periods. They did a good job. We just didn't find a way to overcome it . . . and I think it's a direct result of our start. We got behind and they played their game."

Halak was rock solid for Montreal, stopping all but one shot — a second-period drive by Ovechkin — after his disastrous Game 3 outing.

Instead of advancing and earning some rest, the Capitals had to make their way back to Montreal to face hungry opponents and another loud crowd.

Game 6 saw Halak's best display of the series. He stopped 52 of 53 Washington shots in the 4–1 win.

Montreal built an early 2–0 lead for the second straight game, this time thanks to a pair by Cammalleri, and then Halak held the fort. While the Capitals put shot after shot on the Montreal netminder, the Habs did a good job of keeping most of the chances to the outside. The league's highest-scoring team was clearly frustrated.

"We make goalies feel unbelievable," Ovechkin told AP afterward. "When we played against Philly, [Martin] Biron was good. [Henrik] Lundqvist was good. And this year we just made Halak feel good. It's always this team being good and we'll find a way to break it and win it. No panic, nothing."

But everything that had gone right for Washington all season long was now going wrong. The power play was still struggling, and in general the team was having a tough time lighting the lamp. Now, they'd be forced to play their third straight Game 7 in two years.

Twists and turns help make the NHL playoffs unique: sometimes fates and fortunes change in a hurry. In this case, everything the Capitals had been working on since September was coming apart in a span of just five days.

Marc-Andre Bergeron took advantage of a bad Green penalty late in the first, scoring a power play marker with just 29.1 seconds left in the period. It was what Montreal needed. Halak kept Washington at bay for most of the night, and then Travis Moen iced the game with 3:36 to play.

Brooks Laich did manage to set up a frantic finish when he potted one with 2:16 left. Then a late Montreal penalty set up a 6-on-4 as Washington pulled its goalie. But the team that had proven so resilient during the regular season couldn't pull another comeback out of the hat.

The game wasn't without some controversy. An apparent Ovechkin tally in the first minute of the third was disallowed by referee Brad Watson, who ruled that Mike Knuble committed a crease violation. "That's a violation that hasn't been called all year," an angry Knuble said later. "I felt all night that I wasn't a crease presence, as far as being in the blue paint. I was right on the edge where I should be, and we talked about it, the referee and I . . . You haven't seen it all year and now it comes out in Game 7."

Of course, there was much more to the Capitals' demise than a questionable call. The league's best power play finished the series at a woeful 1-for-33, and, worse, Washington could muster only three goals in the final three games of the series — all of them coming after Montreal had built at least a 2–0 lead.

For a team that had been making such progress, this was a big setback. And the 2–1 loss certainly struck the players hard.

"If someone came to your work and stepped on your desk or punched you in the head . . . that's how I feel," Jason Chimera said in a subdued Caps locker room. "You come for a long playoff run, and it doesn't happen . . . it's tough. Right now it's weird."

"It's not fun at all," Nicklas Backstrom said. "We have been working hard, we thought, this season. Maybe we didn't work hard enough. We were scoring a thousand goals in the regular season and we can't even score in the playoffs. That's . . . not acceptable for our team . . . Of course, I feel bad for the fans that have been supporting us this whole season. I guess that's hockey."

"When you have a 3–1 lead in a series, you think there's no way you are going to drop three straight, especially [with] two of those games at home," Mike Knuble said. "It's the most disappointing for a team that is known for . . . goal scoring. The amount of offense that we can provide . . . to come up short and not get the goals in a timely manner when we have done it all year . . . It's extremely disappointing for us."

"I think we are all disappointed, but you know, I really have nothing to say right now," Ovechkin said. "We all know we have a pretty good team, but we didn't win when we have to win."

"There wasn't much I could tell them," Bruce Boudreau said of his disappointed team. "I told them I felt exactly like they did. I thought we had a good chance to win the Stanley Cup this year. I would have bet my house that they wouldn't have beaten us three games in a row, and that we would have only scored three goals in almost 140 shots. But I told them there was no sense in me saying anything right now because we all feel as low as we can possibly feel."

Some of the Capitals seemingly had been looking ahead to the second round before the series was finished and lost focus on the task at hand following the Game 4 win. And according to the *Washington Examiner*'s Brian McNally, the ramifications loomed large. "Whatever you want to say that it was a fluke, they were still that much better than everyone else offensively," he said two years later. "To not win, and especially when you have a chance to win and have a chance to finish your opponent off, when you're a competitor, that's when doubt starts creeping into your mind a little bit.

"The path was open, and they were playing at a high enough level, but they didn't go through. That'll never go away. I'm sure if you ask them 10 years from now, that'll haunt them."

Two years after the fact, Ted Leonsis still ruefully looked back at the loss to the Canadiens as his "greatest disappointment."

"That was very, very disappointing. That year that team just could exert its will on anyone it played. We were proportionately better, and, in hindsight, we were spoiled. It was too easy, too open, we could do whatever we wanted. Our power play was world-class. If you played us tight and we were on the power play, it was in the back of net.

"When your power play is working like that, it really changes everything. Your best players are on the ice all the time, you just kind of go into it with so much confidence . . . I think we were 24 to 25 percent [effective on the power play]. And then we went into the playoffs and Montreal put the sleeper hold on us. That's literally what it was. And there were some games they were taking nine shots on goal, and we weren't patient enough and had a terrible performance on the power play. I think we were for 1-for-33. If you look back, if we were 6-for-33 we would have won the series easily."

CHAPTER 17

CAPTAIN
AMERICA ARRIVES

While the Capitals' dream season came to a crashing end, the team's AHL affiliate once again offered hope for the organization when a trio of young prospects showed off their skills in the Calder Cup playoffs.

Goaltender Michal Neuvirth and defensemen Karl Alzner and John Carlson had certainly played well in both Washington and Hershey, and the three were an important part of the Bears' successful Calder Cup defense.

While Neuvirth was impressive in net, and Alzner was quietly solid as a shutdown defenseman, Carlson had quite a start to 2010, scoring the game-winning goal in Saskatoon for USA Hockey's World Junior Championship team — stunning the host Canadians on January 5.

"I said, 'If you guys were to tell me at the beginning of the tournament that we'd be here right now going into overtime for the gold medal, anyone in the locker room would have taken it,'" Carlson told TSN after the game. "So I think the camaraderie really helped and we really pulled together there and squeaked out a win."

"The thing I remember first and foremost was him leaving for Team USA, and his first game back in Hershey was in Winnipeg," former Bears play-by-play voice John Walton recalled. "He goes into MTS Centre, and as I'm walking out of the team hotel, and I look at the *Winnipeg Sun* in the box, and the entire front page is a photo of John Carlson and his medal and the headline is 'PUBLIC ENEMY No. 1.' And he did not touch the puck that night where he wasn't booed like crazy."

The *Patriot-News'* Tim Leone felt the experience helped Carlson adjust to what would be a much brighter spotlight in Washington later on. "The big turning point for Carlson — you can tell, because first-year defensemen struggle [in the AHL] — is he was *average*," Leone said. "And to say that, as a rookie or a junior-eligible player, he was really *good*. To be average is to be good. But it was easy for him and he was 19. He was obviously young; you could tell there was an adjustment going on.

"I think the big thing for him was going to junior worlds. He was the magic man there, scored the winning goal — with huge amounts of media attention. He's right in the middle of it. I noticed immediately when he came back how much more at ease he was at dealing with us in the media and being in the spotlight and seizing the mantle, so to speak. He was excellent, all-rookie. Which is remarkable in this league for a true rookie to play that well."

Carlson's penchant for big moments followed him to Washington for a stint with the Capitals. His first Stanley Cup playoff goal forced overtime with just 81 seconds left in Game 2.

"There's just something about him — I mean, glory follows him," Boudreau said after the game. "Some guys get that. I've said it before. They come up in the ninth inning with the bases loaded, and they're the ones that do the damage. I think John Carlson in his career is going to be like that."

Like the Capitals, the Bears were dominant in the regular season, becoming the first AHL franchise ever to win 60 games, and they collected a franchise-record 123 points. Like the Caps, the defending Calder Cup champion Bears didn't see a whole lot of adversity all season long.

The Bears even got an indirect boost from the Penguins' front office. When Pittsburgh tried to send Chris Bourque — a player they claimed from Washington off waivers just before the regular season started — down to the AHL, the Capitals reclaimed him to get him back in Chocolatetown.

"When he got claimed, and he was going to the NHL — it's unfortunate it didn't happen [in Washington] — but that's the way it works," Walton said. "When Pittsburgh put him on waivers, there was a phone call from Chris to our trainer, Dan Stock, and it was relayed to me — and I can hear it in a Boston accent — 'Tell me they're not going to send me to Wilkes-Barre/Scranton!'

"Because it's one thing to be [in Pittsburgh] for the NHL, but he did not want to go [to Wilkes-Barre/Scranton] — that was something when he came back to Hershey.

"[Claiming Bourque back from the Penguins] was the spark. [The Bears] went on a tear that the team never did even under Bruce [Boudreau] or Bob [Woods]. From the first week of December to the end of the year, it was winning like I'd never seen it. To win 60 games and be the first team in AHL history to do that, Chris Bourque had everything to do with that, because when he came in, things were good. But with Chris to go with [Alexandre] Giroux and [Keith] Aucoin and the rest, they were absolutely unstoppable."

Michal Neuvirth was involved in his second playoff run for Hershey, biding time in the minors while Jose Theodore was in the last year of his two-year deal.

"This team has no holes, and [Neuvirth played] with swagger like I haven't seen," Walton recalled. "Even though it needed a turnaround in the finals . . . he goes to a whole different level. He has the attitude of 'I'm not going to let anyone beat me' . . . When he's ready to go, I'd never bet against him."

The team knocked out Bridgeport in five games, then got Alzner and Carlson back from Washington after the Montreal series to take out Albany in a sweep. Still, according to Walton, the series was tougher than it might appear in hindsight. Hershey dispatched Manchester in six games, but then fell behind 2–0 in the Calder Cup Finals at home against Texas. It was a deficit that had never been surmounted in the history of the Calder Cup Finals.

"There wasn't much adversity in 2010, but it hit hard when it hit," Walton recalled. "I think of Bryan Helmer, a guy who won it in his first two years pro and went 14 years before he won another one. The morning of Game 3 in Texas, he said, 'Coaches, out. Broadcaster, out. Trainers, out. I don't care. It's just us.'

"He took charge, and to this day, I don't know what was said. But I know that after the first period of Game 3, Texas was never in it . . . When you're down 2–0 — after what happened at home — [it] was stunning.

"There were so many contributions from so many different guys, Carlson and Alzner and the rest . . . you can't put a price tag on that. The Bears don't win without Bryan Helmer as a leader. I firmly believe that."

The Bears rallied, capped off with a Calder Cup–winning goal from none other than Carlson in the deciding game back at Hershey's Giant Center — the first time since 1980 the Bears had won the championship on home ice.

"He's obviously a very special player," Walton said.

"It was huge," Carlson said on the ice following the clincher over Texas. "We had won three straight, so we wanted to keep that momentum going in our favor. I think that was a huge goal, not just because I scored it. It's unbelievable. It's what you play for as a hockey player. It never gets old. Every time it is just a thrill. It's unbelievable."

For the Capitals, while the sting of losing to the Canadiens was tough for the big league club, there was hope in the experience of three key pieces for next year; Karl Alzner, John Carlson and Michal Neuvirth would help the team deal with losing Jose Theodore and also add some depth on defense.

"When Carlson and Alzner were paired together for the Conference Finals and [Calder Cup] Finals, they were a tough combination to beat," Walton recalled. "They logged a ton of minutes. Neuvirth already had one Cup to his credit, and by getting another one, there was nothing left for him to accomplish at the [AHL] level."

Alzner later said his development in Hershey was key to his successful transition to full-time NHLer.

"It's nice, it's good development [in Hershey]; you get to go down there and get to try things you might not try up here, like carrying the puck or handling the puck a bit more," Alzner said. "For me, that was the main thing, getting confidence to make plays and . . . believe in myself."

He also said that coming into the NHL with a partner like Carlson was a big part of his successful transition.

"It helps a lot," he said. "A guy closer to my age . . . That helped a ton . . . to go out there and have fun. If he makes a mistake, that's OK, I'm not going to be mad at him, and vice versa. That's something as a young guy you really need . . . to grow and have confidence on the ice . . . it always goes back to that in this league, and you need that to be good."

DEFENSE
FIRST

After a year when they had shattered franchise records for regular-season success — but couldn't get out of the first round of the play-offs — the Capitals adopted a different mindset. Instead of putting a lot of stock in regular-season accomplishments — either as a team or as individuals — they seemed to just want to get through the regular season unscathed. Despite wearing T-shirts at training camp that said "Stay Angry," the organization had its sights set on the distance and a run deep into the playoffs.

"They got to camp, and nobody wanted to be at camp. They wanted to be in the playoffs," the team's then–vice president of communications Nate Ewell recalled. "It was just a long preamble you had to get through."

"I think the Caps were totally focused on what they could do to be better once the playoffs started," Ed Frankovic of WNST in Baltimore said of the team's mood as camp opened. "It was clear that the regular season didn't matter much to them. George McPhee said that to me on Media Day. He said the only thing that mattered to him was a long playoff run. So if the man at the helm is saying that, then the players were likely thinking the same way."

Washington's season would still be unique. Not only was the team a part of the NHL's New Year's Day outdoor game, its Winter Classic in Pittsburgh, the Caps and the Penguins were also featured in an HBO reality series — a first for any pro hockey team.

Although the premium cable network had already produced its *Hard Knocks* series, chronicling the training camps of various NFL teams, this show involved cameras being encamped for a month during an NHL regular-season stretch — it was something the Capitals management was enthusiastic about.

"The meetings I had [with Boudreau] lasted about 10 minutes," Washington general manager George McPhee told reporters when the series was announced. "It's great for our team and it's great for our sport. HBO is very good. It's like I told Bruce and the players, 'Just be yourselves. Don't worry about whether it's good TV, just be yourselves, and they'll make it good TV.'"

"The one thing that I was concerned about was that they would be showing us cutting players because that's a very personal thing," Boudreau explained. "But I think they'll be very respectful of what we have to do."

There were roster changes. Jose Theodore's departure via free agency meant Michal Neuvirth came up from Hershey. With Semyon Varlamov, he became part of a very young goaltending tandem. Brendan Morrison and Eric Belanger also left as UFAs — the latter in a fairly ugly public spat with the club as Belanger's agent accused the club of failing to fulfill a verbal promise to sign the veteran — and that meant the Capitals were fairly thin at center.

Marcus Johansson, the team's first-round pick in the 2009 NHL Draft, was vying to make the roster as a 20-year-old rookie. Matt Hendricks, who was given a tryout after being cut loose from the Avalanche, was also added to the mix. Finally, the pair of young defensemen who had helped Hershey three months before — Karl Alzner and John Carlson — were ready to step into their roles full-time.

The Capitals clearly had a younger look about them as they opened the season in Atlanta on October 8. And after falling to the Thrashers, the Capitals returned home to earn a wild 7–2 win over the Devils. The contest, which featured the strange spectacle of Mike Green and Ilya Kovalchuk dropping the gloves, was blown open late by Washington.

"The difference was that [the game in Atlanta] was an embarrassing night for us and we just regrouped and watched video," Ovechkin said. "Everybody played bad last night and tonight we moved our legs and finished our checks; [we] played better in the neutral zone, defensive zone.

"I think guys like Brads [Matt Bradley], Chimmer [Jason Chimera], Greenie [Mike Green] and [Matt] Hendricks do unbelievable jobs protecting our guys and protecting themselves. It was a pretty big step for us tonight."

The game also featured John Carlson scoring on the goaltender he grew up watching in New Jersey, Martin Brodeur. "It was pretty cool," Carlson said afterward. "It's definitely one of the ones I'll remember."

Although the Capitals started off strong enough — they were 7–4–0 in October — many observers still felt they were inconsistent. Some nights they only seemed capable of putting in 20 or 30 minutes of effort, and they were leaving Michal Neuvirth — who had taken over as the starting goalie role with Semyon Varlamov battling injuries — to fend for himself in some contests. But that didn't seem to faze the young Czech netminder: he was named NHL Rookie of the Month for October.

"He's incredible," Green said. "I don't want to pump him too much but he's been outstanding for us. As a defenseman I feel so comfortable with him behind us. There's already a mutual bond that we feel even though he's only been here a short period of time."

"We're asking a lot of him for a first-year guy to come in and stand on his head, and he does," Boudreau said. "That's why he was Rookie of the Month."

After ending the first month with a 7–2 win in Calgary, the Capitals played well through November, opening the month 7–0–1. But the team showed began to show strange inconsistencies before the calendar turned to December, getting blown out by Atlanta and New Jersey, two of the league's weaker clubs, by identical 5–0 counts.

With the team not quite getting the offensive production of the year before, one player stood out. Alexander Semin set a new franchise record by recording three hat tricks in a span of 35 days, capping off the achievement in a 6–0 win over Tampa Bay on November 26. "I haven't changed anything, and I'm not going to change anything," Semin said through a translator. "I'm just going to continue doing the same thing."

"He's an unbelievably skilled guy," Nicklas Backstrom said of his teammate. "I don't know if I've seen anyone more skilled than him, to be honest with you. He can shoot from every angle. That's pretty impressive. I'm just glad he's on our team."

The Capitals made a trade at the end of November too. Looking to upgrade their defense for the playoffs, they acquired Scott Hannan from the Avalanche for Tomas Fleischmann.

Then, December. With winter coming the Capitals' season would take a dramatic turn. First, the HBO cameras arrived to film *24/7: Penguins-Capitals*, and then the team went through its longest losing streak since Boudreau took over as coach. As the Caps returned to Washington after a tough loss in Dallas, they readied for a month with cameras and microphones everywhere — even following players and management into their homes.

In their first game back, the Capitals lost 3–1 to Atlanta. Concerns about their once-potent offence had resurfaced.

"We didn't work hard enough out there," Nicklas Backstrom said. "In this kind of game, we have to score on the power play. We have to look at some tape and see what we did wrong."

"It happens to every team and every player," John Carlson added. "You just have to work through it, battle through it. There are no excuses. We're a good enough team that we can't feel sorry for ourselves."

"I think it's a lack of commitment to paying the price to score," Bruce Boudreau said. "We're all wanting to score. But we're staying on the perimeter hoping to get the puck rather than being the guy that's going to the puck."

It was the first time the team had lost back-to-back games in regulation time since October — and things were going to get a whole lot worse before they got better. Worse still, everything was about to play out in front of HBO's cameras.

"It was shocking," Nate Ewell said of HBO's arrival. "They do a good job of kind of blending into the background to the point where you'll see them around and you kind of get used to it. Then you'd turn the corner into the training room or weight room and forget they were going to be there, and they're there.

"There were three guys traveling with each camera — a cameraman, an assistant and a sound guy, so everywhere you go it's noticeable. The good thing was the crew was such a good group of guys, and they've done *Hard Knocks* so they knew how to act around a team . . . After a few days you'd get more comfortable, but you'd never get to the point where we'd be completely comfortable."

The next game, on December 6 against Toronto, was one of the worst losses of the season. The Capitals were in full control as the third period started, up 4–1 against a bad team, but somehow they allowed the Maple Leafs to rally and force overtime. Then they dropped the extra point in the shootout.

"It's frustrating anytime you give up a 4–1 lead in the third period; you're going to be angry," Boudreau told the media. "It doesn't happen and it's not supposed to happen."

"We quit playing in our zone," he added. "We just wanted to play safe. You can't just allow a team to come into our zone all night long. When they were in our zone, our positioning, by both defensemen and forwards, was really bad."

"I don't know what happened [in] the last 10 minutes. It started with our line when Grabovski scored," Alex Ovechkin said. "[A] 4-to-1 lead after two periods is pretty big. Losing a game like this is pretty bad for us. It's a lesson and it's good we have another game soon."

Even with the HBO cameras in the house, the coaching staff elected to make a rather radical change to the team's style of play. Bruce Boudreau — who had ample success with a rather loose and offensive-based system since coming to Washington in 2007 — decided to try to make the team more responsible defensively. "We didn't attempt to do anything early on in the season," Boudreau later explained. "Those guys, they're such a good group of players that they would have bought into whatever I was trying to sell, because they want to win. Once it got to that point in the middle of the losing streak, we said we had to tweak things . . . They were not radical changes.

"We didn't say we were going to stop scoring [by introducing the defensive system] — we just *weren't* scoring.

"We could tell from the beginning of the year that we weren't getting the same [scoring] production we had in the past. If we weren't going to score four goals a game, we better not give up more than two."

"Whether they were the perfect players [for the system] or not, they all bought into it; they became the best defensive team in the league from January on," Boudreau pointed out after the season's end. "You sacrifice maybe a couple of 2-on-1s here, or a couple of scoring chances there, to make sure you aren't scored upon. I thought they did a fabulous job with it and grew."

In the short term, however, the losing continued. Washington was blanked 3–0 by Florida in a game that saw them yield a last-second goal to end the second period. The error fueled an expletive-filled tirade by Boudreau that was captured by HBO's cameras. "So shit's not going right," he said. "It's not fucking working the last 10 days . . . Get your heads out of your asses and fucking make it work by outworking the opposition. You kill two fucking men [disadvantages] and then we stand around and watch it while they fucking score here.

"Outwork guys! If you want it, don't just think you want in, go out like you fucking want it. But you're not looking like you want it; you look like you're feeling sorry for yourselves. And no one wants anybody who's feeling sorry for themselves. You got 20 fucking minutes and you're down by one fucking shot. Surely the fuck [you know how to] deal with this."

The losing skid hit five on December 11, with a 3–2 loss to the Avalanche. It was the first time the team had lost five in a row since November 2007 — a streak that had cost Glen Hanlon his job.

Things got worse the next night in New York. A 7–0 loss to the Rangers left Boudreau searching for answers. And even veteran New York hockey scribes were asking the Washington media what was going on in the nation's capital.

"I don't have an answer right now. I've got to think about this," a somber Boudreau told reporters in a small room underneath Madison Square Garden. "It is unfamiliar territory, and I think we have a lot of people feeling sorry for themselves . . . But as you can tell, when you get down, teams aren't feeling sorry for you. They're pushing and piling it on. We have to figure out a way to get out of this before it's too late."

"The losing streak was as bad as I've ever seen it," Brian McNally of the *Washington Examiner* recalled. "Then that builds on the playoff disappointments . . . we can't even win in the regular season. How are we losing games 5–0 in New Jersey? What is happening? The doubt was there, and sometimes you just need to get lucky."

After an overtime loss to Anaheim, the Capitals headed up to Boston in what was one of the strangest games in recent Capitals history. Washington fell behind 3–0 in the first period but poured a ton of pressure on Bruins goaltender Tim Thomas — setting a team record with 26 shots in the final period — only to fall short in a 3–2 decision.

"To go through that third period in Boston and not tie it was absolutely ridiculous," Ewell remembered. "This is not hockey anymore; this is absurd. You can't possibly have a period like that and lose."

The Caps then flew up to Ottawa. On an eight-game losing skid, the team was in its biggest funk in years and searching for any way to stop the slide.

"Incredibly difficult. Painful. Physically painful," Ewell described of the mood heading to Ottawa. "[Even] the HBO crew was miserable. They hadn't won since [HBO] arrived. [The crew] didn't know at what point they were going to say, 'The hell with you guys, "Get off the fucking plane — stay away from us!"'

"I was lucky enough to be on that trip," Ewell added. "I remember the flight to Ottawa. That was absolutely painful."

But, according to McNally, the worst point of the streak actually showed the team they could compete. "The low point was the Boston game . . . They played well enough to absolutely destroy the Bruins the last two periods of that game. But after that, they realized they could play at that high level again. And they came out and won the next night."

Against the Senators, the Capitals once again fell behind early, but this time the team was able to rally. A 3–2 win gave them the much-needed two points. The end of the losing streak set off a playoff-type celebration.

"We felt like we won a championship," Mathieu Perreault told reporters. "We needed that . . . for our confidence. That was a huge win for us."

And it wasn't just the players who were happy. "[The HBO crew was] so happy when we won," Ewell said. "They were happier than the guys. They felt like they had cursed the team."

With the streak over, the Capitals began to slowly return to their winning ways, playing a different brand of hockey. After beating the Devils at home, in a preview of the Winter Classic just before Christmas, the Caps and Pens battled to overtime in an entertaining contest; Pittsburgh prevailed in the shootout.

After wins over the Hurricanes and Canadiens, Washington was ready to head to Pittsburgh for the team's biggest regular-season game in years. There would be a sold-out crowd at Heinz Field, home of the NFL's Steelers, and a large, nationwide audience watching on television.

Both the league and fans of both teams were excited about the rivalry hitting the big stage — and so were the players. "We have to feel like we have over the last week, where we keep building and building," Mike Green said. "We still have a lot to learn, but at least we get to play in a great event like Saturday."

"It will be exciting," Mike Knuble added. "It's one of those things we just want to take in — enjoy the game and just have fun with it."

The Winter Classic also showed how far the Capitals' fan base had come. In years past, supporters from Pittsburgh were famous for invading the Capital Centre and the Verizon Center. This time around, an estimated 30,000 Caps fans — with an estimated 20,000 seats going to the team's season-ticket holders — made the trek north to Pittsburgh to become a very vocal minority.

Reebok manufactured 38,000 retro jerseys for both teams, and 40 percent of those were replicas of the Capitals' original red, white and blue uniforms. They completely sold out.

The game, which was originally scheduled to start at 1 p.m., had to be pushed back due to heavy rain. The result was to give the day a very football-like feel, under the lights on a soggy night in the Steel City.

When the puck finally dropped, the two teams battled each other and the sloppy conditions. It was a slow-paced game, with all the water that had fallen on the ice surface. Evgeni Malkin finally put the Penguins up 2:13 into the second period with a shot that beat Semyon Varlamov.

Mike Knuble managed to tie the score on a power play less than five minutes later, poking the puck past Marc-Andre Fleury. The equalizer created a sizeable reaction from the red-clad fans in attendance.

"You can see, you can hear when we score goals how many people [were] fans of Washington," Ovechkin said afterward. "I can see a thousand people in one spot, a thousand people upstairs, it was really unbelievable. When it was the national anthem, and they were screaming, it was unbelievable. The fans support us all over the place. So it's good."

A miscue by Fleury led to a Washington go-ahead goal, as Johansson stole the puck from the Penguins netminder behind the net and then fed Eric Fehr in front to put the Capitals on top with 5:15 left to play in the period.

Toward the end of the frame, one team's season — and some might argue the entire history of the league — took a dramatic turn. As usual, the two rivals' fates seemed inexorably intertwined. This time, it was Pittsburgh's future that was altered.

As the period wound down, Sidney Crosby collided with David Steckel in the Penguins' zone. The Pittsburgh star's head collided hard with the Washington center's shoulder. The hit sent Crosby reeling and left him with a concussion. The injury was exacerbated a few days later when he took another hit, this time from Tampa Bay's Victor Hedman. The combination knocked Crosby out of action for the rest of season.

The Penguins' star missed a good portion of the 2011–12 season as well, suffering from post-concussion syndrome.

As rain fell harder during the third period, the Capitals were able to put the Penguins away. Eric Fehr got his second of the game on a breakaway to give the Capitals a 3–1 Winter Classic victory.

"I think both teams were just so excited, and it was pretty fun," Ovechkin told reporters at the postgame press conference. "The first period was good weather. The second period was a little bit of rain, and third period was lots of rain . . . [The] weather changed all the time and we handled it, and it was a pretty good game."

"It felt unbelievable," Fehr told reporters. "The first time we came out, the fans were loud and it was just everything you dreamed of. It was a perfect night. Nice and dark outside — with the lights, it was great."

"It was one of the best feelings in my life," Ovechkin said. "When you see it's sold out, it's like I can't imagine . . . Football players play every game like this. [You want to] go out and play like this all the time. And your family watching, your friends, and a million people watching you. When you get success, you get two points, you get excited and you just feel good about yourself and about your team."

"It was pretty cool," Bruce Boudreau said. "When you walk out and see those people, whether they're booing or cheering, it's an experience I'll never forget. And when you come into this kind of atmosphere and you're playing arguably the best team in the league and you win, it was more than just a game."

"This is as close to the Stanley Cup as we've gotten," the coach added. "We are not denying that it was more than just two points. It was a fabulous game."

It was also the end of the reality series. After the cameras had left, Boudreau said he was happy with the experience. "Now that it's done, I think it's great. The amount of people who watched that show . . . The way they did it — it was so professionally produced. It made the bad times look not so bad and the good times look euphoric, and it was entertaining."

Still Boudreau learned all about the dangers of having a microphone on you all day. "As soon as you walked in the building, they were putting mikes on you, and you had it on until you were leaving," he said. "Sometimes you forget and think, damn, what was I saying?

"Thankfully we got good guys and they were respectful of what should be said and what shouldn't be said — especially when we were in the middle of that eight-game winless streak. You say things in between periods that you didn't want other people to hear, but you said, damn, I was miked. I forgot, so they were good about it."

Ted Leonsis wasn't quite as happy with the experience, although he did say he was glad to help the league promote itself. "I don't think it helped the franchise. I think it helped the league, and that's why we did it. But we were already sold out for every game, we already had a great brand and so there was nothing it could do."

One thing that neither Leonsis nor Ewell were happy about was an interview that appeared in the program's first episode. It featured the owner, lit by bright lights in front of a dark background. "I thought the way they shot that interview with Ted was pretty embarrassing," Ewell said later. "I thought that was made to put him in an evil light."

"We helped to feed the monster," Leonsis said. "Personally, I agreed to do whatever they wanted. They asked me to come and speak . . . I have two offices: here [at Verizon Center] with huge windows and at Kettler . . . the sunniest, brightest offices you've ever been in.

"They filmed me in the basement of Verizon Center, with the lights off, and my face literally this close to the camera. So they filmed me like that and I asked why. It's supposed to be unfettered access . . . And the only time you're talking to me . . . [it's in] the least natural atmosphere? It's not in my office . . . not with interaction . . . Who speaks to someone in a wooden box, with the camera right in front? And then it ran, and I said, 'OK, they're telling a story.'"

Leonsis added he wasn't too happy with how his game-day experience at Heinz Field — being followed, constantly, by HBO's cameras — was reduced to a brief clip.

"We get to the game day itself, and the 24/7 cameras follow me and my family — wife, son and daughter . . . From the moment I arrive in

Pittsburgh . . . we walk into the locker room . . . we walk outside — I'm in awe of everything. They have a camera in my face — they come into the box, which didn't ruin the day — to watch all of my reactions. We win the game . . . then stroll through the building down to the locker room . . . There's a little bit of celebration and then that episode runs. They must have shot seven to eight hours of film, and I think I was in it for three seconds.

"It was a lot of work, and I thought the last episode was herky-jerky because we didn't follow the script. And so it was great television, it won Emmy Awards, but there's usually not happy endings in reality television. I would do it again to support the league, but it wasn't a great experience."

With the Winter Classic behind them, the Capitals still had business to attend to: there were still 42 games left before the team would get another crack at the playoffs.

There was a hangover after the Pittsburgh win, and the Caps went just 4–3–4 in the month following the Winter Classic. Tampa Bay knocked them off their perch atop the Southeast Division in mid-January. The team was struggling without a true second-line center and still adjusting to the new defensive style. For a team used to being dominant, a 6–5–1 in February, including some head-scratching efforts in an early month homestand, was troubling.

The lackluster play and the obvious hole at center led management to make a splash at the trade deadline. They picked up veteran center Jason Arnott from the Devils in exchange for David Steckel and a draft pick. The addition of Arnott sparked the team to a strong finish, and the Capitals wrapped up the regular-season 15–3–1 and re-passed the Lightning for the Southeast Division title, as well as the Flyers for the Eastern Conference's top seed.

The veteran Arnott made a quick impression on Alexander Semin, encouraging the sometimes enigmatic and quiet Russian to be more vocal on the ice. Something clicked, and Semin responded with improved play, reaching levels he hadn't managed since his hot start to the campaign.

"We're talking a lot on the bench," Arnott said. "If we keep that up, hopefully our chemistry will keep going."

"I especially like Arnott and Semin and [Brooks] Laich," Bruce Boudreau said of his new line. "They like playing with each other."

"He's been around this league for a long time," Boudreau said of Arnott. "He's being used in a different situation than he was for most of the year [with the struggling Devils], so I think he's excited about playing."

With the team surging and able to pass the Lightning for the Southeast crown, management opted to let Arnott and Ovechkin undergo procedures — minor knee surgery for Arnott and reportedly the same for the team's captain — to get them ready for the postseason. Despite taking a cautious approach into the final stretch, they reeled off a nine-game win streak even without Ovechkin, Arnott and Backstrom for some of those games.

They were once again playing well, but Boudreau said he wasn't concerned with landing the top spot: "I don't want to think about [the number one seed]. To me it is a nice feather in your cap and we got a nice trophy for winning last year, but in the end I don't care if we're first or eighth — I got to believe the eight [seed] can beat the one . . . It has happened, I think.

"The playoffs are a different animal. This is still the regular season. You want to play as hard as you can, all teams are trying to position themselves, but unless you have been in the playoffs . . . once it hits there, it ramps up an awful lot more — no matter who you are going to play."

Washington finished the regular season with 107 points — 14 off the year before, but just one off their pace of two years earlier, despite having to fight through an eight-game losing streak. Their reward was another date with the Rangers, a team that had handed the Capitals two of their worst losses of the year — 7–0 at Madison Square Garden in December and 6–0 at Verizon Center in February. The 82-game preamble was over. The Capitals were finally getting a chance to wash away some of the bitterness they'd carried since last spring's loss to the Canadiens.

CHAPTER 19

ONE STEP FORWARD, TWO STEPS BACK

One of the things that makes the Stanley Cup so hard to capture is that while regular-season standings are used to pair teams up in the post-season, the second season is really about how teams match up against one another . . . and their strengths and weaknesses.

"You have to look at where our league is now and how competitive it is," Capitals general manager George McPhee explained. "There isn't much of a difference between teams. That's the great thing the league has done. Since coming out of the lockout, how close everyone is.

"Everybody's in the race, it's a race all year long to get in the playoffs. We were the number one seed, we're playing the number eight seed, and we had four more wins than they did. That was it over the whole season. The difference between number one and number eight was four wins."

The Rangers had been a thorn in the Capitals' side all season long. New York's Swedish superstar Henrik Lundqvist — their goaltender who nearly engineered the Caps' playoff upset two years before — had blanked them twice. For its part, Washington was putting its faith in young Michal Neuvirth, who was making his first run in the Stanley Cup playoffs after two successful Calder Cup campaigns in Hershey.

"[There's a] big difference between these leagues . . . the NHL is a better league," the goaltender said. "But there was a lot of pressure down in Hershey, pressure to win."

The series began in Washington on April 13, and the two sides were tentative. The Rangers wanted to slow down the pace to keep the series low scoring, but Washington had prepared since December to play this type of game.

Neuvirth was strong in net for the Capitals, matching his counterpart Lundqvist save for save.

"Yeah, obviously [Lundqvist is] a good goalie, and we want to beat them," Neuvirth said after Game 1. "I got to be as good as he plays."

Although he was making his Stanley Cup playoff debut, the young netminder said he was confident.

"To be honest, I wasn't nervous at all," Neuvirth said, laughing. "I had a good nap . . . I felt good the whole day."

Neuvirth held the Rangers off the board for 40 minutes, including a spectacular save on New York sniper Marian Gaborik.

"He was very calm and very focused on the puck and in the game," Alex Ovechkin said of Neuvirth. "In the second period Gaborik had a great opportunity to score . . . and [Neuvirth] made a huge save to keep us in the game."

New York finally jumped on top at 1:56 of the third on a Matt Gilroy goal. And after being blanked for over 180 minutes dating back to the regular season by Lundqvist, concern began to grow on Washington's bench. But the Caps pressed for the equalizer, and the team was finally able to break through on a scramble in front, with Ovechkin poking in the puck.

"I was pleased we got a goal — at one point I didn't know if there was ever going to be a way to beat that guy," Bruce Boudreau said at his postgame presser. "Sometimes you need a greasy goal like that to spark your team."

"Well, I didn't see the puck, I just try [to] get something," Ovechkin explained afterward. "It goes in. I didn't see . . . I saw Sasha was like screaming, 'Goal, goal' so I was excited and start celebrating."

"Henrik Lundqvist is a great goalie and it's very difficult to score an easy one on him . . . We couldn't get a nice goal on him, so we scored a 'junk' goal — just pushed it in — whatever worked," Semin said via translator Slava Malamud.

The low-scoring game continued into overtime, and it was decided when Arnott was able to intercept a Marc Staal clearing attempt. The veteran gloved the puck down to his stick and then quickly passed it to Semin, who scored his first goal in 15 playoff games (dating back to the strange double-deflection he put in during Washington's Game 7 win over New York in 2009).

"I just saw the puck get intercepted [by Arnott]," Semin said via Malamud. "It's just a situational play. I tried to get open and shoot as soon [as] possible because the defenseman was right there."

"We're not getting anywhere without Alex Semin scoring," Boudreau said. "I could barely see [the shot]. I thought Arnott made a great play to keep it in and he didn't hesitate. It was a great shot."

Considering the fact that they'd dropped the first two games to the Rangers at Verizon Center in 2009, the Caps were more than pleased to take Game 1.

"It is huge for us," Mike Green said. "Obviously it is a seven-game series and anything can happen, but we wanted to get off to a great start and especially in our building here. We have home ice advantage, and we need to take advantage of that."

"I thought we were doing a lot of good things," Mike Knuble said. "It was a big relief when Alex [Ovechkin] scored to tie it up. Then we played a pretty strong overtime — [we] got a turnover there — and Alexander [Semin] scores. It's always great to get the first win of the series."

New York came out strong in Game 2, outshooting Washington 13–7 in the first, but Michal Neuvirth was able to hold the Blueshirts off the board. The Capitals took command early in the second, when Jason Chimera scored 2:11 into the frame, sending the sellout crowd at Verizon into a frenzy. Less than two minutes later, the team's dormant power play finally awoke, ending the 0-for-19 slump that dated back to the previous year's series against Montreal. The goal itself was a tad fluky: Green wound up from the point but the puck redirected off the stick of Matt Gilroy and caromed across to Jason Arnott, with Lundqvist well out of position thanks to the strange bounce.

"I was kind of in the right spot at the right time," Arnott told reporters. "In the first period we were a little too fancy [with the first power play] and we wanted to get more shots on net.

"I saw [Green] wind up and shoot it and it got deflected, and it happened to land on my stick. I knew [Lundqvist] was down and out, and that's the only way we can beat him. He's a phenomenal goaltender."

"Special teams are going to win you games," Boudreau said. "We got a lucky break, it deflected onto [Arnott's] stick. But it was a great shot and we deserved to score."

All the Capitals were happy to convert with the extra man.

"Last year's last year; this year's this year," Green said. "It's important to take advantage of the power play no matter what.

"You're not going to win games if you don't score on your power play and you don't get many chances. When we do, we better take advantage of them."

With their new defensive commitment, the Capitals were content to sit on the 2–0 lead as the game headed into the third. They were able to make it stand up and took a 2–0 series lead.

"I think we were a little lackadaisical in the third," Arnott said of the finish. "We were panicking a little bit. That's normal with young guys, but we have to do a better job if we're getting the lead going into the third. We have to keep forechecking, keep shooting pucks. They took it to us."

The Caps only allowed one goal in the first two games, and even though New York wasn't one of the league's best offensive clubs, the result showed a marked improvement.

"They've been buying in since the middle of December," Bruce Boudreau said. "They just want to win. The important thing is that they get success. We've got a lot of guys who've won a lot of [individual] awards and that doesn't mean anything to them now."

"It goes back to the games we play in the regular season," Mike Green added. "We've been in the position a lot this year. It hasn't been blow out games, whether we've been blown out or blowing other teams out. It's been comforting to know that we've played enough games to know what to do now."

Still, the trip to New York threatened to derail the Capitals' push, and the team faced real adversity at the Garden. Both teams had to deal with a quick turnaround and a Sunday afternoon game that would be broadcast nationally on NBC. They battled to a scoreless first, but after that the Rangers seemed to have the hockey gods on their side.

Just 5:30 into the second, Erik Christensen shot a puck from the boards that fluttered under Michal Neuvirth and somehow made it into the cage. The Caps' netminder was solid after that, however, and Alex Ovechkin was able to tie up the contest with a goal of his own with 59.2 seconds left. Then, in the dying seconds of the period, a Ruslan Fedotenko shot deflected off John Erskine's skate just as time expired, apparently giving New York the 2–1 lead. Video review from the NHL's offices in Toronto determined that the clock had expired just a fraction of a second before the puck crossed the line, negating the tally.

Washington wasn't able to cash in on the break, and the Rangers jumped back in front in the third when Vinny Prospal scored with 11:59 left, banging in a Gaborik rebound. The Caps were able to tie it up again with 5:12 left, but paid a fairly steep price.

Washington was on a power play as time wound down when a Mike Green slapshot went off Mike Knuble's thumb, shattering it in the process. Knuble was able to corral the puck and beat Lundqvist to square the score, but the veteran forward was knocked out for the rest of the series with the injury.

The Rangers were able to grab the win and climb back in the series on another strange tally. As the game wound down, a Brandon Dubinsky shot from the side of the cage went off Karl Alzner's back, then tipped in off Ovechkin's stick as he was trying to prevent the puck from crossing the goal line with just 1:39 to play.

"All three games have been wars," Boudreau told reporters afterward.

"It's not a question of throwing different strategies at them. We know what they're going to do. I don't think we're going to change overnight."

"They played hard, and we played hard too," Ovechkin told the media. "It was kind of a tight game. We knew . . . that the first 10 minutes of each period they were going to come hard, and we tried to handle it. The results were not on our side."

Three nights later it appeared that the Rangers were going to square the series. New York was able to build a 3–0 lead after 40 minutes, once again getting fortunate bounces along the way.

First, an Artem Anisimov centering feed deflected past Michal Neuvirth, putting the Capitals in a 1–0 hole early. And then a horrible seven-second span in the second put Washington in a three-goal hole. With 6:20 left in the middle frame, Gaborik was able to double the Rangers lead when he took a Fedotenko centering feed and banged it in. Seizing momentum, the Rangers charged in the Washington zone off the ensuing faceoff, and Dubinsky was able to sneak in and score. New York would carry that momentum into the second intermission.

The Capitals' season appeared to be unraveling once again, but in between periods and early in the third, things turned Washington's way.

"[Boudreau] was pretty calm and said let's build momentum," Jason Chimera told the media. "It is a long [series] and let's just play our game. We said it again and again, 'We've got the horsepower to do it. Let's just get one and get rolling.' We had a great effort in the third period.

"Once we got one, we kind of felt them sit back a bit. Everyone does it. When you're up 3–0 you sit back a little bit and we took advantage of it."

Washington's first break came when Ryan McDonagh's pass attempt was intercepted by Alexander Semin, who broke in and beat Lundqvist 2:47 into the third.

Then, just 57 seconds later, Marcus Johansson took a Brooks Laich pass and beat Lundqvist with a shot that deflected off his pad to cut the deficit to 3–2.

"In between periods, we never gave up," Bruce Boudreau told

reporters later. "You get one and you never know. When we got both goals really quickly, I thought we believed we were really in it."

The Capitals eventually tied it up with 7:53 left in regulation, as John Carlson's long shot eluded Lundqvist and squared the score.

With an important goal looming, the two teams were cautious as the game headed into overtime. Another strange goal would decide everything.

With the Capitals breaking into the Rangers zone as the second overtime was winding down, Johansson dropped the puck for Chimera, who wound up. His shot was blocked by Rangers defenseman Bryan McCabe and bounced toward the Rangers netminder. Gaborik went back to try to aid Lundqvist in gathering the puck, but he accidentally popped the puck loose and up into the air — right toward Chimera, who was standing alone in front of the New York net.

"It hit my chest and went down," Chimera told the press. "It felt like forever until it went down to my stick."

It was a huge goal, giving the Capitals a 3–1 series lead for the second time in two years. At the same time, it was a devastating loss for the Rangers, who had played well through four games but were on the verge of elimination against a team whose talent simply overmatched them.

"It was a good effort by us in the third period and what a comeback," Chimera told reporters. "There was no quit. Once we got one, we felt them sit back a bit. We took advantage of it."

"It was an exciting game," Ovechkin said. "It changes our mentality right away. If we play the same way that we did in the third period in overtime, no one can stop us."

"We looked nervous," John Tortorella told the media afterward. "We felt better once we got through [the third period] and got to overtime. We still had chances we didn't make. We got beat by a goal that is a nothing goal.

"It is just a nothing play that turns into something — obviously something big."

Having learned not to take a potential clincher lightly after dropping

Game 5 against Montreal the year before, there was no doubt how the Capitals would come out of the gate with a chance to clinch on April 23.

"Last year, when we had the lead 3–1, we thought it was over, and it was not over," Ovechkin said. "We relaxed. Right now, everybody focused and nobody relaxed."

Washington swarmed early, outshooting the Rangers 13–6 in the first 20 minutes. Mike Green put the Capitals on top, taking an Alex Ovechkin faked shot and beating Lundqvist.

In the second period, Ovechkin put an exclamation point on the series with just over seven minutes gone. The puck was in the corner of the Caps' end when Nicklas Backstrom quickly fed Brooks Laich, who then hit Scott Hannan. Hannan then spotted Ovechkin streaking down the side and gave him the puck. Ovechkin turned on his speed, outraced Marc Staal, and then cut in front of Lundqvist to deposit a backhander for the 2–0 lead.

"We blocked the shot, I just turned and [Laich] and [Hannan] gave me a pass," Ovechkin said. "It was kind of a rush play . . . it was important to score and [build] the lead."

"The pass made the slot, my first read was his speed and watching him a little bit," Staal said in a subdued Rangers locker room. "I got to watch him first and started retreating. I didn't have enough legs to get back."

"I think I have pretty good speed," Ovechkin said. "[Hannan] gave me a pretty good pass and I just do what I have to do to score goals. It's my job."

"We knew [Dan] Girardi and Staal logged a lot of ice time," he added. "When I scored, Staal was a bit tired, and I had a chance to make some moves."

With the Rangers' offense sputtering and Neuvirth playing well, the Capitals closed out the series in five games. Alex Semin added an insurance goal with 3:37 left. Michal Neuvirth's shutout bid was broken with just 31.5 seconds remaining — the only mistake he made on 27 New York shots.

For Washington, who had played in four straight seven-game battles under Boudreau, finishing in five was a unique experience.

"We've never done it," Bruce Boudreau said afterward. "It is one of those things . . . I'll have to give my head a shake tomorrow morning and wonder where we're supposed to be.

"It is good because we have a lot of guys hurt, so you need the time off just to recuperate. That was a really tough series. It was done in five, but I think John [Tortorella] would say the same thing, that either team could have won all five games."

The Rangers later admitted that the third period of Game 4 proved to be the turning point, and that once the Caps rallied, the series was all but over.

"It really bugs me the way we didn't find ways to win those games where we had great opportunities to win," Lundqvist said.

"I thought our first shift was pretty good [but] they came back with some good ones," Brian Boyle said. "[The Capitals'] power play, they were swarming. They kept the momentum [and] the building was rocking. It was hard to get it back."

After a less-than-inspiring effort with the opportunity to close out an opponent the year before, the Capitals were much more focused in this Game 5.

"I thought that we came out like a ball of fire," John Carlson said. "In front of our fans, they've been so good to us in the playoffs and the regular season. It was good to get out to a lead and not sit on it but keep pushing forward. I thought we did a great job of that."

"I think we learned our lesson," Nicklas Backstrom said. "That's what we've been talking about. People were so disappointed with last year. This is only the first round. We have higher goals than this. It is fun tonight, but tomorrow we have to regroup and think about round 2."

The team had to wait to learn who their next opponent was, and this presented logistical problems. It first appeared that the Capitals' would face the Buffalo Sabres, but they lost a lead in Game 6 and fell in seven to Philadelphia. If Montreal had been able to knock off Boston, there would have been a rematch of the previous year's first round, but the Bruins bested the Habs in overtime of Game 7. That meant the Caps would face the winner of the Pittsburgh–Tampa Bay showdown — a contest that also went to seven games.

The Lightning went on to beat the Crosbyless Penguins in Game 7 at Consol Energy Center, rallying from a 3–1 series deficit. A 1–0 shutout by Dwayne Roloson set up a rematch of the 2003 series that began the Capitals' rebuild. Due to the strange nature of the Rangers series, the team had played just three games in a week, and then had to wait another six days before the next round began.

The Lightning arrived in Washington in the early morning after knocking off the Penguins, travel-weary but on a three-game win streak.

Dwayne Roloson, acquired from the New York Islanders on New Year's Day, had played well against Washington in the regular season, recording a pair of shutouts. The wily vet posed a serious threat if Washington failed to crash the net and create pressure.

Just 2:12 into the opener, Sean Bergenheim put Tampa Bay on top. Alexander Semin answered less than two minutes later, taking a Marco Sturm feed and beating Roloson. Washington pressed hard for the go-ahead goal, but Roloson was able to hold the game even. Eric Fehr did manage to put the Capitals up 2–1 1:51 into the second off a Jason Chimera feed, but the team's strong effort unraveled quickly and the Lightning cashed in on a fluky tally.

With just over three minutes left in the middle period, Steve Downie made a centering feed that deflected off Hannan's stick past Neuvirth, squaring the score and changing the complexion of the series.

"They got a lucky goal," Johansson said. "It went off one of our guys and into the net. That got them back in the game."

"I thought we were in control . . . until the Downie goal, and that gave them life," Boudreau said. "But you can't play river hockey. This wasn't the way we play. It was reverting back . . ."

Shortly after the equalizer, Chimera was sent off for roughing. The Lightning cashed in when Steven Stamkos buried a shot with 31.6 seconds left in the second. Tampa had a 3–2 lead.

Using a 1–3–1 defensive alignment in the third, the Lightning frustrated the Capitals. The team had become accustomed to late-game heroics, but Washington wasn't able to break through for the equalizer. An empty-netter gave the Bolts a 4–2 decision.

"[The Lightning] make it frustrating," Bruce Boudreau said. "They just hang back . . . And they are very good at it. That's why when they get a lead — and they got a lead against Pittsburgh — they hold onto it."

"We just got away from our game plan," Jeff Schultz said later. "They turned it up a notch. Two quick goals put us back on our heels and we couldn't catch up. That's exactly how we expected them to play and we had a really good game plan and we had it going for a while, and we kind of gave up on it and things didn't go well after that."

Down 1–0 in the series, the Capitals came out firing in Game 2, outshooting the Lightning 11–4 in the first 20 minutes. But it was Tampa that got on the scoreboard first, when Vinny Lecavalier buried a Martin St. Louis feed with just 59 seconds left.

Washington came out in the second even more desperate, outgunning the Lightning 16–3. They finally drew even with 5:08 left in the frame when Brooks Laich tipped in a Nicklas Backstrom feed. With the shot counter reading 27–9 after 40 minutes, however, there was bound to be a push back from the Lightning. That's exactly what happened in the third.

Martin St. Louis put Tampa Bay in front with 12:25 left in the period when a pass went off Mike Green's skate past Michal Neuvirth for another fluky goal.

The Capitals were able to answer this time. Ovechkin jammed the puck past Roloson with 1:07 left in regulation to force the extra session and send the sold-out crowd at Verizon into a frenzy.

"I thought we had the momentum, quite frankly, for about 45 minutes of that game," Bruce Boudreau said. "I felt very comfortable going into overtime."

The game — and likely the series — was decided on a bad line change with six minutes left in the first overtime.

Randy Jones cleared the puck out of his own end with the Caps trying to get fresh legs on the ice. Teddy Purcell gobbled up the pass, and he and Lecavalier broke in on Mike Green. Vinny Lecavalier took Purcell's pass and made no mistake. Tampa was heading home with a 2–0 series lead.

"Yeah, it is [frustrating]," Jason Arnott said afterward. "It's playoff hockey and Roloson played real well and the team played pretty well in front of him. We've got to hand it to their goaltending tonight. He played extremely well."

Heading south for a must-win Game 3, the Capitals came out strong, but once again fell behind when Bergenheim staked the Bolts to a first-period lead. With their season essentially on the line, the Capitals came out firing in the second, and Knuble was able to take an Ovechkin feed just 59 seconds into the period to tie the game.

Carlson then gave Washington its first lead since Game 1 when his long blast eluded Roloson with 7:58 gone in the period — a stretch where the Capitals were outshooting the Lightning 7–2. Even though the Lightning tied the game a few minutes later on a Lecavalier goal, the Capitals took advantage of a late 5-on-3 to grab a 3–2 lead on an Alexander Ovechkin marker.

Things came undone in the third. The Capitals sat back — and it cost them dearly. Tampa outshot Washington 15–5 and cashed in to grab a commanding 3–0 series lead.

With just under five minutes gone, a Eric Fehr clearing attempt was blocked by Victor Hedman, then picked up by the always dangerous Steven Stamkos. He buried it with 14:37 to play.

"We just gave them lifelines," Mike Knuble told reporters afterward. "I think we played well. We played the game that we wanted to play. We gave them a lifeline when we were leading and they tied it to make it 2–2. We go up 3–2 and we gave them another lifeline."

According to Erik Erlendsson, who covers the Lightning for the *Tampa Tribune*, that third goal marked the beginning of the end.

"You start to wonder about a team like Washington . . . I was like a lot of people, I didn't think Tampa had much of a chance — coming

off a seven-game series in Pittsburgh, with the quick turnaround —
to withstand the onslaught that Washington put on them in that first
period of Game 1, and to win the game.

"I wonder if it put doubt in Washington's mind. Tampa controlled
most of Game 2 — obviously Washington scored late, but gave up the
winning goal in overtime. Then . . . Game 3 — a game that they had to
have. Ovechkin said before the game, 'We're going to win' and when
Tampa scored that third goal, you could see it in their faces, in their
eyes, in the way they played, you knew they were done.

"You talk about how winning can be contagious, but losing and
disappointment can be contagious too. It takes a special leader to pull
guys out of that spiral downward . . . Sometimes it's infectious."

Just 24 seconds after Stamkos's tally, Ryan Malone scored. The
goal gave Tampa a 4–3 win. The Capitals' season was all but done.

"It's tough to say, I don't know exactly, I can't really put my finger
on it," Karl Alzner later told reporters. "I thought we were playing good
but just started to get a little too complacent. We just took our foot off
the gas for a little bit.

"I don't really know [why]. I wish I knew. I just don't know what
to say."

"We weren't supposed to play safe," Boudreau told the media. "We
knew they were going to come out because they've come out in the
third in the two previous games. We knew we had to keep pushing."

"We need to learn to play a full 60 minutes and not give up odd-
man rushes," Jason Arnott said. "We can't give up back-to-back goals
like that either. When they get a goal, we need to be even more prepared to have a big shift after that.

"We get up for a certain amount of time and I think that our guys
think the game is over. The guys just relax a little bit and then they just
come. In the playoffs you need to be focused and ready on every shift.
If you aren't, bad things happen."

The next night, Tampa completed the sweep with a stunning 5–3 win.

"They just beat us in four straight so I think they were [the better team]," Boudreau told reporters. "It wasn't by a big margin, but we're still done in four games, so I'd have to say they were better."

"This is the first team we've played in a while that has three lines that really come at you. Their so-called third line. I think Downie had 12 points, Moore and Bergenheim had at least six goals, so that's pretty good for a third line. They never quit."

The next morning, the Capitals disappointedly cleaned out their lockers for the summer. Once again their season went south in the span of less than a week.

"I thought our opponent played really well," George McPhee said. "They came back from a 3–1 deficit [against Pittsburgh] — we were prepared to play anyone in the second round, but you play a team that comes back from a 3–1 deficit you expect them to be flying — and they were."

"We didn't handle them as we wanted," a dejected Nicklas Backstrom said. "They got confidence from that, that's the hardest part of the playoffs. Once you get on a roll, it's hard to stop."

"I think everyone in the organization is shocked we lost 4–0, but I don't think we deserved to lose 4–0," Alex Ovechkin said. "We want to win . . . it's something hard for us, they played their game, they played well, they played hard, and right now, they deserved to win."

"It's quick," Mike Knuble said. "I touched on it [after Game 4], to think you'd be swept in the second round was the furthest from everybody's mind. We envisioned a long series and successful playoff run. I thought we had the guys to do it, and still do.

"Somebody was asking to compare it to the loss last year [to Montreal]; I don't know, every year's different. I feel bad because sports fans around here will say, 'It's the same, it's another year, typical.' That's what's frustrating as a player."

"It's a shock, I think a lot of us are in a little bit of disbelief," Karl Alzner said. "We realize we have a strong team but we came up really short . . . but it's tough to handle . . . you don't get too many opportunities with really good teams. The last two or three years . . . to have exceptional teams . . . it's tough to let it slip away like that."

For Erlendsson, the Capitals' inability to handle adversity in the series cost them dearly.

"For Tampa, to have won that series, and to have swept that series, was a complete surprise . . . Even to someone like myself, who watched the [Lightning] all year.

"I thought this was Washington's year. They made all those moves at the deadline, they got tougher to play against, their goaltending was pretty good, and they suffered so many disappointments in the past — they were doing the right things.

"Coming back against New York in the first round was a huge key, I thought that would be big. But the first sign of adversity that crept in during the Tampa series, it seemed like it took over."

CHAPTER 20

NEW SEASON, NEW OPTIMISM

More than seven years — nearly 2,750 days — had passed since that March 2004 pitting the Capitals and the Penguins in a battle of bottom-dwellers. The atmosphere in Verizon Center for Washington's 2011–12 season opener had changed completely.

Hours before the opening faceoff, fans wearing red Capitals jerseys and T-shirts walked around Washington's Chinatown, jamming the restaurants and bars that had sprung up in what was now one of the city's trendiest neighborhoods. In the dressing room, a few new names were stitched to the backs of the red Capitals jerseys that hung in the players' lockers — top talent now lobbying to come to Washington via trades and free agency.

Capitals general manager George McPhee — who had to shed most of the team's stars in 2003–04 and agreed to players' demands to be dealt to other teams — said it best when he stated that his club now had "become one of those destination teams."

Tomas Vokoun, one of the top goaltenders on the free-agent market, took a pay cut and a one-year, $1.5 million deal to come to town: he wanted to make a run at a Stanley Cup after spending time in Nashville and Florida.

"I think we have a great team, and a chance to hopefully go through the 82-game season to build a foundation . . . We want to go far in the playoffs," Vokoun said in training camp. "I think nobody here is setting goals for the regular season. The message was pretty clear over the summer . . . it's a great team, and we improved on that. It's up to us players to perform to our capabilities and hopefully we're able to do what we want to do.

"This is a chance I never had in my career, and you never know, you may not get another one. So I'm going to do everything I can to take advantage and not to waste it. I'm glad I got a chance to play for a team like this and at this point of my career, I didn't think it would be possible, but hopefully it's a refreshing thing for me."

Jeff Halpern, the Maryland-born forward who survived the team's fire sale and the lockout, signed a one-year deal to return after playing elsewhere for five seasons, looking to make history in his hometown.

"I would say in the back of my mind, I had always hoped to come back," he told reporters at training camp. "Every year I've played since I had left here, I wanted to win a Stanley Cup, and always felt like it would be a great city to win it in.

"But, in the back of my head, it would be a tremendous opportunity to win a Cup in Washington, and the best place for me to win it. To come back . . . to see the team and have the opportunity, at least on paper . . . This team has a great chance to win."

"It feels great," he added. "I had a lot of great years here, and a lot of friendships and teammates. The organization and city is at a whole new level as far as how they support the hockey team. It's fun to be a part of. It seems like there are more fans and more passion for the team . . . Not just the hockey fans, but the casual fan as well. I think the biggest thing is the product that management's been able to put on the ice is . . . pretty exciting. With the top-end talent that this team has, it makes it easy to support."

Another player who outlasted the fire sale to become part of the rebuild was former goaltender Olie Kolzig, who returned to the team in 2011 as a goalie coach. Since leaving, after the 2007–08 season, Kolzig almost couldn't believe the changes that had taken place. "It's crazy," he said. "You go out there and see a sea of red. You see how far D.C. has come to become a hockey town. It's incredible. I knew the team was going to be good, but I didn't foresee the support and the amount of fans that they were going to generate."

When asked about the team's off-ice success since taking over as coach in 2007, Bruce Boudreau said he just felt lucky to be part of it. "My arrival is just coincidental with the way the marketing has taken off, and Alex becoming the focal point of hockey, and Ted taking over and getting a lot of colorful players," he said. "I was just the lucky recipient.

"I think Washington is a tremendous hockey city, and it's growing by leaps and bounds every day and getting bigger. And the more success we have, the bigger it's going to get."

From a management standpoint, the organization's goals had changed in recent years. Where they were once just looking for progress, now the team had lofty aspirations.

"We weren't happy with the way the season ended last year, but that's a sign of progress," Ted Leonsis said. "That we can finish first in the East, and win a playoff series, and sit back and say it wasn't a successful season . . . I'm happy we're at that point in the development, and we want to go deeper into the playoffs and be more competitive. And that's what everything is working toward."

Leonsis could finally tap into the revenue generated by the building his team plays in, benefiting from the revenue generated by club seats and suite sales. He took control of the Verizon Center and the NBA's Wizards in 2010, following Abe Pollin's death. That wasn't the case during the first decade of his ownership. As a result, the NHL franchise is a more attractive investment, with *Forbes* magazine estimating the Capitals franchise worth at $225 million in November 2011, up more than 100 percent from a low of $110 million in 2004.

As the red-clad opening night crowd slowly filled purple seats that once outnumbered fans, the anticipation of a new season began.

There would soon be 18,377 people in those seats — the club's 107th straight sellout — a number the franchise didn't reach from its inception in 1974–75 until 1989–90. The entire 2011–12 season was sold out, with a wait list for season tickets.

"Obviously, they're a lot more passionate fan base [now]," Erik Erlendsson of the *Tampa Tribune* explained when asked to compare 2004 and 2011. "You can tell they're really into it because they're cheering and booing at the appropriate time instead of sitting on their hands.

"The red helps — I love the new reds. It brings out passion, it's one of those feng shui colors. It's a big, big difference from six or seven years ago — you can tell they really care. It's good to see."

Interest in playing the sport was way up as well. According to Chris Peters, who tracks USA Hockey registration numbers for the United States of Hockey blog, the spike in local hockey participation from 2009 to 2011 was equivalent to that in a city that had won the Stanley Cup.

"The Potomac Valley is following some of the trends established in Carolina when they won the Stanley Cup, the membership blew up," Peters said. "It's similar here — without a Stanley Cup — just the excitement of the team . . ."

High up in the building, what used to be a sparsely populated press box was now filled nearly to capacity — even with the Hurricanes in town.

"Off the ice, the marketing of the team is great," Capitals radio voice John Walton said. "There's been such a good job done . . . and the new media is part of that. It's a tech-savvy region; I came from a more traditional market [in Hershey], but a lot of people are on Facebook and Twitter . . . and follow hockey that way . . . You can go back and forth, you can take ownership of that, when you're a fan.

"You can say I follow John Carlson. I follow John Walton. I follow [WashingtonCaps.com writer] Mike Vogel. I follow media people, front office people and players. That's what Ted has done here, they were doing this before a lot of other teams were, and look at the dividends it's paid . . ."

The difference seven years had made really was striking.

"If you watch videos from [coming out of the lockout], it's incredible," Nate Ewell said. "Everything looks different now, the product on the ice looks different, both from a hockey standpoint and a color standpoint. The arena looks different, the fans all look different. It's really done a complete reversal — from one of the most lackluster environments in the league to one of the best."

On the ice, the Capitals were once again expected to be one of the league's top teams. Pundits believe they'll remain in the hunt for several years with their core of players. In the preseason, *The Hockey News* picked Washington to win the Stanley Cup.

Of course, there was still anticipation — and frustration. Trying to capture a franchise's first Stanley Cup is like that.

"I think a lot about the disappointment in Washington . . . It feels like times have been so tough . . . that you haven't broken through and won," Ewell said. "It's no different in Vancouver. It's a difficult game and just one team wins.

"A player like Ovi is going to win in his career. If you look at anyone who is half as good . . . he wins a Stanley Cup. When they signed him to a contract in January of 2008, I thought, 'Well, Washington's won a Stanley Cup.' Because there's no way he doesn't win one."

McPhee put it succinctly months earlier. "Unfortunately the playoffs can't go well for 15 of the 16 teams that get there," he said. "We've won four consecutive division titles, we've won the conference twice, and we've won the Presidents' Trophy. We keep putting good teams on the ice and hope one of them can go far."

"Sometimes in the playoffs, it's just about the matchups," Capitals newcomer Troy Brouwer — who won a Stanley Cup with Chicago in 2010 — explained. "It doesn't matter what you do in the regular season, if you don't match up well against someone, you're going to have a tough time . . . It is one of those things you kind of wonder why

[Washington hasn't done better], but we've made some good moves and we're happy as players and as an organization and we feel it will help us win in the playoffs.

"I'm not worried about what happened here in previous years, we've got a team that wants to win and we have a great opportunity, so we're going into this season with a new mindset."

The long-term question is whether the Capitals can finally break through, and whether, off ice, they can build off the strides the franchise has taken since the lockout.

"You're going to have a sustained period of success," Brian McNally of the *Washington Examiner* said. "Whether or not they win a title, they're drafting well enough, even . . . when Ovechkin isn't there anymore, to have a competitive team. The growth of the sport . . . it's huge. Winning is always going to be central . . . If not winning, the impression is that it's a well-run team.

"You can't have a Baltimore Orioles situation — where not only are you losing, but the fans think you have no idea what you're doing . . . That was the risk [the Caps took] in 2003 and 2004. But the advantage of the Caps have [now] is people have a sense that it is a well-run organization . . . The scouts know what they're doing, and George knows what he's doing . . ."

Winning had clearly helped the team build its fan base; a Stanley Cup would go a long way toward keeping the team at the forefront of Washington sports.

"They have a window, they're going to be a playoff-contending hockey team for a while, but it would help if they capitalize," Tim Lemke said. "There is still somewhat of the bandwagon effect . . . If the Wizards get better, or the Redskins contend again, or the Nationals become good, there's a lot of competition for the sports dollar in Washington.

"They're in a good position to remain in the forefront . . . They're probably never going back to the dark days of 2003–04 — they would have to be pretty bad to go to that."

"You have to win games . . . have some entertainment level to sell the NHL in a market where it's not the number one sport," McNally said. "It's a basketball region — the Redskins have 80 years of history. If the Nationals do well, and they have some star players, you're competing with that too. You have to find a way to retain confidence . . . Long-term, the hockey prospects are good, because you have more schools play and kids coming out and playing at a high level."

"It's a bandwagon kind of town," Yahoo!'s Greg Wyshynski said. "It's a transient town, a government town. Everybody here, especially young kids, have Ovechkin jerseys and Capitals jerseys . . . Is this the beginning of a generational thing? Or are they government families . . . here for just two years, and if there's a change in the White House they won't be here anymore? Are we seeing something that will last for 20 years?

"I don't think it's going to be temporary. I say that because it's a party, it's become a thing. It's an entertainment option in this part of town . . . I think it's going to have a sense of permanence about it."

When asked to compare the state of the Washington to other markets around the NHL, Ewell was very succinct.

"I think it's going to be somewhere literally and figuratively north of Carolina and Tampa Bay, more solid in support . . . But is it going to be as consistent as Philadelphia?" he said. "I'm not sure."

"Maybe when things are going well it's a better fan base, but I think there are a lot of comparisons to Pittsburgh," Ewell elaborated. "That wasn't a good hockey market for the years they were bad. But it's a heck of a hockey market when they're good.

"I think Washington, because of the size of the community and the economic strength, may be able to weather the bad years better than Pittsburgh."

Ewell also believed the team had a window for on-ice success. "I think they're going to be a contender for two or three years or more," he said. "The fact is, in the end, only one team wins.

"Would it be more gratifying to be in the fourth round and lose? The Montreal series was a perfect example. Bad things happened in a stretch of five days. If you do advance, who knows what happens; but the fact is, Montreal was a really good team and ended up beating Pittsburgh in the next round.

"Last year, I watched the whole Boston–Tampa Bay series, and I still don't understand how Boston beat them. I can't figure it out. Tampa was a better team."

After the player introductions and "The Star-Spangled Banner," the 2011–12 season began. Carolina jumped on top in the second, and then the Capitals responded with a pair that sent the home crowd into a loud roar.

The Southeast Division rivals battled back and forth in the third. Eric Staal scored just 18 seconds in to equal the score, then Brooks Laich appeared to give Washington the win with 3:45 left.

Carolina forced overtime late, and then Mike Green sent the crowd home happy with an overtime winner. It was the sixth of his career — he trailed just Ovechkin in the stat among current Capitals.

Underneath the stands, while the capacity crowd emptied into the night, the man who scored the game-winning goal admitted to opening night jitters. "I think we started a little bit slow," Green said. "It seemed like we were a little bit nervous. I think that is because we were in our own building. Once we settled down and we started finishing our checks and getting on the forecheck, we tired them out and I felt that paid off in overtime."

"First win of the year," Ovechkin simply said. "It's nice. The atmosphere was great, and the fans support us all the time . . . Everyone was missing hockey here, and it's nice to come back."

Outside, past the visitors' room and left down the hall, adjacent to the Verizon Center's media room, cameramen, writers and bloggers gathered to ask the coach his thoughts. "It was the first game," Boudreau said. "The crowd's into it, there are a lot of new guys. Nerves were there. It's like the first day on the job and going into the office. You're nervous whether you're a 20-year veteran on the job, or just brand new."

As the buzz of opening night faded into the 82-game, six-month grind of the regular season, the 2011–12 Capitals were poised to take another dramatic turn. In the process, they parted ways with a key component of their recent history — and brought back one of the iconic faces in franchise history.

HUNTER

Four red retired number banners hang near the American and Canadian flags at the south end of Verizon Center. One bears the number 32 and the name "Hunter," paying tribute to the former captain who embodied what it meant to be a Capitals player for more than a decade during the late 1980s and 1990s.

Dale Hunter was acquired from the Quebec Nordiques in the 1987 NHL draft as a badly needed postseason sparkplug. The Capitals had just blown a 3–1 series lead to the New York Islanders in the Patrick Division Semi-Finals, including a legendary 3–2, four-overtime loss in Game 7 on Easter Sunday that left both teams spent. Hunter, a Petrolia, Ontario, native, brought ample skill and grit to Washington. He made an immediate impact with his new team.

"He was such a character player at that time, and a character person," said former Capitals coach Bryan Murray. "Dale came in and gave us a whole new way of playing the game.

"He was hard, competitive, but had a good skill level, passed the puck real well. Whoever played with him would benefit from his competitiveness and his ability to make plays and score goals. I think it just turned the franchise into a position where we could compete every night and have a chance to be one of the top teams in the league every night. And we were for a while."

Hunter scored arguably the most important goal in franchise history at 5:57 of overtime in Game 7 of the 1988 Patrick Division Semi-Finals against Philadelphia. Taking a pass from Larry Murphy, he broke in on Ron Hextall and beat the Flyers' netminder through the five-hole to send the Capitals into the second round. While there may be bigger goals in franchise history — John Druce giving the team its only Patrick Division playoff title at Madison Square Garden in overtime of Game 5 in the 1990 Patrick Division Finals, or Joe Juneau beating Dominik Hasek for the 1998 Eastern Conference crown in Game 6 in Buffalo — Hunter's goal was picked for the NHL's "History Will Be Made" campaign during the 2011 playoffs.

"Dale . . . battled so hard. I think he challenged [Philadelphia's Rick] Tocchet right away . . . He did just so many things," Murray recalled. "I just remember the goal against Philadelphia to knock them out . . . he just buried it. He was one of those guys who put excitement and jump in everything he did."

Ed Frankovic, who worked for the team during Hunter's tenure, and who now covers the Capitals for WNST in Baltimore, thinks Hunter's tally ranks as the top goal in the franchise's 38-year history. "The Hunter goal was the big one. It was all Redskins, Redskins, Redskins around here, and it was always a fight for the second team in town — and that even includes the Orioles . . . You're looking at a Caps team that won just two playoff series before that . . .

"They lost a seven-game series the year before to the Islanders after getting a 3–1 lead — they go out and get Dale Hunter. I was at all those games in 1988 . . . That series should have been 2–2, but the Caps blew a 4–1 lead in Philadelphia in Game 4, and Murray Craven won the game in overtime. The Caps came back here and crushed them in Game 5 at the Cap Centre. The big play in Game 6 is Bobby Gould drawing Dave Brown into a five-minute major and the Caps go on the power play. If you remember that game, the Caps were down 3–0, and came back . . . It was a great pass by Murphy. That is the biggest goal in Capitals history in my mind.

"After the game, everybody went over to Langway's [bar in Alexandria, Virginia], and you couldn't move. All the players were there. It was a huge win, huge for the franchise, because it took them to the next step. If you look at the attendance figures those next few years, it bore that out. They were selling out a lot of games."

According to Frankovic, Hunter helped them compete with the more-rugged team up Interstate 95 in Philadelphia.

"When he came over from Quebec in the draft day trade in 1987, the Capitals had a really good team . . . They were very similar to [today's] team — they didn't win [Patrick Division titles] because there were the Islanders and the Flyers [in the same division], but they were 100-point teams. They had very successful regular seasons and then failed in the playoffs. They could really never match up and beat the Flyers. The Flyers had their number for a couple of years.

"Dale Hunter comes in . . . and it was totally different playing the Flyers. You go up there, the Caps suddenly were in the game. You could tell, the Flyers fans even knew who he was from some of the playoff battles the Flyers had with Quebec. Philadelphia fans are very knowledgeable, they knew what type of player Dale Hunter was. The Flyer fans are focused on Hunter . . . and there's a whole different buzz when you go into that building.

"We all know what happened in the playoffs. Down 3–1, and the Caps come back and Dale Hunter scores the game-winner. The best thing I can say about Dale Hunter is he's a guy with an unbelievable work ethic. You could say he lived to do two things: farming and hockey."

Frankovic recalled Hunter was a student of the game even as a player. And he was a big presence in the Capitals' dressing room — before he was ever named team captain. "He always had a smile on his face, he always cared about what was going on. He'd always want to know his faceoff numbers after every game, and he usually knew if they were good or bad. That's the type of guy he was. Focused on hockey, just a team guy all around. Everyone on the team respected him. Assistant captain right away when Rod Langway was here . . . Then he became captain. He's a leader, but a man of very few words. When he talks, he's pretty powerful."

Hunter was part of the franchise's only two trips to the conference finals, in 1990 and 1998, and he raised the Prince of Wales Trophy when the Capitals earned their only trip to the Stanley Cup Finals in 1998 with a Game 6 overtime victory at Buffalo's Marine Midland Arena.

"He kind of represents the old Caps, for sure," the *Washington Examiner*'s Brian McNally said. "The team was undermanned, didn't really have the talent that Pittsburgh did back in the day. But they still found a way to make a battle of it. I think that's why people respond to him. A classic underdog . . . They didn't have [Mario] Lemieux here, but Hunter was the guy who could keep them in games . . . who was willing to do anything it took to keep them in games against better teams.

"It never worked out, they didn't have the goaltending for whatever reason . . . but he gave them an effort. In 1998, he was at the tail end of his career . . . But to captain that veteran group to the Stanley Cup Finals cemented his legacy, even if they didn't win the whole thing."

Hunter parted ways with the Capitals franchise less than a year after their lone Stanley Cup Finals trip, when general manager George McPhee sent him to Colorado at the 1999 trade deadline in an attempt to get the veteran's name on the Stanley Cup. That final run fell short — the Avs eventually lost to the Stanley Cup champion Dallas Stars in the Western Conference Final. Hunter hung up his skates that summer at the age of 39. He'd spent 19 years in Quebec, Washington and Colorado without getting his name on Hockey's Holy Grail. He remains the only player in NHL history to record over 1,000 points and 3,000 penalty minutes during his career.

When his playing days were over, Hunter spent time with the Capitals as a scout, then went on to purchase the Ontario Hockey League's London Knights with his brother Mark. He coached that franchise to the Memorial Cup title in 2004–05.

As the 2011–12 hockey season opened, Hunter was still with the Knights. He later said he was still following the Capitals on tape, during the long bus rides between Ontario Hockey League venues. Down south, Bruce Boudreau and the Capitals were unexpectedly running into problems.

The year began well, perhaps too well. The Caps followed the season opening win over the 'Canes with victories over the Lightning, Penguins, Senators, Panthers and Flyers, then beat the Red Wings 7–1 on home ice. It was the first 7–0 start in franchise history. While things seemed perfect as they embarked on a two-game trip to Western Canada at the end of October, the seams of the team were beginning to fray.

"I think they got off to a good start and were scoring goals . . . But if you look back at it, there were some games they weren't playing well," Ed Frankovic of Baltimore's WNST explained. "They were winning close games, but giving up chances . . . the defensive zone was really deteriorating.

"I think a lot of players didn't want to keep playing the way they were playing the year before. A lot of them had down years offensively . . . This is a business. People want to score; they want to get points. Guys are coming up on new contracts . . . At the end of the day, [Boudreau's] message wasn't getting to them."

"It was a tale of two teams. They weren't as strong as you thought at 7–0 . . . parts of their game weren't tip-top . . . But I don't think anyone expected the fall they had. Some tough teams, some tough losses . . . But once it snowballs in the NHL, it really goes downhill quickly."

Washington suffered its first loss of the year on October 27, a 2–1 squeaker decision in Edmonton. They looked ragged in a 7–4 loss to the Canucks, the defending Western Conference champs, as October drew to a close.

Things became turbulent in November. The month began with a home game against Anaheim in which Alex Ovechkin was left on the bench during the critical last minute of regulation as the Capitals were trailing. Cameras caught Ovechkin apparently mouthing an expletive while sitting on the bench in front of Bruce Boudreau. It was becoming clear to observers — and club management — that the message the coach was trying to convey was no longer getting through.

"When you have the same voice telling you stuff for four years, I think that happens," Sky Kerstein, Capitals reporter for Washington's 106.7 The Fan observed. "Here, your star players weren't being the star players. They were 8–0 with Mike Green [in the lineup], but he couldn't stay on the ice. Ovi and Semin just started losing the message and doing their own things . . . They didn't really care what Bruce was saying.

"We saw that when Ovi got benched . . . The not-so-nice comments about Bruce . . . You can't just suddenly come in and make everyone accountable. We were talking to [former Capital] Eric Fehr, and Fehr said that he thought they were going to make everyone accountable last year — and they didn't. In your fifth season with the team? You can't start doing it then. You have to do it right away."

Ovechkin wasn't showing the jump he had in the first years of his career, and the media was starting to make him the focus of the team's woes. While he was typically known as one of the team's hardest workers, observers began noting the team wasn't getting the same hustle from the Moscow native.

Following a 3–2–1 start to November, a fateful three-game road trip put the wheels in motion: Boudreau's four-year stay in Washington was about to end, and Dale Hunter was about to become the prodigal son.

On November 15, Washington blew a late lead in Nashville, then they were soundly beaten by the Jets in the team's first visit to Manitoba since 1995 two nights later. Finally, playing on CBC's *Hockey Night in Canada* against an injury-ravaged Maple Leafs team featuring seven players called up from the AHL's Toronto Marlies, they were crushed 7–1. What was most worrying was how the game resembled some of the ugly lopsided losses the Capitals had suffered the year before.

Washington returned home and rebounded briefly to beat Phoenix and Winnipeg before Thanksgiving. But, after the holiday, the team reverted to the poor effort on display in Toronto. They were rolled 6–3 by the Rangers at home on November 25. Only Ovechkin's solid effort kept the game from being a complete rout. The next night they traveled to Buffalo, and despite playing a team missing nine regulars, they were no match for the shorthanded Sabres. The 5–1 loss would close the book on the Boudreau era.

"Four years [coaching] in the NHL is above the norm . . . It was time," Frankovic said of the change. "The players had tuned him out in Winnipeg and Toronto. After the Buffalo game, the writing was on the wall."

Boudreau, who had come down from Hershey to take over the Capitals reins four Thanksgivings earlier, was fired two days after the loss to the Sabres. Dale Hunter was brought in by his old general manager to do what he was asked to do 24 years before as a player — get the team over the playoff hump.

"Dale's a Washington Capital," Ted Leonsis said a week after the change. "When he retired, he spent some time coaching and scouting for us. I would see Dale when he would come here and at the draft, since he goes to the draft a lot . . . He's a hockey guy . . . He watches the Caps all the time.

"He and George spoke all of the time — Dale knew we needed help right now, and I mean that. He watched our games, and we were all concerned. It just didn't look like our team was our team, so when George reached out to him, he made a great sacrifice. He's got a great, great platform up there [in London] . . . He owns the team, making a lot of money and coaching . . . He literally had to drop what he was doing to come in."

Considering Hunter's investment in London, the Capitals had to be sure he would leave the Knights behind in the care of his brother while Dale would look to grab that elusive Stanley Cup ring in Washington. The team returned from Western New York in the early hours of Sunday morning; general manager McPhee returned after watching a Bears game in Hershey. The decision was made to make the change the next day.

"Sunday afternoon George called me with Dick [Patrick] and said, 'I have to do something,'" Leonsis said. "I said, 'What's your plan B?' He said, 'Stay tuned — I'm going to call Dale. He's coaching a game [at Brampton] right now.' He literally came in on Monday."

Hunter agreed to take the Capitals' job that evening, on a one-year deal to allow Hunter to eventually return to juniors if he didn't want to continue in the National Hockey League, or if the Caps felt it wasn't working in Washington. Hunter, whose last two deals as a player with the Caps were one-year deals, took the same deal from his former GM to see if he could turn around the NHL franchise he felt a deep connection with. As for the team's soon-to-be-former coach, at 6:15 a.m. the next morning, McPhee called Boudreau and asked him to come to his house. He gave him the news immediately and in person.

Owner Ted Leonsis was banking on Hunter to bring the Capitals postseason success. "One thing Dale said to me made me feel this was the right thing to do . . . We weren't as successful as we should have been in the playoffs. Our style of play in the playoffs has been different than in the regular season . . . And Dale's comment to me was 'I don't believe you can change your style of play in the playoffs. You have to play the regular season the way you play the playoffs, so that it's second nature.'

"And that's risky now for us, but Dale is going to implement a new system for the rest of the season . . . And we're going to learn if we have the players for that system . . . We're playing man-to-man defense. You've got to backcheck and make your offense off turnovers. You've got to grind and that's going to take some getting used to . . . We still have 56 games left — it's a dramatic change, but it's like 'Go to bed early, eat your vegetables, drink a lot of water . . .' You don't like it, but it gets you healthy, and that's what we have to do right now. We have a lot of work to do to turn this season around."

A feisty and familiar figure ran the drills on that last Monday in November. The players were used to seeing Dale Hunter's large photo on a banner at one end of the Capitals' practice rink, and now he was in person, looking much greyer than on his last tour of duty, his familiar steely glare and gravelly voice preparing the Caps to try to turn around their season.

"The reason for the change was we weren't winning," McPhee said. "This wasn't a slump. You can ride out slumps. This was simply a case of the players no longer responding to Bruce. And when you see that, as much as you don't want to make a change, you have to make a change.

"Bruce did a terrific job here. We're proud of the work he did. But when the players aren't responding, you have to make a change."

McPhee noted that he started to see problems as early as training camp, but that everything became clear on the three-game road trip through Tennessee, Manitoba and Toronto.

"It's something you see," he explained. "You can tell when your players are playing through a slump. But you can see when the players aren't performing the way they should be and aren't responding."

"Every time we lost two in a row for the last year, people were saying it was going to be coming," Boudreau told the Associated Press. "You never think it's going to come . . . But we lost some games in the recent weeks by scores that we were not accustomed to. That hadn't happened to us before. I didn't know where we were at or what was going to happen, but it wasn't fun."

The players also acknowledged that change had become necessary.

"I feel like our room is better . . . I feel like it wasn't him," veteran Mike Knuble said. "I like to think we were more in charge of ourselves . . . Being a veteran group, [it wasn't] him so much trying to prod us to play well. The pressure would have been in the room . . . I don't know why, it was pretty evident in our play the last few days. I don't know why it happens."

Hunter, who left behind a successful run with his junior club, also praised Boudreau. "Bruce has been here a long time, did a great job," Hunter said. "Sometimes the players hear your voice every day, and the players don't execute as well as they should."

For Hunter, it was a chance to get the one National Hockey League coaching job he truly coveted: back in the city where he spent the majority of his 19-year career. "This has been my team," Hunter told reporters his first day back in Washington. "Well, it's Ted's team, but it feels like my team because I played here so long and have good memories here. And as far as the question about why now? My kids are grown up. When they're younger, it's a little tougher . . . But now, I can have a full commitment and spend the hours to try to win hockey games."

"I played a lot of hockey here, and I've been cheering for the Caps since I left," he added. "I taped every game for the last how many years . . . You follow them and watch the game. In junior, you're riding the buses, you put in the tape and watch the game and it kills a lot of time."

Bryan Murray, who as the Senators' general manager had looked into making Hunter his team's coach years earlier, said he believed the only NHL job Hunter would leave his successful junior team for was in Washington. "It was only going to be Washington — and I thought good for him if they were going to have another coach come in," Murray said. "We certainly had great consideration of Dale [as Ottawa's coach] a couple of years ago but things happened and it didn't work out, and I had a feeling at that time he wanted to stay in London. Good for him to take a challenge on here and rectify a problem."

One thing Hunter noticed right away was that a fan base had grown. "We had good fan support when I was here but now it's unbelievable," he said. "I'd like to create a winner. It starts out by making the playoffs, because it's a tough conference; but once you get in, anything can happen."

"When I came down here a couple of years ago for a playoff game . . . the fans were going crazy," he added. "That's great to see. It improved when we built the rink downtown, but I can't believe how many red jerseys are in the stands now. They have a good team here and they're proud of it."

GM George McPhee had both played against Hunter and employed him. He had stayed in touch with his former captain since trading him to Colorado a dozen years earlier, and hoped that some of his feistiness and desire would rub off on Washington's new players.

"[Hunter was] an intelligent player who had talent — and he was tough, downright mean at times. We probably won't see a player like that again for a while; you won't see numbers like the numbers he had. He played 19 years in this league, and the best thing you can ever say about Dale Hunter, whether the game was home or away, whether he was injured or healthy, whether we were winning or losing, is the guy played the same every night.

"He really had a great NHL career, played a heck of a lot of playoff games, and then went back like a lot of guys do and started coaching at the junior level . . . And no one's been better at that level. In that Ontario Hockey League . . . he has the best winning percentage of all time. It's not a flash in the pan, one or two or three years . . . It's over 11 years — he turned that franchise into the best junior franchise.

"He's a terrific coach . . . Anyone who played with him admired him . . . This is the only pro team he's ever wanted to coach. He's had opportunities with other teams, but this is the one he's wanted. We've talked consistently for 12 years, and I've always hoped that Dale could coach this team . . . Timing is everything, and the time is right now. His kids are grown up; his franchise is in great shape; so he's available to, and ready to, help us now. The only way he wanted to do it is if he could go full bore. In his words, 'I've got to be able to go full bore.' He's ready to go."

Dennis Wideman, who played for Hunter in London, recalled that his coach told him how much he enjoyed playing in Washington, even back then.

"When I was in junior with him, we talked about it . . . about playing here. Obviously, he loved it here, and I'm sure he's extremely excited to be back in Washington."

"I think he'll get us playing the way we need to play, getting pucks in deep, going to work," he added. "With his history, it's going to be good and it'll create some excitement around this city."

Boudreau, who compiled a 201–88–40 record in Washington over his four years, became the fastest coach in NHL history to earn 200 wins. Boudreau earned a lot of praise for his work despite being let go. His work with the Capitals didn't go unnoticed around the league either, as he was hired two days after the Caps dropped him, replacing Randy Carlyle as the Anaheim Ducks' head coach.

"Bruce is a great coach . . . I think he did everything in his power to get this team to win," Mike Knuble said. "I think his four years were good for the Capitals. He achieved a lot. You could say, 'He didn't win the big game,' but there's been a lot of forward progress. He left it a different organization . . . for the better, I think."

Now, with a familiar face behind the bench, the Capitals looked to take Boudreau's successes further and capture hockey's elusive Holy Grail.

Hunter finally got his first NHL coaching win against the Senators.

"It feels good," he said afterward. "It's one of those things you want to get over with right away. You hope it's the first game — but it ends up being the third. It's one of the things you want under your belt."

WASHINGTON'S WILD RIDE

Dale Hunter brought in a new system. For the players, adapting to Hunter's tight-checking defensive philosophy took time and had mixed results.

Some nights, the Caps played strong defensively and secured a hard-fought victory. On other evenings, they allowed early goals and seemed to wilt in the face of the deficit. Washington was still one of the league's best teams at home, despite the transition to a new style of play, but finding a way to win away from Verizon Center proved difficult.

Just 30 days and 16 games before the end of the regular season, Washington found themselves four games above .500 with a 32–28–6 record. The 70 points they'd earned in the season's first five months was good for 9th place in the Eastern Conference, and the Capitals sat two points behind the Jets, with the Sabres, Lightning, Maple Leafs, Islanders and Hurricanes all within seven points of the final playoff spot.

Despite embarking on a five-game homestand, after Ovechkin's dramatic winning goal over the Islanders on the last day of February, the team dropped three straight to the Devils, Flyers and 'Canes. On

March 8, the surging Tampa Bay Lightning paid their final visit to Verizon Center, looking to tie the Caps in the standings.

The game got off to a rocky start. After Keith Aucoin — recalled from Hershey to fill the void created by Nicklas Backstrom's injury — staked Washington to a first-period lead, the Bolts scored a pair of goals. Trailing 2–1 after 40, during intermission, the Capitals' new bench boss, who normally didn't preferred to let his assistants and actions do the talking, delivered a fiery speech to his troops. The season really was hanging in the balance.

"His message was . . . just to man up," defenseman Karl Alzner said afterward. "Play hard and play as a team. . . . [It was] pretty much one of the first times he ever yelled at us, and the guys just snapped out of it."

Facing the 1–3–1 system the Lightning had used to knock Washington out of the playoffs the spring before, the Caps pushed for the equalizer. Marcus Johansson delivered what proved to be one of the most important goals of the campaign with 3:58 left in regulation.

After the Caps stopped an Eric Brewer clearing attempt, Dennis Wideman freed the puck and it deflected over to Johansson, who beat Tampa goaltender Dustin Tokarski.

"We played one of the best periods we have played in a long time and it was good to see that we could turn it around as a team," Johansson said after the game.

The win meant the Caps had the valuable point in the standings for forcing overtime in their pockets. The five-game homestand ended as it began against the Islanders — with an Alexander Ovechkin OT winner. Under a minute into the extra session, young defenseman Dmitry Orlov fed Ovechkin, who beat Tokarski for the victory. The two points brought them into a tie with Winnipeg for the final playoff spot in the Eastern Conference.

For Hunter, the win was pivotal. He felt his team had finally implemented his system. "There were a couple of games where we were being too fancy and trying to outscore teams, instead of outplaying teams and playing at both ends," the coach said after the season. "But we came back and we beat Tampa Bay one game and we had to grind it out to do it. They were playing that defensive role, that defensive style of game, so the guys had to chip it in and chase and the guys got it done. And then each game we built and got better and better from it."

According to the *Tampa Tribune*'s Erik Erlendsson, the win was not only a boost for the Caps, it also helped knock the Lightning out of contention.

"[The Capitals] entered that period down a goal and reeling a little bit, and Tampa was making a push. It was Tokarski's first NHL start, and they had a lot of good things going on . . . But in that game I thought Tampa sat back too much in the third . . . As much as we want to talk about the changes Dale Hunter [implemented] . . . when a team sits back and allows the Capitals to impose . . . they're a highly skilled team. That came through.

"When you have game-breakers like the Capitals have, you can sometimes afford to play a more defensive-minded system, since all you need is a couple of opportunities to break through. That's probably [the game] where Washington started to see the two styles . . . blend."

Two days later, on the heels of the critical comeback win, the Capitals paid their first visit of the season to the home of the defending Stanley Cup champion Boston Bruins. Tomas Vokoun was stellar as the Capitals took a 2–0 lead on goals by Alexander Semin and Matt Hendricks. With just six seconds left in the first, however, a Milan Lucic goal changed the momentum.

"It's a coach's worst nightmare when a team scores late in a period like that," Hunter said. "They came out and tied it up too, but we just kept pushing."

Jay Beagle and Brooks Laich eventually answered back, and then Washington hung on for a 4–3 win.

"We are worried about our overall record and it is what it is," Laich said. "We've just got to . . . focus on today . . . and try to get the job done. I'm happy with the guys; I thought we played a really good game. We'll get out of here, get back and then do it again [tomorrow]."

Washington returned home the following afternoon to beat the

Maple Leafs thanks to a 2–0 shutout by Michal Neuvirth, before embarking on a five-game road trip. It proved to be the stretch that definitively changed the course of the Capitals' season, both in the standings and in terms of their roster.

Despite falling behind 4–1 to the New York Islanders on March 13, the Capitals rallied to earn a shootout victory. The team then headed to Winnipeg in an important divisional showdown. They not only lost the game but their starting goaltender.

In front of a rabid crowd of 15,000 at MTS Centre, Vokoun played well in defeat. He stopped 25 of 28 Jets shots and earning the game's third star. But the veteran also suffered a groin injury in the setback. The Capitals had to call upon one of their young prospects to fill the void. Braden Holtby, the 22-year-old Saskatchewan native who had played well in 14 games with the Capitals the season before, was recalled from Hershey.

Holtby didn't think he'd be with the big club for long. He'd backed up Dany Sabourin in Hershey's shootout win over the Albany Devils on St. Patrick's Day and then got up early the next morning to catch a flight for Washington's game against the Blackhawks on March 18. He parked his car in the more expensive short-term parking at Harrisburg International Airport, just to save a half-hour of sleep.

"I thought I'd chance it with day-to-day parking . . . it's collecting a pretty big [bill] there right now," he joked a week later.

The roster move proved to be very significant. When Michal Neuvirth was injured as well, Holtby assumed the starter role for the Capitals by default. He kept the job with strong play in the postseason. And though he did eventually get his car back from the short-term parking lot, he never returned to the Bears.

Capitals radio voice John Walton, who had seen the young goaltender play in Hershey the year before, wasn't shocked that Holtby grabbed the opportunity with both hands because of "the swagger he always carried, and the ability he's always had, even from the first day he walked into Hershey as the third-string and the Black Ace when the team won [the Calder Cup] in 2009.

"I don't think I'm the only one who would say that. I think people in the organization would as well. The makeup of his character and his ability . . . it's a rare thing to be able to step in and do the job he did, particularly against the competition . . . on the other side. If there was a guy who was capable of doing that, it was Braden."

Although Holtby didn't play in the loss to Chicago, he did author a 4–3 win with 30 saves against the Red Wings at Joe Louis Arena on March 19, the first time Washington had won at Detroit since 2003.

After a shootout loss in Philadelphia on March 22 to end the road trip 2–2–1, the Capitals suffered two tough losses in the ensuing three-game homestand that knocked them out of playoff positioning.

Washington roared out to a 3–0 lead over Winnipeg in the first 26 minutes of the contest the night following the loss to the Flyers. But the Jets rallied and eventually won the game in overtime.

"To have a commanding lead, a 3–0 lead and then to make a couple of mistakes . . . We've got to play with a little more composure than that and protect that lead and win that hockey game," Brooks Laich said afterward.

The Caps beat Minnesota to take the middle game of the homestand. The showdown on March 27 with Buffalo would allow one team to take control of their playoff destiny with just four games left. But the Capitals quickly fell behind 3–0; Sabres goaltender Ryan Miller was on top of his game, and Washington was handed a very tough 5–1 defeat.

"It was one of those games where both teams came out and it wasn't a cat and mouse game; it was wide open hockey game and we took the brunt of it," Hunter said afterward.

"[The Sabres] are playing very well in front of Ryan [Miller] and if he gets a glimpse of the puck, he'll make the save," Mike Knuble said. "That's what you need out of your goaltender this time of year and they're getting it."

"The Buffalo game, in retrospect, was probably rock bottom," Walton said after season's end. "But you saw a team that banded together after that to find a way to get in."

Trailing Buffalo by two points with five games to play, on March 29 the Capitals headed to the TD Garden for the second time in less than three weeks.

Early in the contest against the Bruins, Vokoun tested his injured groin. He was able to play just 18:25 of the first period before being replaced by Neuvirth. The veteran had signed a below-market $1.5 million, one-year deal with the Caps in order to get the chance to play in the Stanley Cup playoffs, something he hadn't done since 2007 with Nashville, but he was done. It turned out to be Vokoun's final appearance in a Washington sweater.

Holtby had been readying for a return to the AHL should Vokoun remain healthy, but he was going to be up with the club the rest of the way. The next time the Capitals were in that building, he was the team's starter.

After battling the Bruins through a scoreless 47 minutes, Dennis Wideman gave the Caps the lead, and then Johansson converted on a 2-on-1 with Ovechkin to put Washington ahead 2–0.

Boston battled back, erasing the Washington advantage in the final 3:10 of regulation. Facing Tim Thomas, one of the best goaltenders in the NHL, it seemed the Caps' playoff chances were once again in jeopardy.

But thanks to a nifty shootout goal by Matt Hendricks, along with tallies from Alexander Semin and Brooks Laich, the Caps pulled even with the Sabres in points and had four games remaining.

Two nights later, the Capitals got a boost with the return of Nicklas Backstrom. The standout center had missed 40 games after a January 3 elbow thrown by then-Calgary Flames forward Rene Bourque left him with a concussion. The team faced Bourque's new club, the Montreal Canadiens. In part thanks to their star center returning, Washington took back control of its playoff destiny with a 3–2 shootout win.

"Everyone's pumped," Dale Hunter said. "You get Nicky Backstrom back. There was a lot of excitement in the room."

Michal Neuvirth, who was Washington's playoff starter the year before, seemed ready to take the team's starting role in postseason once more. But fate thrust Holtby to the forefront.

After failing to clinch a spot after a 4–2 loss at Tampa Bay on April 2, Washington returned home with a chance to pull even in the Southeast Division race against Florida on April 5. It was exactly four years to the day after the team had begun its post-lockout playoff streak with a win over the 'Cats.

The Caps turned in a strong performance and kept themselves alive in the Southeast Division race. They staked themselves to an early lead, thanks to Jay Beagle, who put a Troy Brouwer rebound past ex-Cap Jose Theodore with just 5:42 gone.

But early in the second, another former Cap, Marco Sturm, collided with Neuvirth in the crease. The netminder's hip was injured. As a result of the collision, Holtby came in. The team's playoff hopes now rested on the shoulders of a young netminder.

After the injury to Neuvirth, Washington responded: Ovechkin and Laich scored two minutes apart to give the Caps a lead they wouldn't relinquish. With a Buffalo loss in Philadelphia, the Capitals secured a playoff berth for the fifth straight season.

"It's been a battle," Hunter said after the game. "Through [Backstrom's] injuries and stuff, guys battled. [Green] being out too at different times, and now, goalies going down . . . It made people stronger; it made other people stand up. You got the [Mathieu] Perreaults and the Orlovs, these young guys come in and they play well for us. That's what you need."

Although a fifth straight Southeast Division title wasn't in the cards, they did close out the regular season with an impressive 4–1 win over the New York Rangers at Madison Square Garden. Holtby stopped 35 of 36 shots in the victory. The two goaltenders Washington dressed for the contest — Holtby and Dany Sabourin — had both been in Hershey three weeks earlier.

Despite the rough patches, the Capitals were able to win when it counted. They earned the 7th seed, having the tiebreaker to best Ottawa with 92 points. Washington finished 42–32–8 for the regular season with a 10–4–2 finish that included a much improved 5–3–1 mark away from home.

"Obviously, it was a tough road [to the playoffs], and when they lost that game to Buffalo, it didn't look very good at all," WNST's Ed Frankovic said of the team's strong regular-season finish. "In the past, most Caps teams would have folded the tent, but . . . this group was a little different.

"They went 4–1 down the stretch; they kind of came together and won the games they had to, while Buffalo imploded . . . That last game against the Rangers, they stuck it to them pretty good . . . that gave them some confidence that they could play with anybody."

As the 7th seed, the Capitals drew a tough opening assignment: the defending Stanley Cup champion Boston Bruins.

In franchise history, the Capitals had faced the previous year's Stanley Cup winner in the postseason four times, and they had lost all four series. This year's team was relying on a 22-year-old goaltender with just 21 games of NHL experience to pull off the upset.

"We've done it before, and we have no choice," Capitals general manager George McPhee matter-of-factly said of his goaltending situation at Kettler Capitals Iceplex on the eve of the playoffs.

Washington opened the 2012 playoffs at TD Garden on April 12, playing under the arena's vast collection of banners honoring past Bruins and Celtics. Boston seemed ready to run the Caps out of the building, outshooting Washington 26–7 over the first 40 minutes. But Holtby was able to hold strong, making several spectacular saves to keep the game scoreless.

According to Walton, that showing was important in building the Capitals' trust in their young netminder. "In Game 1, the first two periods, the Bruins had a decided edge in shots and grade A scoring chances — but the game was still scoreless," he said. "I think it was the first time that his teammates felt 'This guy can win us a game,' and that was probably contagious in retrospect.

"The job he was able to do sent the message to the rest of the team that 'We're in this series.' I think he did a magnificent job, and after the first two periods of Game 1, the guys in front of him did a magnificent job."

Washington generated some offensive pressure in the third period and, although Chris Kelly scored early in overtime to give the hosts the first with a 1-0 win, it was clear that the series would be anything but a cakewalk.

"I think he played a hell of a game," Ovechkin said of Holtby. "He kept us in the game, and I think he was nervous, but after the first shot you could see he was calm and he was on his roll."

Two days later, the Capitals pushed back, and after being shut out by Thomas for over 100 minutes to start the series, Brouwer finally got Washington on the board with 2:03 left in the second.

Boston tied it in the third, as Benoit Pouliot took advantage of a rare Holtby miscue, sliding the puck past an overly aggressive poke check to tie the game with 7:47 left in regulation.

Holtby and Thomas battled through one 20-minute overtime, but Nicklas Backstrom proved to be the difference in the second extra period. Off a faceoff in the Bruins end, Marcus Johansson fed the centerman, who beat Thomas 2:56 into double OT. Heading back to Washington, the series was even.

"It feels good," Backstrom said about getting the goal. "But I don't really care who scores in the playoffs. We're a team and we work together and we do everything together. So it doesn't really matter."

The scene shifted to a sea of red at the Verizon Center, and the two teams traded goals in the 4–3 Boston win, which was capped by Zdeno Chara's game deciding marker with just 1:53 left. It was a stinging loss; Washington had held the lead twice in the contest.

"It's tough," Ovechkin said afterward. "Somebody has to win, somebody has to lose and unfortunately we lost. I think we played great today, but we made a couple of mistakes and it cost us a goal. It was a great battle."

"The last goal, that's just a tough break," Holtby said.

To add insult to injury, Backstrom was assessed a match penalty for cross-checking Rich Peverly as time expired. The penalty meant he missed the pivotal Game 4, leaving a club already thin in the middle without one of their best players.

Backstrom's absence did give Mike Knuble the chance to get back in the lineup— he'd been a healthy scratch since the last game of the season — and Holtby once again proved to be on top of his game. Marcus Johansson scored just 1:22 into Game 4, converting a Brooks Laich feed to give the hosts the lead. Still, Boston outshot the Caps 14–3 in the period and tied the game on a Rich Peverly 2-on-1 goal.

The teams traded chances in the second period, and Thomas and Holtby traded saves until Semin was able to put the Capitals in front for good with a perfectly placed snap shot just off the faceoff dot with 1:17 left in the frame.

Boston pushed for the equalizer in the third, outshooting the Caps 13–3, but Holtby held, and Washington squared the series at 2–2.

"It is so fun to see, because [Holtby's] such a great competitor," Johansson said. "He gives everything he's got. Everyone around is giving everything they've got too."

The win wasn't without some mild controversy. While nursing the lead, Hunter elected to sit his captain for all but 13 seconds of the final 11 minutes. Ovechkin sat while the Cap's grinders patrolled the ice.

"At the end of the game there, you've got your shot-blockers out there . . . and you want your best players blocking shots . . . But your offensive guys? You don't want them breaking a foot," Hunter told reporters of his decision the next day.

"It doesn't matter how many minutes I play," Ovechkin said. "Of course I want to be [out] there, but it's his decision."

"If you go back and look at Ovechkin's ice time, it was up when the Caps were even or behind, but when the Caps were winning, or spent a lot of time shorthanded, it was down," Ed Frankovic said of Hunter's strategy. "At the end of the game, if they were leading, Dale Hunter would put out his best defensive players. If they were trailing, they put out their best offensive players."

Game 5 in Boston proved to be a wild ride as the combatants looked to take a critical lead. After a scoreless first 32 minutes, Alexander Semin finally poked a puck past Thomas, and then Jay Beagle scored 3:11 later to give the Capitals control. But Washington's first two-goal lead of the series was short-lived. Boston scored twice in a 28-second span late in the second to erase the deficit and send the sellout crowd at TD Garden into a frenzy.

Despite Boston's quick one-two punch, Mike Knuble was able to put the Caps back in front with 16:39 left to play. The Bruins had an answer for that goal as well; Johnny Boychuk blasted a point shot past Holtby with 11:13 left.

Armed with a late power play, the Capitals took the game, as Brouwer unleashed a shot that Thomas misjudged with just 1:27 left. The Caps had a 3–2 series lead.

"Some relief, that's for sure," Brouwer said. "A lot of joy. Especially late in the game like that, we were getting buzzed a little bit, and I think they had a little bit of momentum off the power play goal. So for us, to get a power play late, create a little bit of offense, ultimately get a goal, it's good."

The defending champs proved their mettle in Game 6 the next afternoon, scoring the game's first goal and then having an answer each time the Capitals tied it up.

With 3:52 left, Ovechkin forced the game into overtime, but young Bruins star Tyler Seguin forced a decisive Game 7 only 3:17 into the extra frame with a goal off a Capitals turnover. Although it was disappointing for the Caps not to close out the series at home, in the post-game press conference, Dale Hunter was excited to see what his team could do in a Game 7.

"Any experiences you get in the playoffs, it just adds to you," he said. "You know what to expect. Game 7s are exciting because it's do-or-die for both teams, and they're awesome to play in."

Hunter knew what he was talking about: he had scored one of the only two Game 7 winners in Capitals history. But the team he coached was facing an opponent that had won three Game 7s the previous spring, en route to their first Stanley Cup since 1972.

On April 25, the Capitals took the ice in Boston looking to make history: they'd never won a Game 7 away from home. The sellout crowd was clearly looking forward to another Bruins long playoff run. But in a tight series that saw the first six games decided by just one goal — the first such series in NHL history — it shouldn't have been surprising that Game 7 was decided in overtime.

Washington opened the scoring when Matt Hendricks tipped a John Carlson shot past Tim Thomas with 8:37 to play in the first. The Capitals sat back with the one-goal lead, seemingly daring the Bruins to beat Holtby. While the young netminder was stellar, Seguin scored another big goal for Boston as he poked home a loose puck sitting in the crease to tie the game with five minutes and change left in the second. Looking to take the lead, the hosts continued to press.

"It was big for us to get out of that second [tied]," Holtby said afterward.

Although Washington was outshot 25–13 in the first two frames, the Caps generated more offense in the third; Thomas, however, was up to the task. Boston got a golden chance to close the series with a late power play, as Chimera was called for a minor with 2:26 left. But Holtby and the Caps rose to the occasion and killed the penalty. They forced Game 7 into overtime, only the third time that had happened in franchise history.

The previous year, Boston had defeated Montreal in a Game 7 overtime in the first round, and they again pressed early, nearly ending it in the first minute with a shot that just missed the post.

Under the banners celebrating 86 years of Bruins history, however, the Capitals were able to author some history of their own. With about two and a half minutes gone, on a play in the neutral zone, the Bruins' Benoit Pouliot tried to dump the puck into the Caps zone to set up a Boston line change. Mike Knuble was able to block the clearing attempt, and the deflection sent the puck into the Boston zone.

"[Pouliot] made the right play," Knuble said. "He was trying to dump it in hard. I was heading toward him and he hit me square in the knees. It kicked out to center ice and caught [the Bruins] in a change . . . a hard rebound coming the other way."

"I went for a change and [Knuble] made a big block there and I assumed we had a little bit of a break," Joel Ward said.

Knuble drove to the Boston net and fired the puck; Thomas was able to stop the initial drive. Ward followed the play and took a swing at the rebound, knocking in the puck past the Bruins keeper to end the series with one of the biggest goals in the team's history.

"I knew he was going to take the puck to the net. I wasn't looking for the pass across, and I was just trying to follow in case there was a puck loose or a rebound," Ward said. "I just saw it there and gave it one of the hardest whacks I've ever given a puck."

"To come out of the pile and can't believe that is where you are on the ice with a 2-on-1," Knuble said. "I was carrying that thing right to the crease, was going to jam it in myself one way or the other. Joel was smart, swings by the net, stops in front of the net. I'm very happy for him."

Unlike Dale Hunter's 1987 goal that sent 18,130 fans at the old Capital Centre into a loud frenzy, as the team flooded out along the side boards to celebrate the 17,565 at TD Garden fell into a stunned silence. Ward joined his coach as the only two Capitals to score in a Game 7 overtime.

"It's very fitting that it ended it overtime," Knuble said. "It's a big thrill for Joel, for me; it's always a big thrill when the fourth-line guys can be the scorers and chip in. It's a great feeling, it's satisfying."

In the small visitors' room underneath the stands, players and team personnel — including owner Ted Leonsis and general manager George McPhee — were packed in with the media throng getting interviews and yelling and celebrating the watershed win.

"The feeling is great," Ovechkin said. "You know, it was a tough series. They played well, but great for us. We kept fighting . . . I cannot say what I'm feeling right now, you know, I'm nervous and I'm pretty happy."

"[I'm] just excited," Laich said. "You're excited you're moving on. It's our dream to play for the Cup. There's been some frustration here in the past — and to move on, to beat a good team and to move on . . . we're excited."

It was the first time the Caps had advanced to the second round in back-to-back years under Ted Leonsis's watch. "Mike Knuble's a pro, he transitioned really well, and all I saw was Joel in the back," he said, surrounded by reporters. "I didn't see the puck but I saw it go into the back of the net, and there was bedlam in our suite."

Leonsis, who had talked five months earlier about playing a playoff-style system throughout the entire season, was pleased with the change on the ice.

"This system seems to be the right system to play in the playoffs," Leonsis added. "We had seven one-goal games and four overtime games. This certainly was the best, most competitive series since I've been here . . . No team deserved to lose this, and we're blessed to have won it. That's a great team over there."

"I think there's a lot more discipline, a lot more dumping the puck and sacrificing their body and all those little things," the owner added.

"This is a series we weren't supposed to win," Mike Knuble said. "We were little bit more of a nuisance to a two seed, being the 7th seed . . . We came in and we felt good how we matched up against [the Bruins.] We were that one or two percent better in the series, and we got the final bounce.

"We felt like we belonged in the series and we proved it every night. Stanley Cup champions don't go out easy."

"We needed to win a series like this," George McPhee said afterward. "Boston's a fabulous organization . . . We played them as hard as we could. I don't know how we did it, but it was nice to see that go in. We needed it."

Ed Frankovic called Ward's goal one of the biggest in club history. "After Dale Hunter's goal against the Flyers and Juneau's goal to get them to the Stanley Cup Finals [in 1998], that might have been the third-biggest.

"The way the team was able to overcome the late power play the Bruins got . . . the way they scored just going to the net, an ugly goal . . . In the old days, it would have been waved off . . . because Knuble was in the crease . . . but that's the way it goes.

"They caught a break for once. But it was a great series, four overtime games, and either team could have won that series. Certainly Holtby was a big factor, but there were a lot of other guys who stepped up and played and to win in overtime was incredible, and to win three games in Boston was amazing."

When asked at the end of the season what the highlight of his year was, Hunter wasted no time picking that moment. "Beating Boston in overtime is always special," he said. "So that was big for us and for [Ward] because they were the defending Stanley Cup champions. It was the quite the achievement to take them to seven games and to go in there and win Game 7 in overtime. I was proud of the guys for that."

Kevin Paul Dupont, the *Boston Globe*'s Hall of Fame hockey writer, was impressed with Washington's defensive play, as well as its depth. "Were the Bruins getting fourth-line production like Washington? No. Were they getting airtight defense from their defensemen? They were getting close, but I think the Washington defensemen did a better job jamming that home plate area. Boston wasn't getting fourth-line scoring. Overall, their scoring disappeared from top to bottom. There was no juice."

Dupont also mentioned the Capitals kept Boston on edge, not yielding the early lead and putting the pressure on Thomas.

"[Washington was] very impressive. I was keeping track of the series in terms of Boston lead time. Boston's lead times were minimal. This was a series with so little room for error . . . the teams weren't able to get comfortable. You hardly saw any two-goal leads . . . I think over the course of first five games, and the Bruins led for 14:53 total — that's trouble. You're not scoring enough, you're not gaining any separation.

"It's putting the series where [the Bruins] were [in their Cup year]. It's all on Thomas. Thomas is an elite goaltender, had a great save percentage even . . . before he got his chance . . . But he wasn't as good as he was last year — and I don't know how he could be as good as he was last year. He was phenomenal. Their win in 2011 was the most goalie-centric I've ever seen."

The Capitals' second-round opponent posted another tough challenge. The New York Rangers had advanced past the Ottawa Senators in a Game 7 of their own. Washington was matched against the top seed in the Eastern Conference, and again had to wage a tight battle with a top team.

Late in Game 1, the Rangers broke open a tie to earn the 3–1 victory. It was the first and only time a Washington playoff game was decided by more than a single goal.

"I thought the Capitals outplayed New York but didn't get the breaks at all," Ed Frankovic said after the series. "In Game 1, they out-chanced them, but Holtby had his worst game of the playoffs. It was his one sub-par game."

"It's a tough game to stay into, mentally," Holtby told reporters after the game, "and I didn't do a good enough job."

Holtby, who hadn't lost back-to-back games since November 2010, bounced back in Game 2. Despite being taunted by the Madison Square Garden crowd for most of the night, Ovechkin delivered the game-winning goal with 7:27 left in regulation. After the tally, the Caps' star cupped his hand around his ear. The series was headed back to Washington, but not without more controversy over Ovechkin's ice time.

The Capitals' star saw just 13:36 of Game 2, a career playoff low. He also played only 23 seconds after delivering the game-winning goal, and he did not touch the ice in the final 5:56 of the game.

"I feel good," Ovechkin told reporters. "You have to suck it up . . . use what time Dale is giving to me. [The] most important thing right now . . . just win the series and win the game. If you're going talk about my game time and all that kind of stuff, it's not [the regular] season. It's the playoffs."

The spectacle of Ovie sitting certainly raised eyebrows among veteran hockey observers. Many believed Hunter was doing the Rangers a favor. "[NBCSN analyst Mike Milbury] said that Hunter had come in and done a good job defensively, and he was doing what he had to do and sat Ovechkin," Kevin Paul Dupont said of the move. "I'm saying to myself, 'You know something, if I've got a team that's sitting Ovechkin? As a general manager, I want a new coach.'

"This is my $10 million player. I want a game that highlights Ovechkin . . . I know he's a liability defensively and got vulnerabilities, but he's one of the top five most talented players in the game."

After the season, Ovechkin described his role under Hunter: "It doesn't matter if I like it or not, because he's my coach and I have to listen . . . He said, 'You have to be a plumber,' so I was a plumber."

The Capitals had a great chance to take the series lead in Game 3, battling New York into overtime. Ovechkin and Troy Brouwer both missed chances to deliver the winner. A Washington defensive breakdown in the third overtime period led to a Marian Gaborik goal, ending the longest game in Verizon Center history with the Caps on the wrong end of a tight 2–1 triple-overtime contest that lasted 114:41 and ended at 12:14 a.m. the next day.

"It was that kind of game," a drained Ovechkin said afterward. "I think both teams fought very well. You just have to use your chances. They had it and they scored. Unfortunately we had it during that 4-on-2 [break] and we didn't."

"Game 3 was very pivotal, the first overtime game of the series," Frankovic said. "Ovechkin hits the pipe, Troy Brouwer had a chance on the doorstep and misses, and you just have to bury those chances against Lundqvist."

The Capitals did rebound nicely from the tough Game 4 loss. Both Ovechkin and Backstrom had tallies, and, with a blast that beat Lundqvist, Mike Green broke open the 2–2 tie with 5:48 left. It marked the first time since Halloween 2010 that the three had scored in the same game.

"Their forwards collapsed . . . I just had to wait out the block, it came across and held across and put it on the crease," Green said afterward. "I know I can still score at least," he added, laughing. "It's been so long."

Boosted by the split in Washington, the Caps returned to Manhattan looking to take their first series lead. The team was within 8 seconds of doing so, but it wasn't meant to be. Game 5 proved to be the lost opportunity; the Capitals could have stolen the quarterfinals.

Tied after 40 minutes, Carlson blasted a one-timer past Lundqvist on the power play to give Washington a 2–1 lead 4:20 into the third. The goal deflated the hosts and quieted the normally boisterous Madison Square Garden crowd. The Capitals pushed for a two-goal lead, getting some prime chances. The Rangers, similarly, looked for the equalizer, but couldn't convert.

The Rangers pushed late. With Lundqvist pulled in for regulation's final minute, the hero of the first round, Ward, took an ill-advised double-minor high sticking penalty with 22 seconds left. The infraction set up a 6-on-4 advantage that New York cashed in on when Brad Richards grabbed a loose puck at the side of the cage and beat Holtby with 7.7 left, forcing overtime and giving the hosts new life.

The Rangers were able to finish the comeback 1:25 into the extra frame. As Ward was ready to leave the box at the end of his second minor, Marc Staal scored the winner on a shot that deflected past the Caps' goalie.

The loss proved to be a tough setback for a team hoping to reach the Eastern Finals for the first time since their 1998 Stanley Cup Finals run.

"I still think the Game 5 loss is the worst in Capitals history, the way they gave it up in the final minute. They can't win a faceoff . . . and, after being the Game 7 hero, Joel Ward takes the worst penalty in franchise history," Ed Frankovic said. "It was just fluky, right before [Richards] scored, Holtby tried to cover it up and creates the hole. It was a whole series of things that doomed the Caps. It just makes you feel the franchised is cursed."

Despite the tough loss, the Capitals pushed back in Game 6 with their best performance of the series in front of home fans. Ovechkin scored 88 seconds in, a one-timer on an early power play. Chimera added a tip-in goal with 9:01 left in the second period. Despite a late Ranger tally, the Capitals earned a 2–1 win to set up the first Saturday night Stanley Cup playoff Game 7 in Madison Square Garden's history.

"We don't want to stop playing," Ovechkin said afterward. "We don't want to finish the season. We knew we could beat them . . . We had our chances, but Lundqvist played unbelievably again in the third period. Same as Holtby."

Although the Capitals had advanced to the second round on a dramatic Game 7 win, the team had never won back-to-back Game 7 series in its history. And, after Richards beat Holtby just 92 seconds into the final tilt, Washington wasn't able to pull even this time around.

While the Capitals pushed Lundqvist in the second, the Vezina candidate showed his mettle, stopping numerous good Caps chances until Michael Del Zotto scored an insurance marker with 9:55 left in regulation.

The Del Zotto tally proved huge; Roman Hamrlik scored with 9:17 left in regulation to bring the Caps within one. Washington could come no closer, however; they were not generating many shots in the final frame and overall were frustrated by the Rangers' ability to hold a lead.

Despite forcing a Game 7, many felt the series was lost six days earlier, when the Caps couldn't hold on to the late Game 5 lead.

"It wasn't lost in Game 7, it was probably lost in Game 5," John Walton said after the season. "If the last 10 seconds in Game 5 had worked out differently, I think it could have been a really special season, and I think that's the hard part in seeing it come to an end.

"It wasn't a series the team wasn't in. Quite frankly, it's a series the team should have won. I think the guys know that, the coaches know that and the fans know that."

Unlike the previous year's second round loss at the hands of the Lightning, the Capitals felt like there were some positives in the team's performance, some things that they could take with them into the future.

"It took a triple overtime for them to win a game. It took them a 6-on-4 and a 5-on-4 goal to win a game," Brooks Laich said after the season. "We were right there. I liked our team at the start of the summer, but I like it even more now . . . I really like the group of guys here."

One of the important things that had changed over the last six weeks of the Capitals' season was how the players came together; the team really bonded as the playoffs rolled on.

"It was the tightest knit group and the hardest-working group," Laich added. "The team that played [in Game 7], I think, was the hardest working team I've been a part of, and the closest I've been a part of. The atmosphere has really changed, and everybody's of equal importance."

Nicklas Backstrom said, "Actually the first game against Boston, we played that way and continued doing that . . . It really changed when we got into the playoffs . . . everyone started to play really good."

"It was an exciting time," Holtby said. "It was a great year, a great experience in life and hockey, and I wouldn't have changed it for anything."

When asked to describe the two months since he boarded a plane from Harrisburg to Chicago for what he thought would be a short stay with the Capitals, Holtby said, "I've imagined it was since I was five. It wasn't that big of a shock [to play in the NHL]; this is the place I wanted to be forever. It's obviously not the result I wanted, but it shows we have the capabilities to win the Cup."

Less than 40 hours after their season came to an end, the team got the news. At 10 a.m. on May 14, two days after the Game 7 loss, head coach Dale Hunter informed McPhee he wanted to return home to his family and business.

Hunter, whose OHL London Knights had advanced to the Memorial Cup Junior tournament in Shawinigan, Quebec, decided that he'd rather be close to his family and team than continue as Washington's coach. Many of the players were disappointed.

"I had to retire [as a player] because I just wasn't that good anymore," Hunter said. "But this was a tough decision. I enjoyed coaching these guys and being back with the team that, I always figured, while it's not my team technically, *is* my team. So it was a tough decision to make, but it was the right thing to do for me and my family."

"It was more something [that we had agreed] we'd revisit at the end of the year and that's what it was — open minded," he added. "We'd see how it goes. I came here, we knew it was just a one-year thing but we'd revisit it at the end of the year and see how I feel, and how George [McPhee] feels.

"I've been home for a while [in London]," he added. "Everybody is a part of the [Knights] there, the farm is there, so we're all a part of it there and sometimes you've just got to go home."

When McPhee was asked how many NHL coaches would walk away from a successful franchise, he simply replied, "One."

"[Dale's a] unique guy," he added. "That's why you love Dale. He's always been really decisive. No grey in his life. When he came into this club and we talked about the job, he said there's one way to play and that's the right way to play and I'll get them playing the right way. He thought he could and he accomplished what he thought he could do with them, and now they're on the right path."

While the players were probably stunned by his decision, they were able to fall back on the lessons they'd learned in the roller-coaster six months under Hunter.

"I think he taught us as much about leadership and respect amongst players and trusting your teammates as he did about hockey," Brooks Laich said. "I said before, it's like having another veteran in the locker room. He was great. He changed the culture here a little bit, which the rest of us really enjoyed and grasped. He's leaving the team in a better state than how he found it.

"He had such a great influence. There were some things culture-wise that had to be adjusted a little bit in order for our team to succeed. I think he did a great job doing that . . . I had a lot of respect for what he did."

"He really came in and kind of changed the identity of the team . . . players helping out, paying the price to win games," Mike Knuble said.

"He's very honest, and he's telling you exactly what he thinks," Nicklas Backstrom said. "That's what I like. He's a hard-working guy himself, and if you want to win hockey games, you have to work hard. It's something I'm always going to remember."

"The transformation of this hockey club stems from him," Green added. "You have to respect the guy. He came into this team and hasn't strayed from his game plan. We all respect him as a coach and played hard for him."

"We [were] a team in the playoffs," Ovechkin said. "I don't know if you guys see that or not, but I was in locker room, I was on the bus, I was on the plane . . . it was a team and you lose like a team and you win like a team."

It certainly was different for the Caps' captain under Hunter. Ovechkin had seen his ice time fluctuate depending on the score. But the team's success, he said, made him a willing participant.

"Wideman and Carlson . . . both know how he was coaching [from their junior days in London]," Ovechkin said. "It was much easier for them to know his system . . . but for me, personally, it was pretty hard. To be honest with you . . . I have to do it because I have to do it for the team."

"Ovi changed some things in his game that made him a more well-rounded player, actually," George McPhee said. "But I don't want to get into [Dale's] impact on individuals, because since he's been here, it's been all about 'team,' which is the way it should be."

Asked if he thought Hunter and Ovechkin could have co-existed long-term, Ed Frankovic said he thought the captain's game could have grown further had Hunter stayed. "Ovechkin wanted to win a Stanley Cup, so he willing to play the way Hunter asked. I think Ovechkin learned quite a bit about how to win under Hunter. And I believe he could have benefited by playing better defensively and scoring more in the transition game."

But after being a little uncomfortable in the bright spotlight of coaching an NHL franchise, Hunter was heading back to London, Ontario. The coach was animated and clearly more comfortable with the press as his time in Washington wound down.

"We knew at midseason it was a trial basis," said John Walton of the change. "Seeing if we fit for him and he fit for us . . . We found, at the end, he became more comfortable with the position and the media, and, quite honestly, I thought some of his best interviews with me and some of his best press conferences with the media as a whole were at the very end."

"Dale is nothing but decisive," Walton continued. "The speed at which it came surprised me, because I thought he might have wanted to build on what was one heck of a postseason run . . . His family is in London, his business is in London . . . and it's tough to be in two places at once, and ultimately family comes first."

Despite it all, Dale Hunter will always be identified with the franchise.

"I thought he enjoyed it, like us," Brooks Laich said. "He's a Capital through and through. He loved being around the rink, he loved being around the guys."

"I'm always with the Washington Capitals," Hunter said. "I'm always a big backer of them and whatever I can do to help them — I'd love to bring a Stanley Cup here . . . the fans deserve it . . . They've been great.

"My dad doesn't travel too much anymore, but he came down during the regular season and couldn't believe how loud it was, so he had to come back down during the playoffs to see it even louder. The fans are great, the team is playing the right way. They're playing Stanley Cup hockey."

"They have a chance to win playing this style," said Hunter, "and you see them taking the top team to seven games and [beating] Boston. If you see the teams that are left, they all play hard and I'm proud of these guys for sacrificing and doing what it takes to win. We came up a goal short but not because of lack of effort."

The players agreed that, despite the result, the team was moving toward its ultimate goal: the Stanley Cup.

"Closer," Mike Knuble said when asked where the team was compared to a year ago. "It's hard to say — you get to the end, everybody's got the microscope — to see what separated this champion from the rest . . . Some people chase that, build their team that way, the flavor-of-the-year changes . . . I think . . . a bounce or two . . . we'd still be playing hockey."

"I believe we're going to win a Cup here, and I want to be part of it," Green added. "We've been improving each yeah, and especially this year, and I feel like we're close. A few more bounces go our way and we work a little harder and focus a little harder, and we'll win it. It's unfortunate it wasn't this year."

"[Hunter] transformed this team into one that works very hard, and other teams don't like playing against," Alzner said. "That's something we can definitely build off, and we're all very happy with that. It's nice to go out and be able to tell yourself that was an honest effort, unlike games earlier in the year . . . I think he put this team on a very good path, and we can continue that next year."

The change was noticed by those outside the team as well. "If you look at the way they played in the playoffs, they definitely showed more heart than they did the previous year," Erik Erlendsson said. "I remember a quote coming out of the Washington room in Game 3, I'm not sure if it was Knuble or Arnott, but Tampa seemed able to score a goal when they wanted. And when you hear a comment like that coming out of a second-round playoff series, that just shows a bit of a defeatist attitude.

"I don't think you saw that this year. They had every reason to fold. They're going into Boston in a Game 7 situation, after a tough series . . . They had every reason to fold up in that game. And against the Rangers they had a reason to fold after Game 5. They had opportunities to fold and they didn't. I think that shows a mental toughness they hadn't displayed before."

"I think you can look at the last two coaches in here and take something from them. Bruce Boudreau in terms of offense and Dale Hunter for defense," John Walton said. "Quite frankly, in my mind, I don't put one above the other. They were different coaching styles, two different philosophies, and there's something to be taken from both.

"I hope, moving forward, [there's] a hybrid . . . that allows your best players to be your best players yet [you're] mindful of playing of playing in your own end and playing the right way . . . That could be a winning combination."

"I think they are closer [to the Stanley Cup] for one reason alone . . . After 2009, Sergei Fedorov left, and they continued to try to play a style that you need two top centers for," Ed Frankovic said. "When you had Nicklas Backstrom and Sergei Fedorov, it makes it harder to key in on Alex Ovechkin, because they could put Alexander Semin with

Fedorov on the second line and Backstrom and Ovechkin on the top line. You could pick your poison. What line are you trying to stop? That's why the Capitals scored so many goals.

"The weakness of that 2009 team was their defense; it wasn't very good at all. [Semyon] Varlamov played well up until that last game, but that defense was leaky. Their defense now is good with Alzner and Carlson and experience to build around. Up front, they need to get another center, but a lot of guys have stepped up. In net, Braden Holtby is the guy. I think they're closer than they were."

In late June 2012, the Capitals hired their fourth coach since the post-lockout transformation. On the very day he was elected to the Hockey Hall of Fame, former Capital Adam Oates was brought in to blend Hunter's defensive commitment with more offensive flair.

"It's an honor to be here today, a day I thought would never happen — I'm a member of the Washington Capitals again," he said at his introductory press conference. "I played my longest time . . . for this organization, and to come back here as a head coach is a huge high for me and my family."

One player clearly happy to see lighting the lamp re-emphasized was the team's captain. "It's not blocking shots, and it's not dump and chase," Alex Ovechkin told the press. "I'm an offensive guy; it's not a secret to anybody. And I'm pretty excited to hear the Caps signed that kind of guy."

Oates had helped mentor and transform Ilya Kovalchuk, Ovechkin's fellow Russian and good friend, into a productive two-way player during his two-year tenure as a New Jersey Devils assistant. Oates also looked forward to working with the Caps' star. "I'm sure when Alex gets back to town for training camp, we're going talk about his game and some of the little things that you might see," Oates said. "He scored 37 goals last year, and the league gets better and better every year. There's not a lot of goal-scoring anymore."

Oates also talked about the physical aspect of Ovie's game. "I think [it's] unprecedented," he said. "I watched [the Caps] play Boston this year, and he's the only guy in the league who can take on Chara, Lucic and Seidenberg and have [a] physical impact. He's a special player. In terms of adding a little bit to his game? I think I can. But he's got to earn my trust as a coach first — along with the rest of the guys — and it'll be a process and I'm looking forward to it."

After spending almost six years in a Caps uniform, the new coach also talked about the change in Washington's hockey culture since he departed in 2002. "Since Ted has taken over, the franchise has changed dramatically in terms of marketing . . . The professionalism — nothing against what we had back then — from where it was when I played, it is a top echelon organization," Oates said. "That's part of the whole environment. It's a top-caliber NHL team and that's what they expect here. That is the code of the business."

He even joked about the obvious increase in media attention, recalling the sparse gathering when he was named captain in 1999: "We did the announcement over by the White House. There was no one there. People were walking by . . . throwing me a nickel."

According to Ted Leonsis, hiring the former superstar demonstrated the team's commitment to winning and high expectations: "I think not only will Adam be a very, very good coach for us . . . he also shares having a chip on his shoulder. When you're captain, and you have the most experience, the players respect you. . . . We're at that point where we have to do better in the playoffs. We have to win the Stanley Cup. That's what our mission is. Adam's now been to the Finals twice, once as a player, once as a coach. We want to win a Cup together. That's our collective goal."

With a blend of skill on the ice and a growing fan base off it, the emergence of hockey in the United States' capital has been nothing short of impressive. All the franchise needs is a Stanley Cup championship to go with it.

"I think . . . there's this vortex that gets built," Ted Leonsis explained earlier in the season. "The last five years, the team's been successful and popular . . . And so youth hockey has become more successful and popular. And you have families more committed to the game . . . And there's a generation of kids who are falling in love with Alex Ovechkin and the team. It's why playoff success and competing and, one day, winning a Stanley Cup is the ultimate for us — not just because it's what every team plays for . . . If we could win a Cup, we could claim a generation of fans.

"Sometimes I hear and read things that are uninformed . . . Sometimes the old-time fans sneer at newbies. If your mom and dad are taking you to play hockey and getting up at five in the morning and taking you to Ashburn Ice House . . . And they're season ticket holders and they're working in Reston and fighting the traffic to get to games . . . And they've been doing that for five years . . . They have a huge, vested interest in our team. They should be respected, admired, loved, welcomed and encouraged . . . I'm happier with the way the business is than the way the team is playing. I hope we can build a team as good as the fan base. This community is one of the fastest growing youth hockey communities in the country, and if we can perform better, we'd be in for some great times."

This book wouldn't have been possible without the help of some terrific folks from around the Washington area and North America.

First of all, thanks to Michael Holmes and ECW Press for taking an interest and giving me the chance to write a more expansive work than my first book, *Transition Game: The Story of the 2010–11 Washington Capitals.*

Thanks are also in order to the entire Washington Capitals organization, from owner Ted Leonsis and general manager George McPhee, to the communications department, led by Kurt Kehl, along with Sergey Kocharov, Ben Guererro, Kelly Murray and Mike Vogel, for their help and assistance during the process. Thanks too to the players who took the time to answer questions and speak with me for the book.

In addition, thanks to the Buffalo Sabres, Carolina Hurricanes, Florida Panthers, Pittsburgh Penguins, Hershey Bears and Hamilton Bulldogs for their assistance in setting up interviews with their players. Thanks also to Ottawa Senators general manager Bryan Murray for taking time to answer questions on Dale Hunter.

Special thanks are also in order to the team's radio voice, John Walton, for his help, both as a member of the Hershey Bears and Washington Capitals organizations, and for giving extensive interviews about both clubs.

I'd also like to thank Comcast SportsNet's Joe Beninati, Dmitry Chesnokov of TSN and Yahoo!'s Puck Daddy, Erik Erlendsson of the *Tampa Tribune*, Nate Ewell of College Hockey Inc., Ed Frankovic of WNST Radio in Baltimore, Jim Iovino of NBC Washington, Tim Lemke of Patch.com, Tim Leone of the *Patriot-News*, Eric McErlain of Off Wing Opinion, Brian McNally of the *Washington Examiner*, Chris Peters of the United States of Hockey and Greg Wyshynski of Yahoo!'s Puck Daddy.

Special thanks also to John Manasso of Fox Sports and NHL.com for helping with the publishing process.

Thanks are also in order to Reed Albers of the *Fairfax Times*, Jack Anderson of XM Radio, John Keeley of On Frozen Blog, Sky Kerstein of 106.7 The Fan, Brian Potter of Comcast SportsNet and Adam Vingan of SB Nation for their assistance with citations and other background information.

Additional thanks are in order to Maria Stainer and Mike Harris of the *Washington Times* for allowing me to research the paper's archives, and thanks also to the fine work of former Capitals beat reporters David Elfin and the late Dave Fay.

Most of all, I'd like to thank my wife, Pam, and daughter, Tori, for being supportive, and my mom and dad for allowing me to do this for a living with their support through the years.

Ted Starkey is a veteran sportswriter and web editor who has been involved in professional sports for over a decade, having worked with Ignite Sports Media, USA Hockey, AOL Sports and FanHouse.com, and most recently with the *Washington Times* as both a sports feature writer and on the paper's web desk.

During his career, he has covered the 2002 Winter Olympics in Salt Lake City and the 2010 Olympics in Vancouver, numerous Stanley Cup playoffs, the 2010 Stanley Cup Finals and the 2011 NHL All-Star Game. He also has covered the NHL, NFL and MLB, and his work has appeared on the web at Rivals.com, BuffaloBills.com, USAHockey.com, AOL.com and FanHouse.com, as well as in print for the *Washington Times* and *Tampa Tribune*.

He also is author of *Transition Game: Story of the 2010–11 Washington Capitals*, which was released in October 2011, featuring the up-and-down season of a team he covered extensively.

A native of Amherst, New Hampshire, Starkey grew up in Vienna, Virginia, attending both Boston University and American University before graduating in 1994.

He currently lives in Ashburn, Virginia, with his wife, Pam, and daughter, Tori.

At ECW Press, we want you to enjoy this book in whatever format you like, whenever you like. Leave your print book at home and take the eBook to go! Purchase the print edition and receive the eBook free. Just send an email to ebook@ecwpress.com and include:

- the book title
- the name of the store where you purchased it
- your receipt number
- your preference of file type: PDF or ePub?

A real person will respond to your email with your eBook attached. And thanks for supporting an independently owned publisher with your purchase!